Human Factors and Typography for More Readable Programs

ACM Press

Editor-in-Chief

Peter Wegner

ACM Press books represent a collaboration between the Association for Computing Machinery (ACM) and Addison-Wesley Publishing Company to develop and publish a broad range of new works. These works generally fall into one of four series.

Frontier Series. Books focused on novel and exploratory material at the leading edge of computer science and practice.

Anthology Series. Collected works of general interest to computer professionals and/or society at large.

Tutorial Series. Introductory books to help nonspecialists quickly grasp either the general concepts or the needed details of some specific topic.

History Series. Books documenting past developments in the field and linking them to the present.

In addition, ACM Press books include selected conference and workshop proceedings.

Production and Copyright Information

Typesetting

Dynamic Graphics Project
Computer Systems Research Institute
University of Toronto

Design and Specifications

The book design is by Aaron Marcus and Associates with the assistance of the Dynamic Graphics Project. The text is set in Times Roman Regular, roman, 12/14. Constructs from the C language appearing within the text are set in Helvetica Regular, roman and italic, 11/14. C program source text (code and comments) is set according to specifications presented in this book.

Trademarks

Many of the designations used by manufacturers and sellers to distinguish their products are claimed as trademarks. When those designations appear in this book, and Addison-Wesley was aware of a trademark claim, the designations have been printed in initial caps or all caps.

Disclaimer

The programs and applications presented in this book have been included for their instructional value. They have been treated with care, but are not guaranteed for any particular purpose. The publisher does not offer any warranties or representations, nor does it accept any liabilities with respect to the programs or applications.

Library of Congress Cataloging-in-Publication Data

Baecker, Ronald M.
    Human factors and typography for more readable programs / Ronald M. Baecker, Aaron Marcus.
      p.   cm.
    Bibliography: p.
    Includes index.
    ISBN 0-201-10745-7
    1. Visual programming. 2. Computer graphics. 3. Human-computer interaction. I. Marcus, Aaron II. Title.
    QA76.75.B34   1990
    006.6–dc20   89-31709
                    CIP

Human Factors and Typography for More Readable Programs

Ronald M. Baecker, University of Toronto
Aaron Marcus, Aaron Marcus and Associates

Assisted by Ilona R. Posner, D. Hugh Redelmeier, Alan Rosenthal, and Cynthia Wong

Addison-Wesley Publishing Company

Reading, Massachusetts • Menlo Park, California • New York
Don Mills, Ontario • Wokingham, England • Amsterdam
Bonn • Sydney • Singapore • Tokyo • Madrid • San Juan

Production and Copyright Information

Typesetting

Dynamic Graphics Project
Computer Systems Research Institute
University of Toronto

Design and Specifications

The book design is by Aaron Marcus and Associates with the assistance of the Dynamic Graphics Project. The text is set in Times Roman Regular, roman, 12/14. Constructs from the C language appearing within the text are set in Helvetica Regular, roman and italic, 11/14. C program source text (code and comments) is set according to specifications presented in this book.

Library of Congress Cataloging-in-Publication Data

Baecker, Ronald M.
    Human factors and typography for more readable programs / Ronald M. Baecker, Aaron Marcus.
       p.   cm.
    Bibliography: p.
    Includes index.
    ISBN 0-201-10745-7
    1. Visual programming. 2. Computer graphics. 3. Human-computer interaction. I. Marcus, Aaron II. Title.
    QA76.75.B34   1990
    006.6–dc20   89-31709
                                         CIP

ABCDEFGHIJ—AL—89

Human Factors and Typography for More Readable Programs

Ronald M. Baecker, University of Toronto
Aaron Marcus, Aaron Marcus and Associates

Assisted by Ilona R. Posner, D. Hugh Redelmeier, Alan Rosenthal, and Cynthia Wong

Addison-Wesley Publishing Company

Reading, Massachusetts • Menlo Park, California • New York
Don Mills, Ontario • Wokingham, England • Amsterdam
Bonn • Sydney • Singapore • Tokyo • Madrid • San Juan

Dedication

We dedicate this book to Karyn Baecker and Leslie Becker Marcus, whose love, patience, and support helped us to complete this project.

Preface

Writing Programs

An *algorithm* is a precise description of a process or method for solving a problem. An algorithm expressed in a notation that a computer can "understand" is called a *program*. The system of notation within which the program is expressed is called a *programming language*.

Thousands of computer languages have been developed in the forty-year lifespan of the modern digital computer (Sammet, 1981). They go by names that range from the serious to the jocular, from those that pay homage to computer pioneers to those that attempt to denote what the language is used for, from acronyms to nonsense words. Typical examples are MAD, FORTRAN, SNOBOL, JOVIAL, MUMPS, PL/I, LOGO, Pascal, and Turing. Languages have progressed over the years from those that directly represent the sequences of binary numbers in a machine ("machine language") to those at progressively higher levels of abstraction ("high-level languages," "very-high-level languages"). Many may be described as "problem-oriented languages" by virtue of their orientation to some domain of problems for which the computer is to be used. Thus COGO and STRESS are used by civil engineers; SPSS and SAS by statisticians; and KEE, LOOPS, and HIRES by knowledge engineers.

Even more significant, however, is the current tendency of interactive application systems designed for modern personal computers to allow their command languages to be extended through what is usually known as a *macro* capability. For example, users of the spreadsheet 1-2-3™, the data base management system dBase III™, and the hypertext system and authoring environment Hypercard™ (Goodman, 1987) can all write programs to modify or extend the capabilities of their tools.

Reading Programs

The result has been an explosion in the activity of programming, one that mirrors the rapid growth of the computer industry over the past forty years and of the software industry over the past twenty years, and the exponential growth of the use of personal computers by non-computer specialists, by executives and middle managers, by accountants and engineers, by writers and designers. Several million individuals are now writing programs in North America. They are also *reading* programs, either those that they themselves have previously written or those that others have written.

The activity of reading programs has always received far less attention than that of writing programs. We teach students how to write programs, but not how to read them. We build tools to facilitate program composition and editing, but not program perusal, browsing, and understanding. Those designing new programming languages have focused on *logical* syntax and semantics, as well they should, but have typically ignored *visual* syntax and semantics, i.e., program presentation and appearance.

Program Appearance

Program appearance has changed little since the first high-level languages were developed in the second decade of computing. With a few exceptions, the most notable of which is APL, programs have been expressed and composed almost entirely out of alphanumeric symbols ("ASCII text"). They are presented in a single typeface, usually without even the use of boldface or italic, in a single point size, with fixed-width characters, fixed wordspacing, and fixed linespacing. Symbols, rules, grids, gray scale, diagrammatic elements, and pictures typically do not appear.

Yet, as readers, we are used to something better. We conduct our professional and personal lives daily with complicated symbolic systems such as circuits, maps, mathematics, and music that have sophisticated and well-developed notations, appropriate diagrammatic elements, typesetting rules, and graphic conventions. There are entire printing and publishing industries dedicated to facilitating effective communication in these disciplines. Furthermore, both experienced computer scientists and novice amateur programmers constantly use pictures and diagrams as tools for conceptualization, thought, and expression.

The impoverished appearance of programs today is an artifact of the technologies available for composing and printing them in the early days of computing, namely, the keypunch, the teletype, and the line printer. These technologies, now obsolete or almost obsolete, have been superseded by the interactive bit-mapped display and current hard-copy devices, primarily the laser printer. Programs can now easily be represented using those elements heretofore omitted, for example, multiple typefaces; variable weights, slants, point sizes, wordspacing, and linespacing; and rules, gray scale, and pictures.

Visual Programming

For over twenty-five years, many who have anticipated this possibility have focused on the vision of replacing the conventional programming language, which is primarily textual and one-dimensional, with one that is primarily visual, diagrammatic, and two-dimensional. This manner of presenting algorithms is called *visual programming* (Raeder, 1985; Myers, 1986; Chang, 1987; Shu, 1988). This is an important and exciting area for research, yet it is one that has so far yielded little of practical utility, little that can be scaled up from limited demonstrations into solutions to real problems.

Early in the 1980's, we were engaged as consultants on an ambitious visual programming project sponsored by the U.S. Defense Department's Advanced Research Projects Agency (DARPA) (Herot, et al., 1982; Brown, et al., 1985). The difficulty of the problem left us frustrated. We turned this frustration into a search for an approach that we thought could yield within a five year time span some significant and practical results.

Program Visualization

The result was a focus on *program visualization. To visualize* is "to see or form a mental image of." *Computer graphics* encompasses the disciplines of typography, graphic design, animation, and cinematography, and the technology of interactive computer graphics. *Computer program visualization* is the use of computer graphics to enhance the art of presenting and communicating programs and thereby to facilitate the understanding and effective use of computer programs by people. Whereas visual programming focuses on input, on the representation and specification of algorithms and programs in a novel form, our program visualization research concentrates on output, on the enhanced presentation of the large body of existing programs, their code, their documentation, and their behavior.

Program visualization's goal, expressed in broad terms, is to facilitate a clear and correct expression of the mental images of the producers (writers) of computer programs, and the communication of these mental images to the consumers (readers) of programs. Our particular approach as described in this book has been to apply the principles of graphic design and the tools of digital typography to enhance the presentation of computer program source text. In order to demonstrate the approach, we have worked with the C programming language (Kernighan and Ritchie, 1978; Harbison and Steele, 1984).

Goals of This Book

The goals of this book in presenting the results of our research are these:

- We intend to show that the presentation of program source text matters, and to demonstrate, by existence proof, that it is possible to produce significantly better program presentation than that to which we are accustomed. Effective program presentation makes good programs more understandable and bad programs more obvious. Effective program presentation helps us deal with a program's complexity. We can emphasize the program's hierarchic structure and the programmer's intent behind that structure.

- Effective program presentation, visually enhanced source code, and improved legibility and readability can be achieved through the systematic application of graphic design principles. We shall show how this can be done.

- The design for the appearance of a language can and should be documented in a *graphic design manual* for that language. We shall illustrate this concept by presenting a graphic design manual for C.

- The fact that principles are applied to achieve a design does not imply that the result is uniquely determined. There are many plausible designs that may be derived from the principles, and they must be evaluated by generating page after page of visual examples and by thoughtful scrutiny and testing of the strengths and weaknesses of each. Examples of these *systematic design variations* for the appearance of C are included in this book. The set of these variations is the first "catalog" of possibilities for the appearance of program source text, and constitutes a set of *template variations* (Marcus, 1987) for the electronic publishing of C programs. We hope that browsing this catalog will stimulate the visual imagination of the programming and computer science community, and lead to an active concern for improving the appearance of program texts.

- Effective program appearance may be automated. Most of the examples included in this book have been produced by a *visual compiler* for the C language, which takes unmodified C source text as its input, and produces as its output high-quality typeset presentations on a laser printer. The SEE visual compiler is also heavily parameterized to allow the customization of text displays to suit individual taste.

- The concepts developed in this book may be applied to other programming languages. In the case of languages similar to C, like Pascal, the principles and specifications are easily extendible; in the case of those more distant, for example, Prolog, there is still much to be learned from the approach and recommendations of this book. Unfortunately, space and time do not allow us to do more than assert this and include one suggestive example.

- Enhanced program presentation produces listings that facilitate the reading, comprehension, and effective use of computer programs. We shall summarize the results of some experiments substantiating this statement. We believe that the results of these experiments lend credence to the following assertion: *Making the interface to a program's source code and documentation intelligible, communicative, and attractive will ultimately lead to significant productivity gains and cost savings.*

- Our approach can be considered part of a broader effort to enhance the art of program writing, documentation, and illustration, an activity that Knuth (1984) has so aptly named "literate programming." We have considered the entire context in which code is presented and used, a context which includes the supporting texts and notations that make a program a living piece of written communication. We seek thereby to enhance programmers' abilities to construct, refine, store, retrieve, scan, read, and manipulate the texts and documents required to do their jobs. Our effort explores an application of the emerging technology of *electronic publishing* to an industry to which it has paradoxically not yet been significantly applied, namely, to the software industry. Our work should encourage the manufacturers of technical documentation systems to integrate their functionality with emerging environments and systems for computer-aided software engineering (CASE).
- Finally, although this book is a research monograph primarily presenting original work and results, we do briefly survey and cite relevant research from other investigators. The publications describing this work are widely scattered and not easily accessible. Unearthing this collection has been a slow process; we hope that those that follow after us will have an easier time because of our efforts.

Caveats and Disclaimers

On the other hand, the reader would be wise to remember that:
- We do not assert that the design we present is the best possible design for C. It is a plausible and, we think, compelling design, but other designers may approach the problem from a completely different perspective and achieve very different results.
- Furthermore, we predict that almost all individuals, particularly those who have worked with C for a long time, will find some aspects of our design that they do not like. If this causes them to think how they would have done it differently, then we shall have succeeded in raising the awareness, consciousness, and graphical literacy of the programming community.
- Our work deals with improving the presentation and appearance of C source code, not with the writing of stylistically proper source code. This book is therefore complementary to books and monographs that deal with the latter topic, for example, Plum (1984) and Cannon, et al. (1987).
- Although the presentations in this book are on paper, many of the concepts we present are equally relevant to the design of effective screen displays. Only modest changes in approach are required to account for the facts that the "page size" is different and more variable, the resolution is lower, and the methods of navigation are far richer. We shall report briefly on some preliminary results from a follow-on project designing and constructing an interactive system for the browsing and display of visually-enhanced source code (Small, 1989).
- Although we shall present empirical evidence demonstrating the utility of the techniques, we stress the point that different views of programs are appropriate for different purposes. The *rapid creation* of novel views can be realized through an interactive implementation of a system such as SEE. The *design and selection* of optimal views requires work on cognitive models of program reading and understanding that goes beyond the scope of this book.

Who Should Read This Book

This introduction to the issues, principles, method, and results of program visualization should be of interest and value to at least nine areas of professional practice, research, and teaching:

- Programming
- C Programming
- Programming language design
- Software engineering
- Software documentation
- Human-computer interaction; human factors of computing systems
- Digital typography
- Electronic publishing
- Graphic design

Computer scientists, programmers, and their managers should find the results relevant to their own efforts to improve the readability of their computer-generated documents. Teachers of programming may find that improved appearance of code and documentation helps make the literature and examples more interesting, compelling, and understandable.

The C programming community obviously stands to benefit the most from the recommendations for improved appearance of the language. As the number of programmers has mushroomed in the last decade, it seems inevitable that improved presentation among expert, occasional, and novice programmers will become an essential component of good writing style. This book presents an examination of a candidate for industry-wide conventions that could benefit the entire community.

Unfortunately, the C language does not encourage readability. The preprocessor is a particular culprit because, in effect, it allows the programmer to change the language. Language designers of the future, aware of the visualization possibilities illustrated in this book and more sensitive to issues of effective presentation and communication, will, it is hoped, design languages and their appearances so that they are easier to read and easier to understand. We believe that all future programming language definitions should be accompanied by specifications for functional and aesthetic appearance, and that all future programming language processors should be accompanied by visible language processors that can automate the production of this appearance.

As activity in software engineering increases, professionals are noting that good presentation of code, comments, and documentation are a necessary part of good project management. Software support for document representation, including paper, hypertext, and hypermedia versions, are beginning to emerge. The textual representation of code is not likely to disappear for a long time, if ever, and the conventions presented in this book can provide assistance to software engineers who seek useful heuristics as well as general principles for code presentation.

Another group of readers are documentation specialists: technical writers and editors, graphic designers, and graphic artists. Until now these professionals have not been concerned with the level of documentation that included computer program source code because they could not readily manipulate it. Given the existence of a graphic design manual for a programming language and the software to support it, documentation specialists can now help programmers meet the visual requirements of good programming "literature" without taking too much time away from program development.

The human-computer interaction community of human factors, psychology, design, and computer science professionals should derive concrete knowledge that will aid them in improving the user interface to code and document depiction specifically, and to text depiction in general. As bit-mapped high resolution displays become commonplace in all application areas, almost every screen will require the analysis of content and typographic representation that this book demonstrates. Although the subject matter and details of presentation may differ, the principles presented here may be of value to improving the graphic design of interactive documents.

Digital typography researchers and professionals should be intrigued by the many challenges to good font design and font management that the code depiction established in this book suggests. An entirely new family of fonts might emerge that is optimized for code depiction.

The field of electronic publishing, whether for low-cost desktop publishing or for more elaborate, high-quality production, whether oriented to paper documents or hypertext/hypermedia interactive screen documents, should find much of interest and value in the suggestions for document design and the depiction of complex text. Researchers will find many challenging display conditions (e.g., parametric adjustment of detailed spatial positioning for multiple-font text) that go beyond the capabilities of most current commercial products.

Finally, graphic designers will benefit from the examples and process that achieve logical, systems-oriented book design, page layout, and typography. This approach to graphic design was foreseen by the Swiss graphic designer and theoretician Karl Gerstner (1965), who proposed an algorithmic attitude to type design, photography, spatial layout, and color selection long before computer technology became widespread. The style of design extends and validates the principles of the so-called Swiss graphic design approach to a new area of visual communication.[†]

In summary, program visualization is a topic of importance to a wide variety of professionals concerned about improved communication through visible language, the literature in which we convey the structures and processes of daily life.

[†]   Design professionals have already acknowledged the value of our approach through an award presented by an Industrial Design magazine in its 1986 Annual Design Review. (*ID* (*Industrial Design*) 33(4), 1986, pp. 133–134.)

Acknowledgments

HCR Corporation, Toronto, Ontario, Canada, and Aaron Marcus and Associates (AM+A), Berkeley, California, U.S.A., carried out the original program visualization research on which this book is based. The work was then continued, expanded, and refined by the Dynamic Graphics Project of the Computer Systems Research Institute of the University of Toronto.

Ron Baecker, founder and Chairman of the Board of HCR, and Professor of Computer Science, Electrical Engineering, and Management at the University of Toronto, and Aaron Marcus, Principal of AM+A, were co-principal investigators, conceptualizing, structuring, and supervising the research. Michael Arent, while he was Design Director of AM+A, played a key role in the first phase of the research and in the development of the initial C language specifications. Ron Baecker, Aaron Marcus, and Michael Arent did the early conceptual work on prototype visualizations for the C language, and were assisted in their preparation by Bruce Browne, Designer at AM+A, John Longarini, programmer at HCR, and Ilona Posner, a student at the University of Toronto. Paul Breslin, John Longarini, Allen McIntosh, Chris Sturgess, and Tracy Tims, programmers at HCR, wrote the software that enabled C programs to be compiled and displayed automatically in the manner recommended by the manual. This work was later carried further by Jin Kang, Hugh Redelmeier, Alan Rosenthal, and Ilona Posner at the University, who all contributed significantly to elaborating the concepts and improving the designs presented in this book. Hugh Redelmeier's deep understanding of the subtleties of the C language coupled with a strong emerging design sensitivity were of special value. David Slocombe of SoftQuad, Inc., Toronto, also added software under contract to HCR.

Ron Baecker is the primary author of the book, with the collaboration and assistance of Aaron Marcus. Aaron Marcus is the primary designer of the appearance conventions, with the collaboration and assistance of Ron Baecker and his staff, particularly Ilona Posner, Hugh Redelmeier, and Alan Rosenthal. Michael Arent and Tracy Tims prepared early drafts of much of the C program graphic design guidelines and specifications. Ilona Posner (with help from Hugh Redelmeier) carefully executed the design variations and then prepared the resulting figures, which appear in Chapter 3 of the book. Alan Rosenthal did an equivalently thorough job for the Eliza program book and for Chapter 5, as did Yari Jeada and Sandra Ragan of AM+A, working under the capable supervision of N. Gregory Galle, for Appendix B. Hugh Redelmeier and Alan Rosenthal were particularly helpful in reviewing and critiquing drafts of the manuscript. Ilona Posner's skilled and diligent maintenance and enhancement of a bizarre and arcane set of TROFF macros is gratefully acknowledged.

The U.S. Defense Department's Advanced Research Projects Agency, System Sciences Division, funded the first phase of the research under ARPA Order 4469. We are indebted to Craig Fields, Clint Kelly, and Steve Squires of DARPA and Andrew Chruscicki of the Rome Air Development Center for their support. Later funding came from the Natural Sciences and Engineering Research Council of Canada under a Strategic Grant. Additional support to our laboratory at the University of Toronto from the Province of Ontario Information Technology Research Centre, from Xerox Corporation, from

Silicon Graphics, Inc., and especially from Apple Computer, Inc., is gratefully acknowledged.

We are deeply appreciative to Michael, John, Tracy, Ilona, Alan, and Hugh, and to Cynthia Wong, my assistant, for the extraordinarily long hours they spent in the final stages of completing the original final report or this book. We would additionally like to thank Edmund Reinhardt, Peter Rowley, Carson Schutze, June Simonsen, Sara Mead, Penny Photopoulos, Lu-anne Lee, Barb McLatchie, Janice Herrington, Karyn Baecker, and Leslie Becker Marcus, who also assisted in the work.

A number of individuals contributed unique and valuable advice with respect to technical problems encountered during the research. Professor Ian Spence helped us in the design, selection, and application of experimental design and statistical methods. Dr. Phil Barnard and Prof. Marilyn Mantei advised us on issues of experimental design. Dr. Bob Sproull made a number of helpful suggestions relating to the pragmatics of writing and maintaining large C programs, in particular, and relating to the entire manuscript, in general.

Mark Green offered some helpful comments on the manuscript at an early stage. Henry Spencer graciously contributed his code for the Eliza program, and undertook a careful review of the manuscript in its almost final state. Marilyn Mantei and Paul Oman made a number of helpful comments on this same manuscript. Ian Small also reviewed this manuscript, and contributed a large number of insightful comments and suggestions. We are thankful for their assistance, and also to the four individuals who formally reviewed and offered valuable feedback on the manuscript: Richard Furuta, Harry M. Hersh, P.J. Plauger, and John M. Nevison.

We owe a hugh debt to Ian Small, George Drettakis, and Carson Schutze for so ably caring for and feeding the Dynamic Graphics Project computer systems. We also thank for assistance in obtaining and preparing illustrations Rick Beach, John Buchanan, Dave Mazierski, Ian Small, and particularly Avi Naiman; and, for the superb job she did on the Index, Cynthia Wong.

Many individuals at Addison-Wesley contributed to the process of the writing, editing, and publishing of this book. We are very grateful to Peter Gordon, Senior Editor in Computer Science, for his interest, support, and patience, to his assistant Helen Goldstein, to Karen Myer, Production Supervisor, and to Mary Dyer, Permissions Editor, who also helped see our book through the final printing stage.

Contents

Figures

Chapter 1   Visualizing Programs

"Nobody can seriously have believed that executives could read programs. Why should they? Even programmers do not read programs."

Gerald M. Weinberg (1971), *The Psychology of Computer Programming*, New York: Van Nostrand Reinhold Company, p. 5. Reprinted with permission.

Section 1.1

Designing Software Presentations

The computing profession is on the horns of a dilemma: More programming is being done than ever before by programmers with varying degrees of skill and commitment to good programming practice and meaningful documentation. Although computer graphics technology has become more powerful, cheaper, and more accessible, program appearance and methods of program presentation have made little use of this technology's potential.

A natural development would be for computer science to learn and apply the lesson that the discipline of graphic design teaches so vividly: *Visual form matters. Effective representation and presentation aids thought, the management of complexity, problem solving, and articulate expression.* In this book we seek to demonstrate and explain how communication about programs and comprehension of programs can be aided by paying attention to the visual schema embodying the programs and the visual appearance of programs.[†]

We begin this exploration into *program visualization* by focusing on every programmer's vehicle of discourse: the program source text, expressed in some computer language and appearing in some form on a physical medium. We employ graphic design and the technologies of high-resolution bit-mapped displays and laser printers to generate far richer representations of program source text than those produced conventionally. Enhanced appearance is achieved using multiple typefaces and fonts, variable point sizes, variable character widths, variable wordspacing and linespacing, non-alphanumeric symbols, gray scale tints, rules, and variable spatial location of elements on a page.

Another way of understanding this approach is the following. We start with the elements of a programming language, such as tokens, expressions, and statements. We add the elements of *visible language*, such as typography, symbolism, and layout. Then, using graphic design principles, we develop a system of mapping elements of the programming language to elements of the visible language in such a way that program appearance is enhanced and essential program structure is made visible.

In this book, we illustrate the approach by applying it to the C programming language. We chose to work with C for three reasons: (1) it is a very important language commercially; (2) its typical current appearance has many aspects in which legibility and readability can be improved; and, (3) we use it heavily.

Furthermore, we can also develop entirely new program representations and methods of presentation that will further aid in bringing out important program structure. These techniques will be introduced and illustrated in Chapter 5 of this book.

[†]   For more detail, see Section 2.3: The Program Visualization Approach.

Section 1.2

Preview of Results

Let's look at an example, to see where we will be heading. The example is a C program that accepts a phone number expressed as a sequence of digits and prints out a list of "reasonable" equivalents with all digits between two and nine replaced by a selection of corresponding letters from a phone dial.[†] The program's definition of reasonable is that the words produced must each contain at least one vowel. Thus, given "765" as its input, the program produces the following as its output: poj, pok, pol, roj, rok, rol, soj, sok, and sol.

The program is first shown as Figure 1.1 on pages 4 and 5 as it is output on a typical dot matrix line printer, a device similar to that used by hundreds of thousands of programmers of microcomputers and minicomputers. Even the lightness of the type, caused by a worn out ribbon, reflects an unfortunate but representative aspect of the way most line printers are used. This light text of course impedes legibility and readability.

The program is presented again as Figure 1.2 on pages 6 and 7. However, this time the program has been output on a modern laser printer, using fixed-width type in a single font at a single point size, and with a format similar to that in Figure 1.1. The result is typical of what would be considered a good program presentation using conventional program-printing technology. Legibility and readability are mildly enhanced over the presentation in Figure 1.1.

Figure 1.3 on pages 9 and 11 shows the output of the SEE processor, a program we have developed that produces enhanced presentations of C source text. The SEE processor drives the same laser printer as in Figure 1.2 but now exploits far more of its capabilities. The phone number program was not modified at all for input to SEE; exactly the same text had been input to the listing program that produced the previous figures. The SEE output was altered only in the addition of some aspects of the headers and the footnotes that are not yet handled automatically by SEE.

Figure 1.1: *The "phone.c" program conventionally formatted and output on a dot matrix printer (see pages 4 and 5).*

Figure 1.2: *The same program conventionally formatted and output on a laser printer (see pages 6 and 7).*

Figure 1.3: *The same program produced by the SEE visual compiler (see pages 9 and 11).*

---

†   The example is not intended to be a paradigm of programming style and virtue, but merely a short, self-contained illustration of fairly typical C code.

Apr 20 12:59 1989   phone.c Page 1

```
/*
 * phone.c - Prints all potential words corresponding to a given phone number.
 *
 * Only words containing vowels are printed.
 * Acceptable phone numbers range from 1 to 10 digits.
 */

#include <string.h>
#include <stdio.h>

typedef int      bool;
#define FALSE    0
#define TRUE     1

char    *label[] = { /* labels on each digit of dial */
    "0",
    "1",         "abc",    "def",
    "ghi",       "jkl",    "mno",
    "prs",       "tuv",    "wxy"
};

#define PNMAX    10       /* max digits in phone number */

int     digits; /* actual number of digits */
int     pn[PNMAX];        /* phone number */
char    *label_ptr[PNMAX];      /* current position in label, per digit */

main(argc, argv)
    int argc;
    char        *argv[];
{
    register int      i;
    bool              foundvowel = FALSE;

    /* For each phone argument ... */
    while (*++argv != NULL) {
        if (!getpn(*argv))
            fprintf(stderr, "PhoneName:  %s is not a phone number\n", *argv);
        else {
            /* For beginnings of label sequences */
            for (i = 0; i < PNMAX; ++i)  /* Reset label_ptr (pointers).*/
                label_ptr[i] = label[pn[i]];
            /* For each combination of characters ... */
            do {
                for (i = 0; i < digits; ++i) {
                    if (strchr("aeiou", *label_ptr[i]) != NULL)
                        foundvowel = TRUE;
                }
                if (foundvowel)  /* Only print things with vowels! */
                {
                    for (i=0; i!=digits; i++)
                        printf("%c",*label_ptr[i]);
                    printf("\n");
                }
                foundvowel = FALSE;
            } while (incr());
```

```
Apr 20 12:59 1989   phone.c Page 2


        }
      }
    }


/*
 * Encode phone number as a vector of digits, without punctuation.
 * Returns number of digits in phone number, or FALSE to indicate failure.
 */

static bool
getpn(str)
    char         *str;
{
    int  i=0;

    while (*str != '\0') {
        if (i >= PNMAX)
            return FALSE;
        /*  Set pn to the digits ignoring spaces and dashes */
        if (*str!=' ' && *str!='-') {
            if ('0'<=*str && *str<='9') {
                pn[i++] = *str - '0';
            } else
                return FALSE; /*not a number or empty*/
        }
        ++str;
    }

    return       (digits = i) !=0;   /*Set digits to length of phone no.*/
}


/*
 * Advance a single label_ptr; return FALSE when done.
 */

static bool
incr()
{
    register int       i;

    for (i = digits ; --i >= 0;) {
        if (*++label_ptr[i] == '\0')
            label_ptr[i] = label[pn[i]];
        else
            return TRUE;
    }
    return FALSE;
}
```

Apr 20 12:54 1989   phone.c Page 1

```
/*
 * phone.c - Prints all potential words corresponding to a given phone number.
 *
 * Only words containing vowels are printed.
 * Acceptable phone numbers range from 1 to 10 digits.
 */

#include <string.h>
#include <stdio.h>

typedef int     bool;
#define FALSE   0
#define TRUE    1

char    *label[] = { /* labels on each digit of dial */
    "0",
    "1",         "abc",   "def",
    "ghi",       "jkl",   "mno",
    "prs",       "tuv",   "wxy"
};

#define PNMAX   10        /* max digits in phone number */

int     digits; /* actual number of digits */
int     pn[PNMAX];        /* phone number */
char    *label_ptr[PNMAX];       /* current position in label, per digit */

main(argc, argv)
    int argc;
    char        *argv[];
{
    register int        i;
    bool                foundvowel = FALSE;

    /* For each phone argument ... */
    while (*++argv != NULL) {
        if (!getpn(*argv))
            fprintf(stderr, "PhoneName:  %s is not a phone number\n", *argv);
        else {
            /* For beginnings of label sequences */
            for (i = 0; i < PNMAX; ++i)  /* Reset label_ptr (pointers).*/
                label_ptr[i] = label[pn[i]];
            /* For each combination of characters ... */
            do {
                for (i = 0; i < digits; ++i) {
                    if (strchr("aeiou", *label_ptr[i]) != NULL)
                        foundvowel = TRUE;
                }
                if (foundvowel)  /* Only print things with vowels! */
                {
                    for (i=0; i!=digits; i++)
                        printf("%c",*label_ptr[i]);
                    printf("\n");
                }
                foundvowel = FALSE;
            } while (incr());
```

```
Apr 20 12:54 1989   phone.c Page 2


                }
            }
        }
/*
 * Encode phone number as a vector of digits, without punctuation.
 * Returns number of digits in phone number, or FALSE to indicate failure.
 */

static bool
getpn(str)
    char        *str;
{
    int i=0;

    while (*str != '\0') {
        if (i >= PNMAX)
            return FALSE;
        /*  Set pn to the digits ignoring spaces and dashes */
        if (*str!=' ' && *str!='-') {
            if ('0'<=*str && *str<='9') {
                pn[i++] = *str - '0';
            } else
                return FALSE; /*not a number or empty*/
        }
        ++str;
    }

    return      (digits = i) !=0;  /*Set digits to length of phone no.*/
}

/*
 * Advance a single label_ptr; return FALSE when done.
 */

static bool
incr()
{
    register int        i;

    for (i = digits ; --i >= 0;) {
        if (*++label_ptr[i] == '\0')
            label_ptr[i] = label[pn[i]];
        else
            return TRUE;
    }
    return FALSE;
}
```

We explain salient features of our design in terms of the example using notes that appear here and on page 10, The reference numbers that appear below, e.g., **(1)** and **(17)**, refer to the small numbers in circles that appear in the right margin of the corresponding pages, 9 and 11. The notes are structured in terms of a taxonomy of C constructs to be introduced in Chapter 3.

The Presentation of Program Structure

The program is presented on loose-leaf 8.5″ x 11″ pages, each of which is separated into four regions, a header **(1)**, a footnote area **(17)**, a main text column for the code and most of the comments **(3, right)**, and a marginalia comment column **(3, left)**.

The listing of each file appears as a separate "chapter" with the filename shown as a very large, bold title **(2)**.

Extra white space has been introduced to provide adequate separation between the *prologue* comments (see below) and the code **(5)**, between function definitions and sequences of declarations **(10)**, between individual function definitions, and between the header and the body within a function definition **(14)**.

Cross-references relating uses of global variables to the location of their definitions are included as footnotes to the source text **(17)**.

The Spatial Composition of Comments

Each file may include, at or near its beginning, a *prologue* comment that describes the purpose of the module **(4)**. The prologue comment is displayed in a serif font laid over a light gray tone. The size of type and gray value have been selected to insure legibility of two generations of photocopies of the original printed pages. There is ample margin allowance around the text to ensure readability.

Comments that are located on the same lines as source code, which we call *marginalia* comments, are displayed in a small-sized serif font in the marginalia column **(9, left)**. These items are intended to be short, single-line phrases.

The Presentation of Function Definitions

The introductory text of a function definition, that is, the function name, is shown as a "headline," in a large sans-serif type **(11)**.

A heavy rule appears under the introductory text of a function definition **(12)**.

A light rule appears under the declaration of the formal parameters **(13)**.

The Presentation of Declarations

Identifiers being declared are aligned to a single implied vertical line located at an appropriate horizontal tab position, 16 picas into the main code column **(7)**.

Initializers are displayed at reasonable tab positions, with the programmer's carriage returns being respected as requests for "new lines" **(8)**.

The Presentation of Preprocessor Commands

The "**#**" signifying a preprocessor command is exdented to enhance its distinguishability from ordinary C source text **(6)**.

Within macro definitions, macros and their values are presented at appropriate horizontal tab positions, 8 and 16 picas into the main code column **(6)**.

The Visual Parsing of Statements

Systematic indentation and placement of key words is employed **(15)**.

Since curly braces are redundant with systematic indentation, they are removed in this example **(15)**. Whether this happens or not is under control of the user.

With conventional program listing technology, it is often impossible to tell without turning the page where a particular control construct (in this case, the *for*) continues on the following page. We solve the problem by introducing an ellipsis, located in line with the *for*, signifying that the first statement on the next page is at the same nesting level as the *for* **(16)**.

explorer:/red/ilona/figs/new   phone.c (1 of 2)   20 Apr 12:54   Revision 1   Page 9

Dynamic Graphics Project   main()   Phone Name   Printed 2 Jun 13:56
University of Toronto, with
Aaron Marcus and Associates
Berkeley

Chapter 1

phone.c

(1)

(2)

(3)

phone.c – Prints all potential words corresponding to a given phone number.

Only words containing vowels are printed.
Acceptable phone numbers range from 1 to 10 digits.

(4)

(5)

```
#include            <string.h>
#include            <stdio.h>
```

(6)

```
typedef int                         bool;
#define      FALSE                  0
#define      TRUE                   1
```

(7)

labels on each digit of dial

```
char                                *label[] = {
    "0",
    "1",     "abc",     "def",
    "ghi",   "jkl",     "mno",
    "prs",   "tuv",     "wxy"
};
```

(8)

max digits in phone number

```
#define      PNMAX                  10
```

(9)

actual number of digits
```
int                                 digits;
```
phone number
```
int                                 pn[PNMAX];
```
current position in label, per digit
```
char                                *label_ptr[PNMAX];
```

(10)

main(argc, argv)

(11)

(12)

```
    int                             argc;
    char                            *argv[];
```

(13)

```
    register int                    i;
    bool                            foundvowel = FALSE;
```

(14)

For each phone argument ...

```
    while (*++argv  != NULL)
        if ( !getpn(*argv))
            fprintf(stderr, "PhoneName:  %s is not a phone number\n", *argv);
        else
```

(15)

For beginnings of label sequences

Reset label_ptr (pointers).

```
        for (i = 0;  i < PNMAX;  ++i)
            label_ptr[i] = label[pn[i]];
        ...
```

(16)

digits→ 2   label→ 1, 2   label_ptr→ 1, 2   pn→ 1, 2

(17)

The Spatial Composition of Comments (continued)

Comments that are *external* to function definitions are displayed in a serif font laid over a light gray tone (**26**).

Comments that are *internal* to function definitions are also displayed in a serif font laid over a light gray tone and appropriately indented to match the current statement's nesting (**28**).

The Presentation of Function Definitions (continued)

The function type specifier, which indicates the type of the value returned by the function, if any, appears on a line by itself above the function name (**27**).

The Visual Parsing of Statements (continued)

When nested statements cross a page boundary, the "nesting context" is displayed in the second column of the header (**19**), just above the code.

The Visual Parsing of Expressions

Parentheses and brackets are emboldened to call attention to grouped items. Nested parentheses are varied in size to aid the parsing of the expression (**25**).

Unary operators such as "++" and the unary "*" are raised (turned into superscripts) to make them easier to distinguish from binary operators (**30**).

The wordspacing between operators within an expression is varied to aid the reader. Operands are displayed closer to operators of high precedence than to operators of low precedence (**29**).

Typographic Encodings of Token Attributes

Most tokens are shown in a regular sans-serif font; reserved words are shown in italic sans-serif type (**20**).

The global variable in C is a fundamental mechanism through which functions can communicate indirectly, and as such also represents a major source of programming errors. We therefore call attention to most uses of globals (but not function names, invocations, or manifest constants) by highlighting them in boldface (**20**).

Macro names, which by C programming convention are all upper case, are shown with the first letter normal size and the remainder of the word in "small caps" (**22**).

String constants are shown in a small-sized fixed-width serif font (**21**).

The Typography of Program Punctuation

In this example the ";" appears in 10 point regular Helvetica type, and thus uses the same typographic parameters as does much of the program code. On the other hand, in order to enhance legibility and readability, the "," has been enlarged to 14 points, the "*" has been enlarged to 12 points, and the "!" has been set in boldface (**24**). Slight repositioning has also been carried out on individual punctuation marks.

The letterspacing between individual characters of multi-character operators such as the "!=", the "<=", and the "++" has been adjusted, to make the symbols more legible as a unit (**23**).

Symbol substitutions are employed where they can reduce the possibilities for error and thereby enhance readability. Since C's two uses of *while* can be confused under some circumstances, we add an upwards-pointing arrow to the *while* that is part of a *do...while* (**25**).

The Presentation of Program Environment

The header describes the context of the source code that appears on the page, including the location of the file from which the listing was made, the last time the file was updated, the page number within the listing, the time the listing was made, and, in the second column, the function name of the code that first appears at the top of the page (**18**).

(18)

while...else...   (19)

For each combination of characters ...

```
        do
            for (i = 0;  i < digits;  ++i)                              (20)
                if (strchr("aeiou", *label_ptr[i]) != NULL)            (21)
                    foundvowel = TRUE;                                 (22)
            if (foundvowel)
                for (i = 0;  i != digits;  i++)                        (23)
                    printf("%c", *label_ptr[i]);                       (24)
                printf("\n");
            foundvowel = FALSE;
        ↑while  (incr());                                              (25)
```

Only print things with vowels!

Encode phone number as a vector of digits, without punctuation.
Returns number of digits in phone number, or FALSE to indicate failure.   (26)

```
static bool                                                             (27)
getpn(str)
```

char	*str;
int	i = 0;

```
    while (*str != '\0')
        if (i >= PNMAX)
            return FALSE;
```

Set pn to the digits ignoring spaces and dashes   (28)

```
        if (*str != ' '  &&  *str != '-')                              (29)
            if ('0' <= *str  &&  *str <= '9')
                pn[i++] = *str - '0';                                  (30)
            else
                return FALSE;
        ++str;
    return (digits = i) != 0;
```

not a number or empty

Set digits to length of phone no.

Advance a single label_ptr; return FALSE when done.

```
static bool
incr()
```

register int	i;

```
    for (i = digits;  --i >= 0;)
        if (*++label_ptr[i] == '\0')
            label_ptr[i] = label[pn[i]];
        else
            return TRUE;
    return FALSE;
```

Section 1.3

Accomplishments and Significance

At first glance, it may seem that we are talking only about work on "pretty-printing."[†] What we shall present, however, goes significantly beyond conventional approaches to prettyprinting in several ways:

- The availability of rich typographic and pictorial representations with many more degrees of freedom changes the nature of the problem to one that is *qualitatively different* from that of prettyprinting on a line printer.
- We have identified basic graphic design principles for program visualization and developed a framework for applying them to particular programming languages.
- We have systematically carried out graphic design experimental variations (see Chapter 3) in order to arrive at a carefully considered set of design guidelines and recommended conventions for program appearance.
- We have formalized these guidelines and specifications in a graphic design manual for C program appearance (see Chapter 4).
- We have developed a flexible experimental tool, the SEE *visual compiler* (see Section 6.6), which automates the production of enhanced C source text.[††] SEE is highly parametric, thus allowing easy experimentation in trying out novel variations, and also suiting the great variety of style preferences that characterizes the community of programmers.
- We have enlarged the scope of the study of program printing from the narrow issue of formatting source code and comments to a far broader concern with programs as technical publications (see Chapter 5). This includes an investigation of methods for designing, typesetting, printing, and publishing integrated bodies of program text and metatext, and also the invention of new displays of essential program structure, which we call *program views*.

In carrying out this work, our goal has been to make computer program source text more effective for the programmer, that is:

- more *legible*, meaning that individual symbols comprising the program should be clearly discriminable and recognizable.
- more *readable* and *comprehensible*, meaning that we should be able to read a text with greater speed and deeper understanding.
- more *vivid*, meaning that the text should be able to stimulate our thoughts and our imagination.
- more *appealing*, so that we enjoy and appreciate the experience.
- more *memorable*, so that we are better able to recognize and recall what we have read.
- more *useful*, in terms of such common programmer tasks as scanning, navigating, manipulating, posing hypotheses and answering questions, debugging, and maintaining the program.

We shall return to these issues, which represent the payoff for program visualization, in Chapter 6.

---

†   For further discussion of prettyprinting, see Section 2.2: Perspectives on the Role of Visualization.

††   Because our prototype is so fragile, we regretfully cannot make it available to other investigators.

Our work demonstrates the benefits of program visualization. The conventions we recommend in this book improve the legibility and readability of computer program source text. The program views we introduce in this book help us to master program complexity. Our approach also provides a paradigm that can be used for exploring program visualization in other languages and enhancing the communication effectiveness of much of electronic publishing. *Human Factors and Typography for More Readable Programs* helps to establish programming as a literary form deserving a mature graphic appearance.

Section 1.4   Organization and Contents of This Book

The remaining chapters of this book present the detailed background, method, and results of our investigation into portraying programs effectively.

Chapter 2: *Background and Motivation* further introduces and motivates our design of an enhanced presentation of C source text by discussing the use of visualization in other disciplines, the nature of complementary work in program visualization, and the method by which we carried out our research and developed our design.

Chapter 3: *Mapping C Source Text to Effective Visual Presentations* begins by developing a taxonomy of C program elements, a taxonomy of visual elements, and a set of graphic design principles. We then present a series of variations in which C constructs are mapped into visual presentations. All the examples are motivated and analyzed in terms of the graphic design principles, so that they can be maximally instructive to those working on their own design of the appearance of C or of any other programming language.

Chapter 4: *A Graphic Design Manual for the C Programming Language* formalizes the set of recommended techniques by developing a set of *guidelines* and *specifications* for source code appearance, which together constitute a *graphic design manual* for the C language. The design manual describes systematically the typographic appearance of each syntactic construct in the language.

Chapter 5: *Programs as Publications* expands our focus from the program code and comments to the entire body of supporting text that results in a documented and usable program, a *technical publication*. Again we develop a taxonomy of documentation elements and a set of design principles. We apply these concepts to a real, medium-sized program, resulting in examples of program views and of a prototype program book.

Chapter 6: *Future Issues in Program Presentation* summarizes the work and discusses experimental validation, implementation, extensions to interactive applications, open research problems, and our conclusions.

Chapter 2

Background and Motivation

"We need to focus research on the problem of source code. We need to get our minds off the abstract and onto the concrete world of real programmers and programming practice..."

Mark Weiser, "Source Code," *Computer* 20(11), p. 73. Copyright © 1987, IEEE. Reprinted with permission.

Section 2.1	# Managing Complex Software

A *program* is a precise description, expressed in a *computer programming language*, of a system, process, or problem solution. Thus we write programs to serve as payroll or inventory systems, as controllers of robots, as "intelligent" tutors, equation solvers, or chess players.

The Software Life Cycle

Large programs typically progress through a "life cycle" (Belady and Lehman, 1976; Aron, 1983), which begins with an analysis of the *requirements* posed by a problem and the definition of a set of *functional specifications* of a proposed solution. The next steps are the creation of a *design* embodying these specifications and the construction of an *implementation* based on the design.[†] Implementations must undergo a phase of *debugging* and should also be refined based on feedback received from users. *Documentation* of the program has to be created. Finally, sustained and long-term use requires that *maintenance* be done throughout the lifetime of the program. Maintenance often consumes from 50% to 75% of the total costs incurred over that lifetime (Boehm, 1981, p. 533).

Incomprehensible Programs

Maintenance is difficult and costly because most real programs are complex and hard to understand. There are many reasons for this:
- We increasingly demand more and more functionality in programs and in *systems* of programs. The result can be systems that are upwards of millions of lines of code.
- The specifications of large programs continually evolve as they are used. Systems must therefore be modified again and again to meet these changing specifications.
- Turnover in the software development and support community is great.

The result is that we have programs of greater and greater size that are incomprehensible, understood neither by their authors nor by their maintainers. In *Computer Power and Human Reason*, Joseph Weizenbaum (1976) asserts that this is a very dangerous phenomenon (p. 236):

"Our society's growing reliance on computer systems that were initially intended to 'help' people make analysis and decisions, but which have long since both surpassed the understanding of their users and become indispensable to them, is a very serious development. It has two important consequences. First, decisions are made with the aid of, and sometimes entirely by, computers whose programs no one any longer knows explicitly or understands. Hence no one can know the criteria or the rules on which such decisions are based. Second, the systems of rules and criteria that are embodied in such computer systems become immune to change, because, in the absence of a detailed understanding of the inner workings of a computer system, any substantial modification of it is very likely to render the whole system inoperative and possibly unrestorable. Such computer systems can therefore only grow. And their growth and the increasing reliance placed on them is then accompanied by an increasing legitimation of their 'knowledge base.'"

Already our society's health is tightly coupled to computer programs that control vital functions such as the financial markets. The design and linkage of computer-controlled financial systems has already contributed to wild fluctuations of the market (Sanger, 1987). This is clearly one of many areas where impervious and imperious code could play havoc with society.

---

† These steps are often intertwined, and some skipped, in what is known as "exploratory programming" (Swartout and Balzer, 1982).

Software Engineering Approaches

The field of *software engineering* concerns itself with the technology and processes of software development, and thus it has approached the problems of software complexity and incomprehensibility in a number of ways.

The most widespread development has been the concern with the logical structure and expressive style of programs, resulting in modern software development techniques such as top-down design and stepwise refinement (Wirth, 1971), structured programming (Dahl et al., 1972), modularity (Parnas, 1972), and software tools (Kernighan and Plauger, 1976).

A second development has been the marked improvement in the clarity and expressive power of programming languages, as can be seen, for example, in Modula (Wirth, 1977) and Turing (Holt and Cordy, 1985, 1989).

Another kind of development has occurred in the organization and management of the team that produces the writing. This has given rise to concepts such as chief programmer teams (Baker, 1972), structured walk-throughs (Yourdon, 1979), active design reviews (Parnas and Weiss, 1985), and defect measurement (Basili and Rombach, 1987).

The fourth development has been enhanced technology that supports the writing and maintaining of programs. This includes high-performance software development workstations (Gutz, et al., 1981) and integrated software development environments (Wasserman, 1981) such as Interlisp (Teitelman, 1979) and Cedar (Teitelman, 1985).

A fifth, related, and more recent phenomenon is the rapidly accelerating activity in the field of CASE — computer-aided software engineering (Dart, et al., 1987; Chikofsky, 1988; Chikofsky and Rubenstein, 1988). Insights derived in the first four approaches are used to produce integrated environments in which programs can be created from specifications that are far terser and higher level than those required by conventional high-level languages.

One other important recent and related development is the attempt to build increasing amounts of knowledge and intelligence into software engineering tools and environments (Balzer, et al., 1983; Barstow, 1987).

The Program Visualization Approach

Despite advances in software engineering, the current appearance of programs:

• Does not contribute positively and significantly toward making a program easier to understand;

• Does not reflect the history of a program as it has progressed through the software development cycle;

• Does not facilitate the transfer of the various strategies and insights achieved by members of the development process to the ultimate readers and maintainers of the program;

• Does not make important program structure as visible as it could;

• Does not deal, therefore, with the fundamental problem of software comprehensibility, that of software *complexity*.

We have therefore in our recent work taken a seventh software engineering approach (Baecker, 1973, 1975, 1981, 1988; Marcus and Baecker, 1982; Baecker and Marcus, 1983, 1986; Baecker, Marcus, et al., 1985), the *program visualization* approach. This approach suggests that we concern ourselves with enhancing program *representation, presentation, and appearance*.

Section 2.2

Perspectives on the Role of Visualization

Visualization is "the act or process of putting into or interpreting in visual terms or in visible form" (Webster, 1981).

First Steps Toward Computer Science Visualization

One of the earliest attempts to improve program appearance was the development of a "presentation," or "reference" form of the programming language ALGOL 60 (Naur, ed., 1963). Unfortunately, with the exception of adopting the dubious practice of putting reserved words in boldface, there has been almost no follow-up of this pioneering effort.

Another idea with a long history is *prettyprinting*, an area in which others before us have worked with more limited graphics tools. The earliest work was done on LISP, so that program readers would not drown in a sea of parentheses. The problems of prettyprinting Pascal have elicited a long correspondence in the ACM SIGPLAN notices (Hueras and Ledgard, 1977; Clifton, 1978; Grogono, 1979; Gustafson, 1979; Leinbaugh, 1980; Bates, 1981; Jackal, 1983; Amit, 1984; Leavens, 1984). With a few exceptions, prettyprinters have done little but systematically indent source code according to the syntactic structure of the program.[†]

Two notable exceptions which have attempted some use of typographic encoding and more ambitious page layout are the Vgrind utility distributed with the Berkeley UNIX system, and the screen typesetting and formatting of the Xerox Cedar language (Teitelman, 1985). Although Vgrind allows some control over program appearance (the default look for C code is illustrated in Figure 2.1) and does allow customization for individual languages, it only scratches the surface of what is possible. Significantly more typographic sophistication has been applied in the design of a consistent publication style for softcopy and hardcopy listings of Cedar programs (see Figure 2.2).

Yet even more ambitious program visualization is a natural outgrowth of the programming process. Programmers have always employed pictures and diagrams informally as aids to conceiving, expressing, and communicating algorithms, as aids to illustrating function, structure, and process. Computer science instructors have long been covering blackboards (as well as themselves) with chalk while drawing intricate diagrams of data structures and sketches of program control flow. If prepared thoughtfully, precisely, and imaginatively, images, words, symbols, and "non-linear typography" can present information more concisely and more effectively than the formal and natural languages typically used by the programmer.

Visualization in Other Disciplines

Other disciplines long ago developed appropriate methods of representation and presentation and have benefited greatly from them. See Figures 2.3 through 2.9.

[†]   Also of interest are more theoretical approaches to this subject. Oppen (1980) discusses prettyprinting algorithms and their complexity. Knuth and Plass (1981) develop a method for breaking paragraphs into lines that considers the paragraph as a whole instead of simply making decisions one line at a time. Mateti (1983) presents a specification schema for indenting programs. Other authors (Rose and Welsh, 1981; Rubin, 1983) have demonstrated methods of extending the syntactic descriptions of programming languages to include their formatting conventions.

phone.c **phone.c**

```
/*
 * phone.c - Prints all potential words corresponding to a given phone number.
 *
 * Only words containing vowels are printed.
 * Acceptable phone numbers range from 1 to 10 digits.
 */

#include <string.h>
#include <stdio.h>

typedef int         bool;
#define   FALSE     0
#define   TRUE      1

char      *label[] = {  /* labels on each digit of dial */
    "0",
    "1",              "abc",       "def",
    "ghi",            "jkl",       "mno",
    "prs",            "tuv",       "wxy"
};

#define PNMAX       10          /* max digits in phone number */

int       digits;        /* actual number of digits */
int       pn[PNMAX];        /* phone number */
char      *label_ptr[PNMAX];            /* current position in label, per digit */

main(argc, argv)                                                    main
    int     argc;
    char              *argv[];
{
    register int              i;
    bool                      foundvowel = FALSE;

    /* For each phone argument ... */
    while (*++argv != NULL) {
        if (!getpn(*argv))
            fprintf(stderr, "PhoneName:  %s is not a phone number\n", *argv);
        else {
            /* For beginnings of label sequences */
            for (i = 0; i < PNMAX; ++i)   /* Reset label_ptr (pointers).*/
                label_ptr[i] = label[pn[i]];
            /* For each combination of characters ... */
            do {
                for (i = 0; i < digits; ++i) {
                    if (strchr("aeiou", *label_ptr[i]) != NULL)
                        foundvowel = TRUE;
                }
                if (foundvowel)  /* Only print things with vowels! */
                {
                    for (i=0; i!=digits; i++)
                        printf("%c",*label_ptr[i]);
                    printf("\n");
                }
                foundvowel = FALSE;
            } while (incr());
        }
    }
}

/*
 * Encode phone number as a vector of digits, without punctuation.
 * Returns number of digits in phone number, or FALSE to indicate failure.
 */
```

Apr 20 12:54 1989 *Page 1 of phone.c*

Figure 2.1: *A fragment of a program formatted with Vgrind.*

The Vgrind utility distributed with the Berkeley UNIX system produces typographic listings of programs in which comments are placed in italics, keywords are put into boldface, and function names are listed in the margin. The example shown above is part of the laser printer output of Vgrind running using its default parameters on the same program that is portrayed in Figures 1.1 through 1.3. Vgrind is "language independent" in that it can be applied to programs in any programming language for which it has been given a list of the language's keywords.

FuglemanClient.mesa
>   *Copyright © 1982, 1989 by Xerox Corporation. All rights reserved.*
>   *Last Edited by Mitchell, August 16, 1982 2:04 pm*
>   *Rick Beach, April 14, 1989 11:19:20 am PDT*

DIRECTORY
>   Fugleman USING [Handle, NewFugleman, Check, SomeProc, FugleFailure];

FuglemanClient: CEDAR PROGRAM
IMPORTS Fugles: Fugleman
= BEGIN

>   TestError: ERROR;

>   **SimpleTest**: PROC ~ {
>   >   *a nonsense program to show how clients invoke operations on objects implemented this way*
>   >   fm: Fugles.Handle = Fugles.NewFugleman[];
>   >   anotherFm: Fugles.Handle = Fugles.NewFugleman[];
>   >   x: INT ← 1;
>   >
>   >   fm.Check[! Fugles.FugleFailure => ERROR TestError]; -- *check the object, convert error*
>   >
>   >   IF fm = anotherFm THEN
>   >   >   ERROR TestError; -- *should get unique objects*
>   >   IF fm.SomeProc[1] = anotherFm.SomeProc[2] THEN x←2;
>   >   };

>   SimpleTest[ ];   -- *call the test procedure*

END. -- *FuglemanClient*

CHANGE LOG
>   Created by Mitchell, March 27, 1980 9:23 AM
>   >   *Produce exemplary template*
>   Changed by Horning: June 7, 1982 2:58 pm
>   >   *Cosmetic changes for conformance with current recommendations*
>   Changed by Horning: June 8, 1982 2:10 pm
>   >   *Insert CEDAR prefix*

Figure 2.2: *A fragment of a formatted Cedar program.*

The Cedar user community has adopted a consistent publication style for its source programs. "This style encompasses choice of typeface, small caps for keywords, italics for commentary, math notation for algebraic expressions within commentary, indentation for subordinate statements within the range of conditional or iterative control structures, spatial separation for procedure declarations, and headings for segmenting the contents of modules." (Beach, 1986) The example shown above was output on a typesetter.

int~sin~x~d x~=~-~cos~x.

int~sin sup 2~x~dx~=~-~1 over 2~cos~x~sin~x~+~1 over 2~x~=~1 over 2~x~-~1 over 4~sin~2~x .

int~sin sup 3~x~dx~=~-~1 over 3~cos~x~(sin sup 2~x~+~2) .

int~sin sup n~x~dx~=~-~{sin sup {n-1}~x~cos~x } over {n}~+~{n~-~1} over {n}~int~sin sup {n-2}~x~dx .

$$\int \sin x \, dx = -\cos x.$$

$$\int \sin^2 x \, dx = -\frac{1}{2}\cos x \sin x + \frac{1}{2}x = \frac{1}{2}x - \frac{1}{4}\sin 2x.$$

$$\int \sin^3 x \, dx = -\frac{1}{3}\cos x \,(\sin^2 x + 2).$$

$$\int \sin^n x \, dx = -\frac{\sin^{n-1} x \cos x}{n} + \frac{n-1}{n}\int \sin^{n-2} x \, dx.$$

Figure 2.3: *Two representations of the same equations.*

Consider, as a first example, how awkward and difficult mathematical expression and reasoning would be if mathematicians needed to deal with a strictly linear format, such as the "eqn" formulation shown in the top of this figure, as opposed to the two-dimensional form to which we have become accustomed (depicted here in the bottom of this figure).[†]

[†]   "eqn" is a program that maps input in the form shown at the top into input for the UNIX ™ typesetting program called "TROFF," which then produces output such as that shown at the bottom. UNIX is a trademark of AT&T Bell Laboratories.

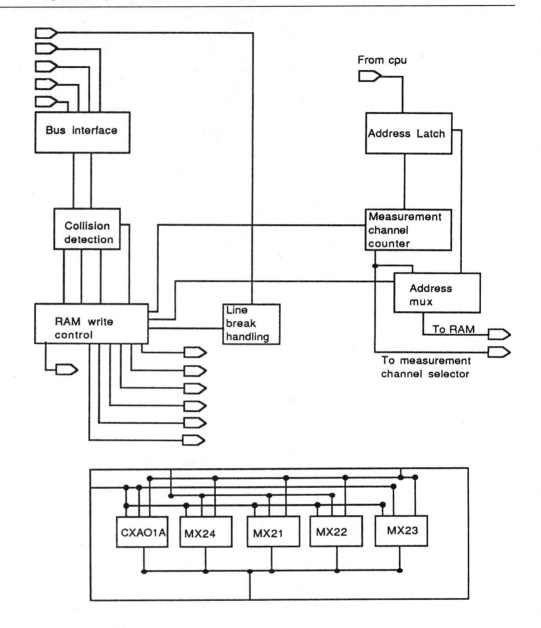

Figure 2.4: *A digital hardware block diagram.*

"Visualization techniques are a way of dealing with complexity. Engineers have invented symbologies and notations in different disciplines so as to communicate complex designs to humans. In some cases, the symbologies go even further and deal properly with hierarchy: the notions of 'bus' or 'bundle' in digital hardware drawings allow a cable that contains many signals to be drawn as a single line, with branches leading off of it to indicate individual wires or sub-bundles. There are other hierarchical conventions, too, like the block diagram. Modern electronic CAD systems embrace quite a refined way of visualizing hierarchy and complexity." (Sproull, 1989) These concepts are illustrated in this figure, adapted from Kurtenbach (1988). In the top of the figure we see a portion of a block diagram of an analog to digital converter controller. The "address mux" block is expanded in the bottom of the figure, which depicts the internals of the address mux block in terms of basic components such as NAND gates, counters, and multiplexers.

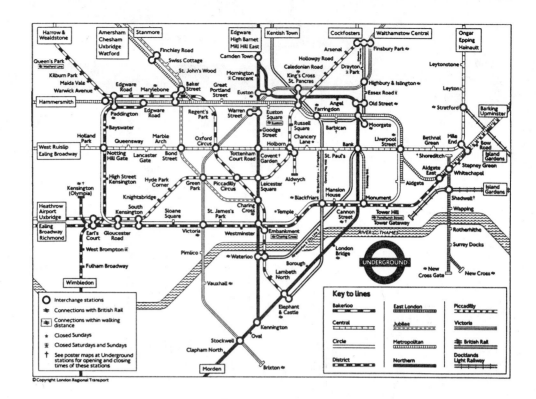

Figure 2.5: *The London Underground system diagram.*

Another obvious example is navigation. Illustrating this concept is the above figure, one of the best designed and most successful diagrams of all time, which portrays the London underground system. Color-coded lines, carefully distorted geometry (a kind of fisheye view, see pages 237 and 240 in Chapter 5), and simplicity of overall design make this diagram clear for the novice and helpful to the experienced user without elaborate supplementary explanation or investment of time in learning.

Johann Sebastian Bach
March in G Major

Event	Pitch	Duration	Next	Comments
1	d5	1/8	1/8	1 sharp; 4/4 time; f
2	g4	1/8	0	
3	d3	1/8	1/8	
4	g4	1/8	0	
5	d3	1/8	1/8	
6	g4	1/8	0	
7	d3	1/8	1/8	
8	g4	1/8	0	
9	d3	1/8	1/8	
10	f5	1/8	0	
11	a5	1/8	1/8	
12	g5	1/8	0	
13	b5	1/8	1/8	
14	e5	1/8	0	
15	c5	1/8	1/8	
16	d5	1/8	0	
17	b5	1/8	1/8	
18	g4	1/8	0	
19	d3	1/8	1/8	
20	g4	1/8	0	
21	d3	1/8	1/8	
22	g4	1/8	0	
23	d3	1/8	1/8	
24	g4	1/8	0	
25	d3	1/8	1/8	
26	d5	1/8	0	
27	b5	1/8	1/8	
28	e5	1/8	0	
29	c5	1/8	1/8	
30	c5	1/8	0	
31	g4	1/8	1/8	

Figure 2.6: *Two presentations of the same musical score.*

It is possible to represent and express a musical score in a linear notation such as that of the figure (top), but the result would be clumsy and undesirable. Clearly, the art of music would have suffered if linear notation were the usual visualization of music, as opposed to the far richer form exhibited by the conventional music notation shown in the figure (bottom).

Figure 2.7: *A visual table of musical contents.*

Individual patterns of music expressed through notation are so clear and distinctive that they may become "icons" or representations of the complete work. Here a non-verbal table of contents (of Beethoven's greatest piano solos) appears that enables the musically literate reader quickly to scan and identify the entries.

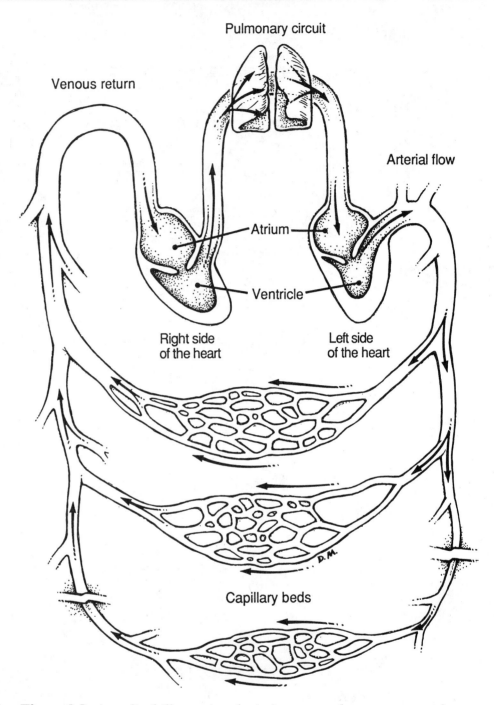

Figure 2.8: *A medical illustration depicting a complex structure and process.*

The science and practice of medicine has benefited from the development of the craft of medical illustration. Imagine trying to present in solely verbal terms the precise visual characteristics that indicate certain physical conditions or the series of actions performed on a complex set of human organs. The diagram presented above portrays both the top-level structure of the lungs, heart, and blood vessels as well as the process of human circulation. The rendering is not strictly a literal one: the heart has been split open for purposes of clarity. Clearly pictorial or diagrammatic illustrations provide effective means to convey structure and process.

From Ackermann, U. The Cardiovascular System. In Ackermann, U., ed. *Essentials of Human Physiology.* Toronto: BC Decker, in press. Reprinted with permission.

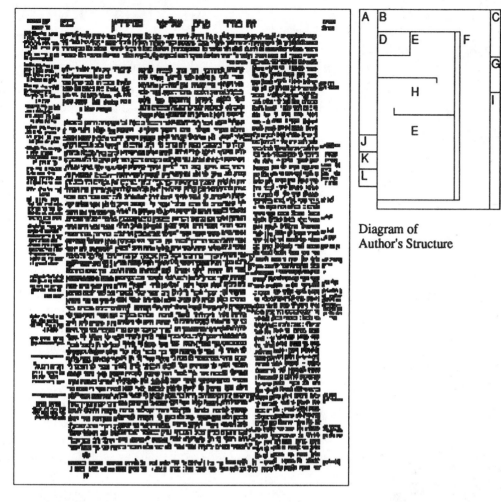

Diagram of
Author's Structure

A	References: Maimonides, Egypt (1135-1204) Rabbi Moses of Coucy, France (13th century) Rabbi Joseph Caro, Palestine (1488-1575)
B	Commentary of Rashi, France (1040-1103)
C	Cross references to other parts of the Talmud.
D	Tosafot (notes by Rashi's disciples).
E	Babylonian Talmud
F	References to scripture
G	Note by Rabbi Elijah Gaon,Lithuania (1720-1797)
H	Mishna
I	Cross references to other parts of the Talmud.
J	Note on variant reading in the Sheelot of Rab Ahai of Pumbdita (8th century).
K	Comment of Rabbi Hananel ben Hushiel, North Africa (965-1055).
L	Comment of Rabbi Joel Sirkes, Poland (1561-1640)

Figure 2.9: *A page of a complex religious text and a diagram of its author structure.*

Another illustration of the inadequacy of simple linear text structures may be found in the field of religious publishing. Most of the world's major religions have encountered the need to present complex commentary in relation to original sacred texts. This need has given rise to numerous conventions for presenting a mosaic of primary, secondary, and even tertiary text elements within a single page. In this example page of the Jewish Talmud (from the Babylonian Talmud, Treatise Sanhedrin, 29a, Romm edition, Vilna, 1895) we show regular appearance conventions for the Torah and commentators' exegeses that were established several hundred years ago.

Section 2.3 The Program Visualization Approach

Program Visualization

To visualize means "to form a visual mental image of something not present before the eye at the time" (Webster, 1981). *Computer graphics* encompasses the disciplines of typography, graphic design, animation, and cinematography, and the technology of interactive computer graphics. *Computer program visualization* is the use of graphics to enhance the art of communicating programs and thereby to facilitate the understanding and effective use of computer programs by people. Our goal is to facilitate a clear, accurate and precise expression of the mental images of the producers (writers) of computer programs, and to communicate these mental images to the consumers (readers) of programs in an attractive and informative manner.[†]

Visualization helps us deal with software complexity (Sproull, 1989; see also Goldberg, 1987). Effective program visualization can aid the work of algorithm designers, system developers and implementers, debuggers, maintainers, managers, teachers, and students. Applications exist throughout the software life cycle: in specification, design, coding, documentation, debugging, performance tuning and optimization, and maintenance. Visualization can also aid in computer science education (Baecker, 1973, 1975, 1981). Examples of program visualization systems are PV (Herot, et al., 1982; Brown, et al., 1985), Tinker (Lieberman, 1984), Balsa II (Brown and Sedgewick, 1984, 1985; Brown, 1988a,b), Animus (London and Duisberg, 1985; Duisberg, 1986), Movie and Stills (Bentley and Kernighan, 1987), the Transparent Prolog Machine (Eisenstadt and Brayshaw, 1987), and LogoMotion (Buchanan, 1988; Baecker and Buchanan, under review).

Visual Programming

Program visualization must be distinguished from *visual programming* (Raeder, 1985; Myers, 1986; Chang, 1987; Shu, 1988), which is the body of techniques through which algorithms are expressed in two-dimensional, graphic, or diagrammatic notations. Examples are Nassi-Shneiderman diagrams (Nassi and Shneiderman, 1973), Warnier-Orr diagrams (Higgins, 1979), contour diagrams (Organick and Thomas, 1974), and SADT diagrams (Ross, 1977, 1985), as well as several dozen others that are catalogued by Martin and McClure (1985), some of which are depicted in Figures 2.10-2.13. PECAN (Reiss, 1984, 1985; Reiss and Pato, 1987) and Garden (Reiss, 1987) are visual programming systems that provide multiple visual representations of programs in conversational syntax-directed development environments. PEGASYS (Moriconi and Hare, 1985a,1985b, 1986) is a visual programming environment in which hierarchically structured collections of pictures serve as formal, machine-processable documentation of systems.

Program visualization focuses on output, on communicating programs, their code, their documentation, their structure, and their behavior to a "reader" or "viewer." Visual programming, on the other hand, focuses on input, on the "writer" or "composer" of programs, but usually provides "feedback" output in the same form as input. Visual programming may appear to subsume program visualization; this is not the case, however, since communicating the structure and process of a program to the reader may need to take advantage of techniques that are not necessarily effective or compatible with those of the writer.

---

† 　　Böcker, et al. (1986) have aptly described the goal of program visualization as a "software oscilloscope."

For example, the ability to display program execution in novel ways is an aspect of program visualization that has no parallel in the world of visual programming. An example of program execution is given in Figure 2.14.

Summing Up

The emphasis in this book is program visualization, not visual programming. Through work in program visualization, we design and build tools to aid the comprehension and use of program specifications, structure, and code; program documentation; and program execution. The examples to be shown will deal primarily with the enhanced presentation of program source text and program documentation. Special cases of the display of program execution will also be discussed.

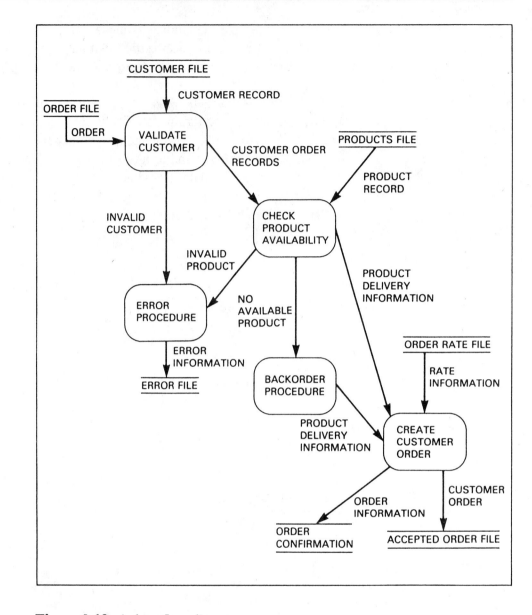

Figure 2.10: *A data flow diagram.*

Diagrammatic notations may be used as descriptions of data and process, as definitions of program structure and program code, as design tools and documentation elements. Martin and McClure (1985) is a recent comprehensive survey of many of these notations, which are increasingly being employed in modern software development environments and computer-assisted software engineering (CASE) tools. This figure (adapted from Martin and McClure, 1985, p. 94) shows a *data flow diagram*, which depicts the overall data flow through the various procedural components of a system or program.

Martin/McClure, *Diagramming Techniques for Analysts and Programmers.* Copyright © 1985, pp. 94, 132, 141, 180, 256. Reprinted with permission of Prentice-Hall, Inc., Englewood Cliffs, NJ.

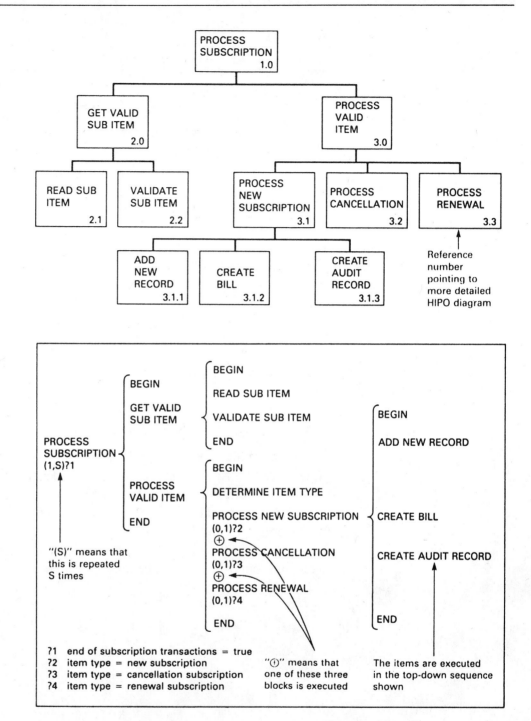

Figure 2.11: *Diagrammatic notations for describing process.*

Two methods of diagramming the hierarchical structure of a program, a system, or a data structure are depicted in this figure. At the top is a HIPO diagram (adapted from Martin and McClure, 1985, p. 132), showing a system's functional components. At the bottom is a Warnier-Orr diagram (adapted from Martin and McClure, 1985, p. 141), diagramming the same system as is shown above, but giving more detail about the underlying control structures.

VALIDATE SUB ITEM:

```
┌─────────────────────────────────────────────────────────────────┐
│ CHECK GENERAL FORMAT                                              │
├─────────────────────────────────────────────────────────────────┤
│                         ERRORS?                                   │
│ NO                                                          YES   │
├───────────────────────────────┬─────────────────────────────────┤
│                               │ WRITE ERROR MESSAGE              │
├───────────────────────────────┴─────────────────────────────────┤
│                                                    DO CASE        │
│                                                                   │
├───────────────────┬───────────────────┬───────────┬─────────────┤
│     NEW SUB?      │     RENEWAL?      │  CANCEL?  │   DEFAULT   │
├───────────────────┼───────────────────┼───────────┼─────────────┤
│ CHECK NAME AND    │                   │ SET CANCEL│             │
│ ADDRESS           │ CHECK FOR VALID   │ FLAG      │             │
│ CHECK FOR NUMERIC │ TERMS             │           │             │
│ ZIP               │                   │           │             │
│ CHECK FOR VALID   ├───────────────────┤           │             │
│ TERMS             │ CHECK FOR PAYMENT │           │             │
│ CHECK FOR PAYMENT │                   │           │             │
├─────────┬─────────┼─────────┬─────────┤           │             │
│  ERRORS?          │  ERRORS?          │           │             │
│ NO      │  YES    │ NO      │  YES    │           │             │
├─────────┼─────────┼─────────┼─────────┤           │             │
│ SET     │ SET     │ SET     │ SET     │           │             │
│ VALID   │ INVALID │ VALID   │ INVALID │           │             │
│ INDICATOR│INDICATOR│INDICATOR│INDICATOR│          │             │
├─────────┴─────────┴─────────┴─────────┴───────────┴─────────────┤
│                    INVALID INDICATOR?                             │
│ NO                                                          YES   │
├───────────────────────────────┬─────────────────────────────────┤
│                               │ WRITE ERROR MESSAGES            │
└───────────────────────────────┴─────────────────────────────────┘
```

Figure 2.12: *A Nassi-Shneiderman diagram.*

Moving from the world of high-level system descriptions to low-level program descriptions, we look at a Nassi-Shneiderman diagram (adapted from Martin and McClure, 1985, p. 180), which was developed as a structured alternative to the traditional flowchart. The example here shows an algorithm implemented with nested selection (IF-THEN-ELSE) and CASE constructs. Clearly diagramming *per se* is no panacea; a well-formatted, well-presented listing in pseudo-code might better convey the algorithm's structure.

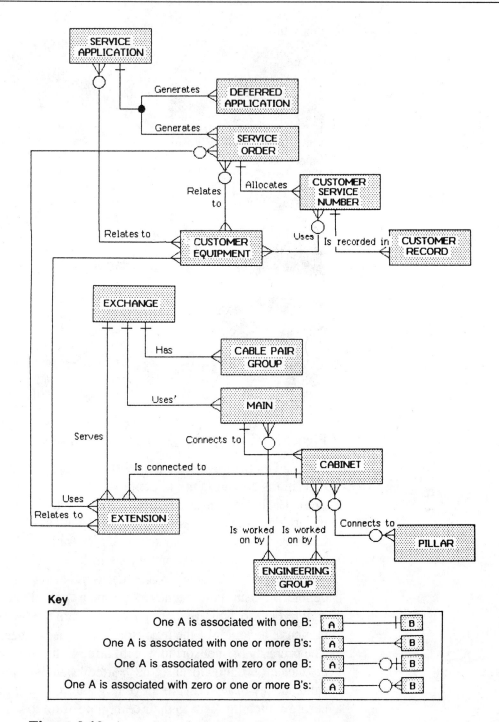

Figure 2.13: *An entity-relationship diagram.*

Finally, we show an example of an *entity-relationship diagram* (adapted from Martin and McClure, 1985, p. 256). The entity-relationship diagram presents a high-level overview of data and its relationships and associations.

Linear Insertion   Bubblesort   Straight Selection

Binary Insertion   Shakersort   Tree Selection

Shellsort   Quicksort   Heapsort

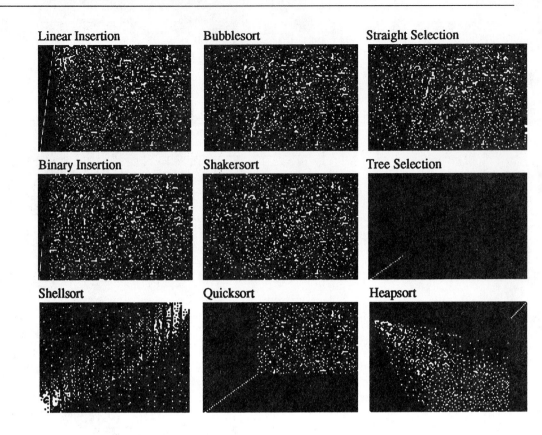

Figure 2.14: *One frame from a race of nine sorting algorithms.*

Sorting Out Sorting (Baecker, 1981) includes a race of nine different sorting algorithms operating upon identical data sets consisting of 2500 data items each. Each data item is represented by a dot. In each of the nine sub-images, unsorted data appears as a cloud, sorted data as a diagonal line. Interesting features of the algorithms are vividly portrayed by their animations, for example: (a) The movement of data is depicted by the movement of dots. A color change (not visible in this black-and-white illustration) is used to denote when an item reaches its ultimate "sorted" position. (b) The five *n squared* algorithms are distinguishable from the four that are *n log n*. (c) The recursive behavior of the quicksort and its use of partitioning are shown.   (d) The property of shellsort in which, through multiple passes, it pushes all of the data closer and closer to the "sorted" state is apparent. (e) The paradoxical tendency of heapsort to move large items closer and closer to the front before switching them to their correct position toward the back of the data is portrayed.

Chapter 3

Mapping C Source Text to Effective Visual Presentations

"When you make a thing, a thing
        that is new, it is so complicated
        making it
that it is bound to be ugly.
But those that make it after you,
they don't have to worry
                about making it.
And they can make it pretty, and
        so everybody can like it
when the others
make it after you."

Picasso (as quoted by Gertrude Stein), as cited in Victor Papanek (1982), *Design for the Real World*, London: Thames and Hudson, p. 131. Reprinted with permission.

I don't know what it means, but I like the way it looks!

Section 3.1	# Design Method

To develop new program visualization techniques, we have followed traditional analysis and design procedures as follows:

Visible Language Taxonomy

We first developed a visible language taxonomy for computer-based documents and publications (see also Gerstner, 1978; Ruder, 1973; Chaparos, 1981). This organization was intended to be a checklist to guide approaches to enhancing source code presentation. The checklist is summarized in Section 3.2: *Taxonomy of Visible Language*, and presented in detail in Appendix B: *Taxonomy of Visible Language*.

C Taxonomy

We simultaneously developed a taxonomy of C constructs, a systematic enumeration and classification of logical components of the language (AT&T, 1985; Kernighan and Ritchie, 1978). This was intended to be a companion checklist for ensuring completeness in the representation of C source text. We subsequently reworked our taxonomy slightly based on the classification schema described in Harbison and Steele (1984). We also added some notions not in the formal description of the language, especially those dealing with various categories of comments. The C Taxonomy is introduced in Section 3.3: *Taxonomy of the C Programming Language*, and is used in Appendix D: *Graphic Design Specifications for C Programs*.

Review of Current Practice

Next, we collected, organized, and reviewed typical mappings from C constructs to visible language constructs, examples abstracted from real C programs prepared by typical experienced C programmers. Because these examples often embody valuable design insights that come from non-designers, they could be termed "folk designs," as opposed to the "professional designs" such as the conventions proposed in this book.

Design Principles

Then, we developed a systematic set of principles that govern the design of mappings from C constructs to visible language constructs. These principles guide detailed visual research into the effective presentation of C source code. We present the principles in Section 3.4: *Graphic Design Principles*.

A New Design

We applied these principles and informally reviewed the merits of interim designs to develop a new set of conventions for the presentation of C programs. The design specifications have been illustrated by applying them to a concrete example in Section 1.2: *Preview of Results*. The complete specifications, or optimized mapping, will be described in this chapter and in Chapter 4: *A Graphic Design Manual for the C Programming Language*.

Design Refinement

To facilitate our systematic approach to the design of program presentation, we constructed SEE, a visual C compiler, a program that maps an arbitrary C program into an effective typeset representation of that program. A discussion of the implementation appears in Section 6.6: *Implementation of Program Visualization Processors*. We have produced numerous examples using this automated tool, which has in turn enabled us to modify and improve the graphic design of program appearance. Some of the examples are collected in Section 3.5: *Design Variations for C Presentation*.

Design Testing

The design was also tested experimentally in an attempt to substantiate and quantify its value. Results of these experiments are reported in Section 6.3: *Experimental Verification*.

Design Formalization

The final specifications (that is, a precise, complete mapping of all elements of C to selected appearance characteristics) were then embodied in a graphic design manual for the appearance of C programs, which appears in Chapter 4 and Appendix D. The general guidelines (sets of rules) for this mapping are described in Section 4.2: *Graphic Design Guidelines*, organized in terms of visible language categories. The specifications, i.e., the details of the mapping organized by reference to programming language constructs, are presented in Section 4.3: *Graphic Design Specifications for C: An Introduction*, Section 4.4: *Graphic Design Specifications for C: Details*, and Appendix D: *Graphic Design Specifications for C Programs*.

Program Publishing

Finally, we shifted our viewpoint away from the details of code appearance and considered the larger issue of the function, structure, contents, and form of the *program book*, the embodiment of the concept of the program as a publication. Although we did not fully automate its production, we developed and have included in Chapter 5: *Programs as Publications* a mock-up of a prototype of a program book.

Iterative Design

We did not proceed through these steps in a linear fashion. The entire process was one of *iterative design*, in which analysis of examples produced with the help of the visual compiler, feedback from members of the project team and other interested parties, and results from experiments were all used in an ongoing process of design refinement and improvement.

Section 3.2

Taxonomy of Visible Language

Graphic Design

Graphic design is the composition of typography and images for the purpose of communicating facts, concepts, and emotions. Communication can be oriented toward three basic kinds of content: information, persuasion, and aesthetics. For information-oriented graphic design, when the amount of content is large and complex, it is typically appropriate to adopt a "form follows function" approach to designing the graphics. The appearance and interaction characteristics (for viewing or reading) develop out of an awareness of the need to establish simple, clear, consistent communication.

The graphic material being designed is often two-dimensional and static, for example, books, posters, and magazines. Dynamic/kinetic and three-dimensional graphic design examples include packaging, exhibits, architectural and environmental signage, product design, television, movies, and CRT display screens. A common thread running though all these presentation media is the use of visible language to represent content. For computer program visualization, the visible language must be easy to learn, easy to use, and easy to display.

Visible Language

A *visible language* is the set of visual signs by which information is communicated from one person to another. The science that studies signs and sign relationships is called *semiotics* (see, for example, Eco, 1976). Human visual communication signs are usually a "universal" and familiar set, such as the characters of an alphabet or a systematic set of symbols. Visible language signs are typically organized in logical, cohesive arrangements such as documents, audio-visual presentations, and signage systems. According to semiotics, these signs may be analyzed in terms of the following dimensions of communication:

> Lexical
> Syntactic
> Semantic
> Pragmatic

Computer scientists should be aware of the fact that these terms are used somewhat differently in semiotics than they are in the study of programming languages.

The *lexical* dimension refers to the set of valid signs and the means for generating or producing them within the communications context. In the case of laser-printed pages, for example, we concern ourselves with the design of appropriate signs and with the hardware and software techniques for displaying representations of these signs as configurations of pixels.

Syntactics refers to the relative visual attributes of signs, including their size, shape, color, spatial grouping and arrangement, and temporal sequencing.

Semantics refers to the relationship between visible signs and the structures or processes to which they refer, i.e., the connection between the sign and the referent or items designated, denoted, or connoted by the sign. It is in this dimension that one can consider the expository, descriptive, and rhetorical qualities of communication.

Pragmatics concerns how signs are consumed and used. Our specifications take into account the display characteristics of different media and their physical effects on visual signs. We have tried to bear in mind legibility and readability criteria for information design and document design derived from human factors research and from perceptual and cognitive psychology. Because of this, we believe that the recommended conventions will improve reading speed and comprehension of programs in the C programming language.

A Visible Language Taxonomy

The following taxonomy seeks to organize the ways in which visible language, i.e., the typographic, pictorial, and ideographic elements of language expression, can be presented on the printed page. This categorization, which is essentially a syntactic structure, is not intended to be exhaustive. The taxonomy is included in this volume as an aid to readers who may wish to extend, alter, or improve upon the typographic and ideographic specifications provided later in the book.

For purposes of practical page design and easily demonstrable examples, the following classification of visible language has been used: [†]

> Page characteristics
> Page composition and layout
> Typographic vocabulary
> Typesetting
> Symbolism

[†]   The Standard Generic Mark-Up Language (SGML) (Goldfarb, 1986) and other approaches to batch processing of textual electronic publishing documents have proposed alternative hierarchies of elements.

Color and texture
Sequencing[†]

Important examples in each category will now be presented. Explanations of terms appear in Section 4.2: *Graphic Design Guidelines*. The complete taxonomy and visual examples of many of its elements are provided in Appendix B: *Taxonomy of Visible Language*. Since, even there, space does not permit us to show all possible attribute selections, emphasis has been placed on providing practical variants.

Page Characteristics

Page characteristics determine the overall visual field within which program visualizations may be constructed.[††]

Page size and proportion
Page orientation
Paper properties
Binding

Page Composition and Layout

Elements are structured within a visual field through the application of a system for locating text elements, blocks of text, and figures.

Grid
Layout

Typographic Vocabulary

Since we are presenting program source text, selection of an appropriate typographic vocabulary is of prime importance.

Typeface
Size
Weight
Proportion
Slant

Typesetting

Elements of the typographic vocabulary are combined into meaningful units through the judicious choice of typesetting parameters. These units include:

Words
Lines
Paragraphs
Lists and tables
Forms

Key typesetting parameters control the following spacing characteristics:

Letterspacing
Wordspacing

[†] Because we are dealing primarily with the production of individual pages, the sequencing of pages is not considered further in this book.

[††] Because we are dealing primarily with the production of paper pages, we do not present a full description of the characteristics of electronic pages.

> Linespacing
> Indentation
> Justification

Symbolism

The presentation of source text can be enhanced by adding symbolism:
> Rules and leader lines
> Pictograms and ideograms
> Figures

Color and Texture

Visible language also includes the capabilities of color and texture:
> Hue
> Chroma
> Value (Tone)
> Texture
> Interaction

Using the Taxonomy

Because the design space is so large, and the content (C programs) so complex, it is necessary to establish principles, guidelines, procedures, and specifications for its detailed graphic appearance. Documentation of our visible language program begins in Section 3.4, but we must first introduce a taxonomy of the programming language which is to be visualized.

Section 3.3

Taxonomy of the C Programming Language

C is a complex and sophisticated programming language. Standard BNF or modified BNF descriptions of the language's syntax (see, for example, Harbison and Steele, 1984, pp. 335–342) run to several hundred lines. The semantics of C contains even greater complexity. We can bring some order out of the apparent chaos, however, by recognizing that the language's constructs may be organized according to a taxonomy that we now present. Its major categories are the following:
> Program structure
> Comments
> Function definitions
> Declarations of identifiers
> Preprocessor directives
> Statements
> Expressions
> Tokens (words)
> Punctuation tokens
> Program environment

These categories are illustrated below. An exhaustive enumeration plus further explanation of each taxonomy item appears in Appendix D.

Program Structure

There are several kinds of top-level structure in all C programs. Of prime importance is that they are organized into *files*. Also vital is that C source text consists of utterances from three distinct languages:

      The C language proper

      C comments, written primarily in English[†]

      The C preprocessor language

Finally, C programs consist of:

      Function definitions

      Declarations of identifiers

Comments

Comments, although ignored by C language processors, are written for the human reader of a program and are vitally important in aiding the comprehension of the reader. They express in English what some portion of the program is intended to do and what design decisions were made in developing the program.[††] We have classified comments into four categories (see Appendix C for a more advanced taxonomy):

      Prologue comments

      External comments

      Internal comments

      Marginalia comments

Function Definitions

To help span the gap between problems and their solutions, *function definitions* are used to define groups of statements that conceptually form separate complete actions. These functions can then be invoked (executed) as single units. Functions in C are composed of the following parts:

      Function type specifiers

      Function declarators

      Formal parameter declarations

      Function body

Declarations of Identifiers

Identifiers are "names" in the C language. They can denote different kinds of C entities, such as variables, functions, structures, and types. *Declarations* are used to establish these associations and sometimes also to define the entity or give it a value. Declarations are constructed from:

      Storage class specifiers

      Type specifiers

      Declarators

      Initializers

[†]   Although comments are an integral part of C, they are expressed in a different language.

[††]   Comments need not be expressed entirely in English, for they can contain non-English strings of symbols, white space, code fragments, pseudo-code, "mathematics," "pictures," or some other natural language.

Preprocessor Directives

The other language that appears within C source text is the language of the C preprocessor. The C preprocessor is a simple macro processor that transforms the source text of a C program before the compiler proper parses the source program and outputs its translation. Its capabilities include:

> Simple macros ("object-like")
> Macros with parameters ("function-like")
> File inclusion
> Conditional compilation

Statements

As in natural language, "sentences," or *statements* as they are called in C, are units of linguistic expression that describe actions upon objects. Statements are composed of *tokens*, which are like "words" separated and linked by punctuation marks. C has several kinds of statements:

> Expression statements
> Labeled statements
> Compound statements
> Conditional statements
> Iterative statements
> Switch statements
> Control-flow-altering statements
> Null statements

Expressions

New values can be calculated in C by combining constants and variables using a wide variety of operators. Such combinations, which represent the "phrases" of C, are called *expressions*:

> Primary expressions
> Unary operator expressions
> Binary operator expressions
> Conditional expressions
> Assignment expressions
> Sequential expressions

Tokens (Words)

C tokens include *reserved words*, *identifiers*, *constants*, and *punctuation marks*. There are a number of different kinds of reserved words:

> Preprocessor command names
> Declarative reserved words
> Control reserved words
> Control-flow-altering reserved words
> Reserved word operators

There are several classes of variables:

> Global variables
> File static variables

Local variables (automatic)
Local variables (function static)
There are numerous kinds of identifiers:
Function names in their definitions
Function names in their declarations
Function names in use
Typedef names
Structure, union, and enumeration tags
Structure and union member names
Enumeration constants
Statement labels
Preprocessor (macro) names in their definitions
Preprocessor (macro) names in their use
There are four classes of constants:
Integer constants
Floating-point constants
Character constants
String constants

Punctuation Tokens

C punctuation marks may be described by the following taxonomy:
Separator symbols
Containment symbols
Simple operators
Compound operators

Program Environment

Finally, C programs cannot be understood and maintained without some appreciation of the context within which they exist. This context may be defined by certain metatext and metadata such as the author of the code, its current location in a storage medium, and the data and time of last update.

Section 3.4

Graphic Design Principles

The conventions that we recommend for C program appearance have evolved through an iterative process guided by the principles of information-oriented, systematic graphic design. These principles are derived from professional practice and are similar to those cited in basic books on graphic design (Dondis, 1973; Ruder, 1977; Maier, 1977; Müller-Brockman, 1981; Carter, et al., 1985; Miles, 1987; White, 1988). For computer program visualization, we postulate ten fundamental principles, and seven secondary principles that follow from the fundamental ones.

**Fundamental
Principles**

The ten fundamental principles are:

• Principle 1 – *Legibility*: Design the individual characters of the textual vocabulary for a program visualization so that they are rapidly and reliably identifiable and recognizable.

- Principle 2 – *Readability*: Design the textual components of a program visualization so that they are as easy to interpret and understand as possible.

- Principle 3 – *Clarity*: Design all non-textual components of a program visualization so that their semantics are as unambiguous as possible.

- Principle 4 – *Simplicity*: Include in a program visualization only those elements that communicate something important. Try to be as unobtrusive as possible.

- Principle 5 – *Economy*: Maximize the effectiveness of a minimal set of techniques or cues.

- Principle 6 – *Consistency*: Observe the same conventions and rules for all elements of a program visualization. Be consistent from visualization to visualization. Deviate from current conventions only when there is clear benefit to be gained in doing so.

- Principle 7 – *Relationships*: Use visible language elements to show relationships among those elements of a program presentation that need to be linked, and to show lack of relationship among those that should not be linked.

- Principle 8 – *Distinctiveness*: Use visible language elements to distinguish important properties of essential parts of a program.

- Principle 9 – *Emphasis*: Use visible language elements to emphasize the most salient features of a program.

- Principle 10 – *Focus and Navigability*: Use visible language elements to position the initial attention of a reader or viewer to the program visualization or one of its components, to direct attention, and to assist in navigating around the material.

Secondary Principles

Application of the above principles yields a set of derived principles or approaches which suggest how to use effectively the elements of visible language.

- Principle 11 – *Page Characteristics*: Select visualization techniques appropriate to the output display technology. In this case, we shall output C program pages on 8.5" x 11" loose-leaf sheets using technology typified by the 300-dots-per-inch monochrome computer-controlled laser printer.

- Principle 12 – *Page Composition and Layout*: Clarify the program structure and emphasize important relationships by carefully organizing the page composition through application of a standardized page layout, through the use of implicit grids, through the application of explicit and implicit rules, and through the inclusion of appropriate white space.

- Principle 13 – *Typographic Vocabulary*: Choose a small number of appropriate typefaces of suitable legibility, clarity, and distinctiveness, applying them thoughtfully to encode and distinguish various kinds of program tokens. Within each typeface, select a set of enhanced letterforms, punctuation marks, and symbols with which to represent the text effectively.

- Principle 14 – *Typesetting*: To enhance readability of the program, to emphasize what is most salient, and to achieve appropriate focus, adjust the typesetting parameters of text point size, headline size and usage, wordspacing, paragraph indentation, and linespacing. Whereas Principle 13 concerns itself with the selection of symbols, Principle 14 deals with their application in clusters. In applying both principles, be careful not to compromise the principles of Simplicity and Economy.

- Principle 15 – *Symbolism*: Integrate appropriate symbols and diagrammatic elements to bring out and highlight essential program structure. In this way we achieve non-textual augmentations of the source code proper.

- Principle 16 — *Color and Texture*: Use appropriate highlighting and lowlighting techniques, such as one or two levels of gray tone as backgrounds, if they assist in displaying meaningful semantic distinctions.

- Principle 17 – *Metatext*: Augment the source code and comments with mechanically generated supplementary text, additional metadata and meta-text that enhance the comprehensibility and usability of the source text.

Principle 17 leads us to the design of pages supplementary to those containing source text, a topic we shall cover in Chapter 5: *Programs as Publications*. In this chapter, we discuss only those aspects reflected in the headers and footnotes of program pages.

Section 3.5   Design Variations for C Presentation

Given the elements of visible language as described in Section 3.2 and the elements of a programming language such as described in Section 3.3, how can we use the visible language to enhance the presentation of programs expressed in the programming language? The brief answer is that we try to apply the design principles of Section 3.4. Yet these principles are general statements of intent, not algorithms, procedures, or deterministic selection rules. The principles can be applied in numerous ways, resulting in large numbers of possible design solutions. We must therefore create and examine many variations, then apply our professional expertise by systematically observing, evaluating, and testing them, before deciding on a particular recommended design solution that is to be systematized and documented in a graphic design manual such as that of Chapter 4.

Creating Variations

The SEE Visual Compiler accepts one or more C source text files as its input and produces enhanced typeset representations of them as its output. SEE has many parameters whose values may be quickly changed, producing a new appearance of the typeset program. With this flexibility of appearance, experiments can easily be performed to determine suitable enhancements.

Some of the more interesting results of these experiments appear on the following pages. Consider all variations relative to the currently recommended form of presentation. Several typical programs, each one or two pages in length, are used. The first was introduced in the previous chapter; the others are introduced when needed. Each excerpt from a program is indicated by the occurrence of a "scissors" symbol depicting a "cut". SEE produced the majority of the examples "almost totally automatically." Electronic adjustments were occasionally used to add or alter tone, rules, symbols, header elements, and footnotes, or to adjust pagination.

Types of Variations

All variations are organized into the ten areas of C programming language constructs already described.[†] In each case, we first enumerate some of the design and typographic possibilities that could reasonably be explored. We then present some of the more interesting variations. These typically fall into one of the following classes:

- Sequences of variations illustrating how the design process progresses from problem statement through initial searching to an ultimate solution, including promising ideas that didn't work.

- Sets of interesting and viable options to design problems that do not seem to admit of obvious unique "right" solutions.

- Solution ideas to difficult design problems that still require more work.

- Interesting ideas pointing in dramatic new directions.

In all cases, the examples are intended to elucidate our design process and decision process, and to teach the readers of this book how better to see and imagine the impact of graphic design choices on the effectiveness of computer program presentations.

The Presentation of Program Structure

A C program consists of one or more C source files. Each source file contains a portion of the entire C program, each comprising some number of top-level declarations. These top-level declarations are either declarations of identifiers used in the program or definitions of new C functions.

Rather than defining all required constructs from scratch, a C programmer typically makes use of a set of included external files (".h" files) which contain declarations of identifiers, functions, manifest constants, and new defined types. Many declared functions generally useful to all C programmers are found in standard libraries of "include files" which are stored on the system. SEE, the visual C compiler, produces a listing of a file with respect to a set of included external files binding the external references.

Enhancing the comprehension of this program structure is a vital task for a program visualizer.[††] We therefore considered and experimented with the use of a number of design and typographic methods.

Page Composition and Layout

One key issue is pagination, including the breaking of pages and the introduction of appropriate amounts of white space separating the key components of a source file (Figures 3.1 and 3.2). In all cases we assume that each new file begins on a new page.

Another important issue is that of navigation through the program. For example, we can add cross-referencing mechanisms to facilitate movement from the use of a global variable to its definition.

---

†   Within each C construct, the variations are presented according to the visible language taxonomy outlined in Section 3.2.

††   We present in this section some methods that result in modifications to the appearance of individual program pages. We defer to Chapter 5 other methods that enhance the display of program structure through the production of new pages supplementary to those listing the program source text.

Pagination and the Introduction of White Space

The problems of breaking pages and of introducing white space are similar. In each, the basic idea is to link sections of code that are related and to separate those that are not. There are two kinds of relationships that may be considered; each leads to a different approach to the problem.

We first consider relationships evident from program syntax. We want to avoid breaking the page in such a way that an external or internal comment is separated from the code following it (to which it typically refers), and to avoid breaking a page in the middle of a comment, function header, type definition, or structure definition. It is also desirable that there should not be less than two or three lines in a related group of lines isolated at the top or the bottom of the page. Related groups of lines of text include sequences of statements, preprocessor statements, or simple declarations. We also want to break the page at a point that is as shallowly nested as possible.

On the other hand, the concept of statements being related often depends intrinsically on the text of the program and on the programmer's intent. Therefore relatedness is not computable from the program. The only solution is to allow the programmer to determine the pagination and not rely upon automation of the process.

The approach that we adopt considers both these aspects. It attempts to do a reasonable job automatically, trying to avoid splitting a function header or a prologue, external, or internal comment. It also introduces extra white space below a prologue comment, and at every transition from top-level declarations to function definitions, and between each pair of function definitions.

Semantics are dealt with by interpreting the programmer's "intentions" as follows. Two consecutive newlines, i.e., a blank line, is considered as a request for whitespace, such as a programmer might want to delimit sections of code not already marked by internal comments. A full line skip results in too large a gap, so we add only an additional half line of white space. A formfeed character is taken to mean a request for a new page, which allows the programmer to control pagination if this is desired.

The above strategy is adequate for most situations; however, a few examples in this book have been adjusted manually to ensure that page breaks occur at better locations in the program.

Navigation

To deal with the navigation problem, we have developed a mechanism in which we add to each program page footnotes that contain cross-references showing where each external identifier used on that page is defined (indicated by a left-pointing arrow) and where each such identifier defined on that page is used (indicated by a right-pointing arrow).[†] Cross-references for file static variables are also included. This produces, in essence, a cross-reference listing distributed throughout the entire program on pages where it is relevant.[††] This technique is illustrated in Figure 1.3 and in the Eliza listing in the sample program book of Chapter 5.[†††]

[†]   See, for example, page 177, which is page E21 of the Eliza program book.

[††]   This approach may be contrasted to WEB (Knuth,1984a), which produces a complete mini-index on each right-hand page of a program book that lists every identifier used on one of the two facing pages that is not also defined on one of these two pages. The mini-index points to the program section where the identifier is defined and indicates the type of the identifier. See, for example, Knuth (1986a,b).

[†††]   Other methods of facilitating navigation through the generation of new pages are presented in Chapter 5.

For each combination of characters ...

```
    do
        for  (i = 0;  i < digits;  ++i)
            if  (strchr("aeiou", *label_ptr[i])  != NULL)
                foundvowel = TRUE;
        if  (foundvowel)
            for  (i = 0;  i != digits;  i++)
                printf("%c", *label_ptr[i]);
        printf("\n");
        foundvowel = FALSE;
    ↑while  (incr());
```

Only print things with vowels!

Encode phone number as a vector of digits, without punctuation.
Returns number of digits in phone number, or FALSE to indicate failure.

```
static bool
getpn(str)
```

char	*str;
int	i = 0;

```
    while  (*str != '\0')
        if  (i >= PNMAX)
            return  FALSE;
```

Set pn to the digits ignoring spaces and dashes

```
        if  (*str != ' '  &&  *str != '−')
            if  ('0' <= *str  &&  *str <= '9')
                pn[i++]  =  *str − '0';
            else
                return  FALSE;
        ++str;
    return  (digits = i)  != 0;
```

not a number or empty

Set digits to length of phone no.

Advance a single label_ptr; return FALSE when done.

```
static bool
incr()
```

register int	i;

```
    for  (i = digits;  −−i >= 0;)
        if  (*++label_ptr[i]  ==  '\0')
            label_ptr[i] = label[pn[i]];
        else
            return  TRUE;
    return  FALSE;
```

✂ --

Figure 3.1: *A program page with too little white space.*

This figure illustrates the inclusion of too little white space delimiting regions of the program. Without skipped lines or fractions of lines to help identify and distinguish these regions, the viewer's eye cannot readily distinguish the program parts. This figure should be compared with Figure 1.3 on page 11 and with Figure 3.2 on the following page.

For each combination of characters ...

```
do
    for (i = 0;  i < digits;  ++i)
        if (strchr("aeiou", *label_ptr[i]) != NULL)
            foundvowel = TRUE;
    if (foundvowel)
        for (i = 0;  i != digits;  i++)
            printf("%c", *label_ptr[i]);
    printf("\n");
    foundvowel = FALSE;
↑while (incr());
```

Only print things with vowels!

Encode phone number as a vector of digits, without punctuation.
Returns number of digits in phone number, or FALSE to indicate failure.

static bool
getpn(str)

char	*str;
int	i = 0;

```
while (*str != '\0')
    if (i >= PNMAX)
        return FALSE;
```

Set pn to the digits ignoring spaces and dashes

```
    if (*str != ' '  &&  *str != '-')
        if ('0' <= *str  &&  *str <= '9')
            pn[i++] = *str - '0';
        else
            return FALSE;
    ++str;
return (digits = i) != 0;
```

not a number or empty

Set digits to length of phone no.

Advance a single label_ptr; return FALSE when done.

static bool
incr()

register int	i;

✂ ---

Figure 3.2: *A program page with too much white space.*

This figure illustrates the inclusion of too much white space delimiting regions
of the program. Too many skipped lines unnecessarily separate the regions of
the program, create disturbing gaps, and also reduce the amount of code that
can be displayed and read on a single page.

The Spatial Composition of Comments

Traditional methods of structuring programs pay little attention to developing and enhancing the content and method of presenting comments in relationship to code. Comments, if included at all, are often an afterthought, an unpleasant reminder that management is concerned about issues of program readability and maintainability. Nor is the process of creating comments and integrating them with code facilitated by the interactive text editors and program development environments commonly available.

In our research we were able to deal neither with the management issues implied by the legislation of adequate comments nor with the literary and stylistic concerns of making comments both appropriate and meaningful. Instead, we have been concerned with presenting comments for maximum communicative effect, both in isolation and in relation to code. In other words, we have attempted:

- to separate comments from code perceptually, since they are utterances in separate languages that should not be blurred together, as they are currently;
- to make code and comments each maximally readable by themselves; yet
- to strengthen the relationship between comments and the code to which they refer; and
- to facilitate the reading of code together with comments when desired.

Satisfying these goals requires applying the principles of Relationships, Distinctiveness, and Emphasis. In doing so, we have found it helpful to divide all comments into four classes:

- *prologue comments* (those at the beginning of a file);
- *external comments* (those outside a declaration or function definition);
- *internal comments* (those within a declaration or function definition and which appear on their own line(s) in the input text); and
- *marginalia* (those that do not appear on a line by themselves).[†]

We have explored comment design variations incorporating several aspects of visible language.

Page Composition and Layout

We have considered comments integrated with code in a one-column format (Figure 3.3) and comments strictly separated from code in a two-column format. Assuming a two-column format, code can be on the right with marginalia comments on the left, or vice versa, and there can be variations in the width of the code in relation to the width of the comments, for example, 2:1 or 3:1. Finally there can be variations in the indentation style of the comments that appear in the main code column (Figure 3.4).

Color and Texture

Overlaying gray scale tints on regions containing different kinds of comments can be very effective (Figures 1.3 and 3.8).

Symbolism

Various kinds of rules, boxes, and symbols can delimit regions containing different kinds of comments (Figures 3.5–3.8). Various diagrammatic notations, such as leader lines, arrows, or connecting braces, can indicate connectivity between code and comments (Figures 3.9 and 3.10).

[†]   See Appendix C for a deeper discussion of comments and ways to categorize them.

Typographic Vocabulary

We can use the same typeface for code and comments, or variations of one typeface (roman, bold, italic), or different typefaces (for example, a serif typeface such as Times Roman, and a sans-serif typeface such as Helvetica) (Figure 3.11).

Typesetting

Finally, there are subtle impacts on readability that depend upon the point size and leading of the comments relative to the point size of the code (Figures 3.12 and 3.13).

Semi-automatic Composition of Comments

Another typesetting issue requires additional comment (pun intended). Although SEE indents and formats C source code according to the syntax of each statement, SEE outputs comments organized into the same lines in which they were originally entered. Spaces and tabs in input lines are also preserved. Thus, by requesting SEE to map external comments into a fixed-width typeface such as Courier (Figure 3.14), we can reproduce tables and "pictures" that appear amidst the English prose of comments without forcing the user to employ a complete typesetting language. Knuth (1984), in his WEB system, takes the opposite approach. His users write integrated text that includes Pascal code and T$_E$X comments. They must work harder than our users do, but they can achieve more ambitious effects. For example, C tokens located within a comment should appear in Helvetica regular, italic, or bold (depending upon the kind of token), and not in Times Roman, so that their status as C constructs is clear. This is possible in WEB, but not currently possible in SEE.

For each combination of characters ...

```
do
      for  (i = 0;   i < digits;   ++i)
            if  (strchr("aeiou",  *label_ptr[i])  != NULL)
                  foundvowel = TRUE;
      if  (foundvowel)          Only print things with vowels!
            for  (i = 0;   i != digits;   i++)
                  printf("%c",  *label_ptr[i]);
      printf("\n");
      foundvowel = FALSE;
  ↑while  (incr());
```

Encode phone number as a vector of digits, without punctuation.
Returns number of digits in phone number, or FALSE to indicate failure.

```
static bool
getpn(str)
```

char	*str;
int	i = 0;

```
while  (*str  != '\0')
      if  (i >= PNMAX)
            return  FALSE;
```

Set pn to the digits ignoring spaces and dashes

```
      if  (*str  != ' '  &&  *str  != '–')
            if  ('0'  <= *str  &&  *str  <= '9')
                  pn[i++]  = *str – '0';
            else
                  return  FALSE;          not a number or empty
      ++str;
return  (digits = i)  != 0;                Set digits to length of phone no.
```

✂ --

Figure 3.3: *A one-column format.*

The use of a variable-width font results in text that appears in a significantly more condensed form than it would if a fixed-width font had been used. Most programmers use 80 characters or less most of the time, and this rarely requires more than 5 inches of column width. Thus the single-column format shown above is wasteful; we need not use the entire width of the page to present C source text. Instead, we can adopt a two-column format such as that shown in Figure 1.3, with the advantage that comments will no longer get lost in the code.

For each combination of characters ...

```
          do
               for (i = 0;  i < digits;  ++i)
                    if (strchr("aeiou", *label_ptr[i]) != NULL)
                         foundvowel = TRUE;
               if (foundvowel)
                    for (i = 0;  i != digits;  i++)
                         printf("%c", *label_ptr[i]);
               printf("\n");
               foundvowel = FALSE;
          ↑while  (incr());
```

Only print things with vowels!

Encode phone number as a vector of digits, without punctuation.
Returns number of digits in phone number, or FALSE to indicate failure.

```
static bool
getpn(str)
```

char	*str;
int	i = 0;

```
     while  (*str != '\0')
          if  (i >= PNMAX)
               return  FALSE;
```

Set pn to the digits ignoring spaces and dashes

```
          if  (*str != ' '  &&  *str != '–')
               if  ('0' <= *str  &&  *str <= '9')
                    pn[i++] = *str – '0';
               else
                    return  FALSE;
          ++str;
     return  (digits = i)  != 0;
```

not a number or empty

Set digits to length of phone no.

✂ --

Figure 3.4: *Internal comments not indented.*

The variation shown above removes the indentation of internal comments so that they no longer align with the code to which they refer. This version is inferior, since the unindented comment interferes visually with the vital movement of the indentation of the code and with the important information it conveys.

```
                        ┌─────────────────────────────────────────────────┐
                        │ For each combination of characters ...          │
                        └─────────────────────────────────────────────────┘
                    do
                        for  (i = 0;   i < digits;   ++i)
                            if  (strchr("aeiou", *label_ptr[i]) != NULL)
                                foundvowel = TRUE;
                        if  (foundvowel)
                            for  (i = 0;   i != digits;   i++)
                                printf("%c", *label_ptr[i]);
                            printf("\n");
                        foundvowel = FALSE;
                    ↑while  (incr());
```

Only print things with vowels!

```
    ┌─────────────────────────────────────────────────────────────────────────┐
    │ Encode phone number as a vector of digits, without punctuation.           │
    │ Returns number of digits in phone number, or FALSE to indicate failure.   │
    └─────────────────────────────────────────────────────────────────────────┘
    static bool
    getpn(str)
    ─────────────────────────────────────────────────────────────────────────────
        char                                        *str;
    ─────────────────────────────────────────────────────────────────────────────
        int                                         i = 0;

        while  (*str != '\0')
            if  (i >= PNMAX)
                return  FALSE;

        ┌─────────────────────────────────────────────────────────────┐
        │ Set pn to the digits ignoring spaces and dashes             │
        └─────────────────────────────────────────────────────────────┘
        if  (*str != ' '  &&  *str != '−')
            if  ('0' <= *str  &&  *str <= '9')
                pn[i++] = *str − '0';
            else
                return  FALSE;
        ++str;
        return  (digits = i) != 0;
```

not a number or empty

Set digits to length of phone no.

✂ --

Figure 3.5: *Boxes rather than gray scale around comments.*

This figure shows the use of boxes around external comments and internal comments, an undesirable variation. The boxes provide too much emphasis for the internal comments and too much separation from the code to which they refer. It is also very ''busy''; there are too many lines distracting the reader from what is essential.

> For each combination of characters ...

```
do
    for (i = 0;  i < digits;  ++i)
        if (strchr("aeiou", *label_ptr[i]) != NULL)
            foundvowel = TRUE;
    if (foundvowel)
        for (i = 0;  i != digits;  i++)
            printf("%c", *label_ptr[i]);
    printf("\n");
    foundvowel = FALSE;
↑while (incr());
```

Only print things with vowels!

> Encode phone number as a vector of digits, without punctuation.
> Returns number of digits in phone number, or FALSE to indicate failure.

```
static bool
getpn(str)
```

char	*str;
int	i = 0;

```
while (*str != '\0')
    if (i >= PNMAX)
        return FALSE;
```

> Set pn to the digits ignoring spaces and dashes

```
    if (*str != ' ' && *str != '−')
        if ('0' <= *str && *str <= '9')
            pn[i++] = *str − '0';
        else
            return FALSE;
    ++str;
return (digits = i) != 0;
```

not a number or empty

Set digits to length of phone no.

✄ ---

Figure 3.6: *Brackets rather than gray scale around comments.*

This figure shows the use of brackets around external comments and internal comments, another undesirable variation. Although less busy than the previous version, it suffers because the brackets provide insufficient emphasis for the external comments and do not separate them well enough from the code.

```
  ┌ For each combination of characters ...
  │
     do
        for  (i = 0;  i < digits;  ++i)
            if (strchr("aeiou", *label_ptr[i]) != NULL)
                foundvowel = TRUE;
        if (foundvowel)
            for  (i = 0;  i != digits;  i++)
                printf("%c", *label_ptr[i]);
        printf("\n");
        foundvowel = FALSE;
   ↑while  (incr());
```

Only print things with vowels!

┌───┐
│ Encode phone number as a vector of digits, without punctuation.   │
│ Returns number of digits in phone number, or FALSE to indicate failure. │
└───┘

```
static bool
getpn(str)
```

char	*str;
int	i = 0;

```
while  (*str != '\0')
    if  (i >= PNMAX)
        return  FALSE;

  ┌ Set pn to the digits ignoring spaces and dashes
  │
    if  (*str != ' '  &&  *str != '−')
        if  ('0' <= *str  &&  *str <= '9')
            pn[i++]  =  *str − '0';
        else
            return  FALSE;
    ++str;
return  (digits = i)  != 0;
```

not a number or empty

Set digits to length of phone no.

✂ -

Figure 3.7: *Boxes and brackets around comments.*

This figure combines the best of the two previous ones. Instead of distinguishing comments by the use of gray tone (Figure 1.3), it employs boxes (prologue and external comments) and brackets (internal comments). Although not quite as effective in achieving perceptual separation of code and comments, this is a very viable alternative when gray tone is not available on one's output device, or in cases where gray areas are intended to be used for some other purpose (such as to denote preprocessor statements, as in Figure 3.34, or to denote code that has been changed since the previous version).

> For each combination of characters ...

```
    do
        for  (i = 0;  i < digits;  ++i)
            if  (strchr("aeiou", *label_ptr[i]) != NULL)
                foundvowel = TRUE;
        if  (foundvowel)
            for  (i = 0;  i != digits;  i++)
                printf("%c", *label_ptr[i]);
        printf("\n");
        foundvowel = FALSE;
    ↑while  (incr());
```

Only print things with vowels!

Encode phone number as a vector of digits, without punctuation.
Returns number of digits in phone number, or FALSE to indicate failure.

```
static bool
getpn(str)
```

char	*str;
int	i = 0;

```
    while  (*str != '\0')
        if  (i >= PNMAX)
            return  FALSE;
```

> Set pn to the digits ignoring spaces and dashes

```
        if  (*str != ' '  &&  *str != '–')
            if  ('0' <= *str  &&  *str <= '9')
                pn[i++] = *str – '0';
            else
                return  FALSE;
        ++str;
    return  (digits = i)  != 0;
```

not a number or empty

Set digits to length of phone no.

✂ -

Figure 3.8: *Gray for external comments, brackets for internal comments.*

This figure shows the mixing of both gray scale and brackets to represent comments, a very viable alternative. It separates external comments from code nicely. It provides strong perceptual linkages between internal comments and the code to which they refer, without breaking up functions visually as much as the gray tone does. On the other hand, we prefer the recommended convention shown in Figure 1.3 because it makes comments more evident, because it allows easier reading of the comments by themselves, and because the presentation is visually more consistent.

Happily Ever After Program

```
#define           No              0
extern  unsigned int              Newlywed;
extern  unsigned int              Single;
int                               weddings,
                                  divorces;
```

really a union!	`typedef struct marital {`	
	`struct human {`	
secs past millenium	`int`	`age;`
m/f/n yes/no	`int`	`sex;`
Canadian dollars!	`int`	`income;`
alive, dead, decaying	`int`	`health;`
	`int`	`status;`
the main squeeze	`struct human`	`*mate;`
your younger sibling	`struct human`	`*sibling;`
	`}`	`husband;`
	`struct human`	`wife;`
a queue	`struct human`	`*rug_rats;`
	`int`	`status;`
	`}`	`MARRIAGE;`
in the beginning	`struct human`	`adam;`

```
MARRIAGE *
courtship(him, her)
```

`struct human`	`him;`
`struct human`	`her;`

`MARRIAGE`	`*m;`

```
if (!compat(him, her) || him.status != Single
   || her.status != Single)
```
The marriage is off!	`return ((MARRIAGE *) No);`

```
if (attracted(him, her))
    while (still_talking(him, her))
        if (asks(him) && accepts(her))
            tell_parents();
```

✂ --

Figure 3.9: *Rules linking marginalia comments to code.*

Next we consider the problem of linking the marginalia comments to the code to which they refer. One solution is the explicit use of rules. Hairline, or 1/6-point-wide, rules are shown above. This can be very effective in certain cases but can become too busy.

Happily Ever After Program

```
#define              No            0
extern  unsigned int               Newlywed;
extern  unsigned int               Single;
int                                weddings,
                                   divorces;
```

```
really a union! ........................ typedef struct marital {
                          struct human {
secs past millenium ........................ int        age;
m/f/n yes/no ........................ int                sex;
Canadian dollars! ........................ int           income;
alive, dead, decaying ........................ int        health;
                          int                  status;
the main squeeze ........................ struct human  *mate;
your younger sibling ........................ struct human *sibling;
                          }                    husband;
                          struct human         wife;
a queue ........................ struct human   *rug_rats;
                          int                  status;
                          }                            MARRIAGE;
in the beginning ........................ struct human           adam;
```

```
MARRIAGE *
courtship(him, her)
```

```
    struct human              him;
    struct human              her;

    MARRIAGE                  *m;
    if ( !compat(him, her) || him . status != Single
       || her . status != Single)
```
The marriage is off! .... `return ((MARRIAGE *) No);`

```
    if (attracted(him, her))
        while (still_talking(him, her))
            if (asks(him) && accepts(her))
                tell_parents();
```

Figure 3.10: *Leader lines linking marginalia comments to code.*

A somewhat lighter touch to the same problem, employing leader lines, is illustrated above. The result is very effective because it provides the necessary linkages in an unobtrusive manner and gives more emphasis to the marginalia comments.

Encode phone number as a vector of digits, without punctuation.
Returns number of digits in phone number, or FALSE to indicate failure.

static bool
getpn(str)

char	*str;
int	i = 0;

```
while  (*str != '\0')
    if  (i >= PNMAX)
        return  FALSE;
```

Set pn to the digits ignoring spaces and dashes

```
if  (*str != ' '  &&  *str != '–')
    if  ('0' <= *str  &&  *str <= '9')
        pn[i++]  =  *str – '0';
    else
        return  FALSE;
```

not a number or empty

✂ --

Encode phone number as a vector of digits, without punctuation.
Returns number of digits in phone number, or FALSE to indicate failure.

static bool
getpn(str)

char	*str;
int	i = 0;

```
while  (*str != '\0')
    if  (i >= PNMAX)
        return  FALSE;
```

Set pn to the digits ignoring spaces and dashes

```
if  (*str != ' '  &&  *str != '–')
    if  ('0' <= *str  &&  *str <= '9')
        pn[i++]  =  *str – '0';
    else
        return  FALSE;
```

not a number or empty

✂ --

Figure 3.11: *A serif typeface for code, a sans-serif typeface for comments.*

This figure reverses the use of the serif and the sans-serif typeface, applying Times Roman to program code and Helvetica to comments. Gray tone is used in the top image; boxes and brackets in the bottom of the figure. Although interesting, the resulting appearance offers only one advantage: because of the lack of serifs, Helvetica is somewhat more legible on a gray background than is Times Roman. However, we still prefer the recommended convention shown in Figure 1.3 for two reasons: (1) Use of a serif typeface for the English prose of comments rather than a sans-serif typeface is more consistent with typographic tradition. (2) Program pages must survive photocopying. A sans-serif typeface is more resilient to this process and thus should be used for the code, where degradation of a character could be disastrous.

Encode phone number as a vector of digits, without punctuation.
Returns number of digits in phone number, or FALSE to indicate failure.

```
static bool
getpn(str)
```

char	*str;
int	i = 0;

```
while (*str != '\0')
    if (i >= PNMAX)
        return FALSE;
```

Set pn to the digits ignoring spaces and dashes

```
if (*str != ' ' && *str != '-')
    if ('0' <= *str && *str <= '9')
        pn[i++] = *str - '0';
    else
        return FALSE;
```

not a number or empty

✄ ---

Encode phone number as a vector of digits, without punctuation.
Returns number of digits in phone number, or FALSE to indicate failure.

```
static bool
getpn(str)
```

char	*str;
int	i = 0;

```
while (*str != '\0')
    if (i >= PNMAX)
        return FALSE;
```

Set pn to the digits ignoring spaces and dashes

```
if (*str != ' ' && *str != '-')
    if ('0' <= *str && *str <= '9')
        pn[i++] = *str - '0';
    else
        return FALSE;
```

not a number or empty

✄ ---

Figure 3.12: *Design variations and the appropriate choice of point size.*

We now illustrate some of the subtleties that occur in the interaction of seemingly independent design conventions — namely, the comment identification style, that is, gray tone or box/bracket, and the selection of point size, for example, 10 or 11 points. 10-point type is used in the top image, and 11-point type is used in the bottom of the figure, for the comments that appear on a gray tone. Our preference is for 10-point comments, because it seems to produce a more even page with more pleasing visual density. The use of 11-point type is a very viable alternative, because the extra size helps the comments stand out on top of the gray tone and helps them survive the degradation of photocopying.

> Encode phone number as a vector of digits, without punctuation.
> Returns number of digits in phone number, or FALSE to indicate failure.

```
static bool
getpn(str)
```

char	*str;
int	i = 0;

```
while  (*str != '\0')
    if  (i >= PNMAX)
        return  FALSE;
```

> Set pn to the digits ignoring spaces and dashes

```
    if  (*str !=' '  &&  *str != '–')
        if  ('0' <= *str  &&  *str <= '9')
            pn[i++]  =  *str – '0';
    else
not a number or empty        return  FALSE;
```

✂ --

> Encode phone number as a vector of digits, without punctuation.
> Returns number of digits in phone number, or FALSE to indicate failure.

```
static bool
getpn(str)
```

char	*str;
int	i = 0;

```
while  (*str  != '\0')
    if  (i >= PNMAX)
        return  FALSE;
```

> Set pn to the digits ignoring spaces and dashes

```
    if  (*str  != ' '  &&  *str  != '–')
        if  ('0'  <=  *str  &&  *str  <=  '9')
            pn[i++]  =  *str  –  '0';
    else
not a number or empty        return  FALSE;
```

✂ --

Figure 3.13: *Design variations and the appropriate choice of point size.*

This figure uses 10- and 11-point type (8 and 9 for marginalia) for the comments in relation to boxes and brackets. 10-point type is perfectly adequate, and it is preferable because it uses less space. 8-point type is adequate for the marginalia.

```
A window looks like:

======================================
|X|              title bar          |X|
|------------------------------------|
|                                  |A|
|                                  | |
|              ooooo               | |
|             o  o  o              | |
|             o  /  o              |V|
|              o = o               |e|
|              oo oo               |r|
|               o o                |t|
|             ooooooo              |i|
|           o o S o o    o         |c|
|            o  o e o  o o          |a|
|          o    o e o    o         |l|
|           o   o  o                | |
|           o ooooo                |S|
|              o      o            |c|
|              o       o           |r|
|              o       o           |o|
|              o      o            |l|
|            o       o             |l|
|            ooo     ooo           | |
|                                  | |
|                                  | |
|                                  |V|
|------------------------------------|
|<-     Horizontal Scroll Bar  ->|X|
======================================
```

```
extern  struct  Window              *NewWindow();
extern  void                        *DestroyWindow();
```

Figure 3.14: *An application of a fixed-width typeface in comments.*

Many programmers are used to designing comments whose readability depends upon the fixed-width characters to which they have become accustomed. SEE provides this link with current custom by allowing the use of Courier, a fixed-width font. Tables and "pictures" included in comments will now pass through SEE and be printed as they were intended.

The Presentation of Function Definitions

We also had to develop mechanisms to highlight the program's constituent structure, that is, its function definitions. The presence of functions help determine for the reader the general sequence and rationale for the program's structure. Making these major "chunks" of the program immediately accessible can contribute significantly to the program's readability. The key is the proper use of white space, headlines, and horizontal rules to highlight the significant components of a function definition. These indicators can be used to highlight the initiation, constituent structure, termination, and separation of the function definitions. Our approach emphasizes initiation and constituent structure.

We experimented with a number of techniques.

Page Composition and Layout

Pagination can be used to minimize the splitting of function definitions across page boundaries in ways that impair readability.[†]

Symbolism

We can use rules of various weights to distinguish the major substructures within a function definition, including the type specifiers and declarators, the formal parameter declarations, and the function body (Figures 3.15–3.20).

Typesetting

Headlines for the declaration of the function name and formal parameter list (Figures 3.21 and 3.22) add useful emphasis.

Page Composition and Layout

Placement of the type of the value returned by the function, if any, on a line separate from the function name and formal parameter list (Figure 1.3) facilitates scanning and reading.

[†]   This topic has already been discussed in the sub-section entitled "The Presentation of Program Structure" which appears earlier in this section.

print out a cast

void
docast(name, left, right, type)

```
    char                            *name,
                                    *left,
                                    *right,
                                    *type;
    int                             lenl = strlen(left),
                                    lenr = strlen(right);
    if (prev == 'f')
        unsupp("Cast into function", "cast into pointer to function");
    else if (prev == 'A' || prev == 'a')
        unsupp("Cast into array", "cast into pointer");
    (void) printf("(%s%*s%s)%s\n", type, lenl + lenr ? lenl + 1 : 0, left, right,
        name ? name : "expression");
    free(left);
    free(right);
    free(type);
    if (name)
        free(name);
```

void
docexplain(constvol, type, cast, name)

```
    char                            *constvol,
                                    *type,
                                    *cast,
                                    *name;
    if (strcmp(type, "void") == 0)
        if (prev == 'a')
            unsupp("array of type void", "array of type pointer to void");
        else if (prev == 'r')
            unsupp("reference to type void", "pointer to void");
    (void) printf("cast %s into %s", name, cast);
    if (strlen(constvol) > 0)
        (void) printf("%s ", constvol);
    (void) printf("%s\n", type);
```

Figure 3.15: *Function definitions with no rule under the formal parameter declarations.*

The absence of a rule under the formal parameter declarations is an inferior variation because it becomes very hard to find the local variable declarations.

print out a cast

void
docast(name, left, right, type)
    char   *name,
                                        *left,
                                        *right,
                                        *type;

```
        int                          lenl = strlen(left),
                                     lenr = strlen(right);

    if (prev == 'f')
            unsupp("Cast into function", "cast into pointer to function");
    else if (prev == 'A' || prev == 'a')
            unsupp("Cast into array", "cast into pointer");
    (void) printf("(%s%*s%s)%s\n", type, lenl + lenr ? lenl + 1 : 0, left, right,
        name ? name : "expression");
    free(left);
    free(right);
    free(type);
    if (name)
            free(name);
```

void
docexplain(constvol, type, cast, name)
    char   *constvol,
                                        *type,
                                        *cast,
                                        *name;

```
    if (strcmp(type, "void") == 0)
        if (prev == 'a')
                unsupp("array of type void", "array of type pointer to void");
        else if (prev == 'r')
                unsupp("reference to type void", "pointer to void");
    (void) printf("cast %s into %s", name, cast);
    if (strlen(constvol) > 0)
            (void) printf("%s ", constvol);
    (void) printf("%s\n", type);
```

✂ --

Figure 3.16: *Function definitions with no rule under the function name.*

The absence of a rule under the declarator and the formal parameter list is an
interesting variation, as it reduces the visual·clutter on the page. However, we
prefer to give more emphasis to the declarator. A number of ways of doing so
will now be presented.

---

print out a cast

void
docast(name, left, right, type)
    char   *name,
                                     *left,
                                     *right,
                                     *type;

---

    int   lenl = strlen(left),
                                 lenr = strlen(right);

if (prev == 'f')
    unsupp("Cast into function", "cast into pointer to function");
else if (prev == 'A' || prev == 'a')
    unsupp("Cast into array", "cast into pointer");
(*void*) printf("(%s%*s%s)%s\n", type, lenl + lenr ? lenl + 1 : 0, left, right,
   name ? name : "expression");
free(left);
free(right);
free(type);
if (name)
    free(name);

---

void
docexplain(constvol, type, cast, name)
    char   *constvol,
                                     *type,
                                     *cast,
                                     *name;

---

if (strcmp(type, "void") == 0)
    if (prev == 'a')
        unsupp("array of type void", "array of type pointer to void");
    else if (prev == 'r')
        unsupp("reference to type void", "pointer to void");
(*void*) printf("cast %s into %s", name, cast);
if (strlen(constvol) > 0)
    (*void*) printf("%s ", constvol);
(*void*) printf("%s\n", type);

✂ ---

Figure 3.17: *Function definitions with the rule above the function name.*

In this example we move the rule above the declarator and formal parameter list, the type specifier (if present), and the associated external comment (if present). Although this variation shows a reasonably strong separation between the individual function definitions, the approach is inconsistent with other uses of rules to underline or underscore an item in order to emphasize it. The rule does not attract the eye to the function name.

print out a cast

void
docast(name, left, right, type)━━━━━━━━━━━━━━━━━

char	*name,*
	left,
	right,
	type;

| *int* | lenl = strlen(left), |
| | lenr = strlen(right); |

```
if (prev == 'f')
    unsupp("Cast into function", "cast into pointer to function");
else if (prev == 'A' || prev == 'a')
    unsupp("Cast into array", "cast into pointer");
(void) printf("(%s%*s%s)%s\n", type, lenl + lenr ? lenl + 1 : 0, left, right,
    name ? name : "expression");
free(left);
free(right);
free(type);
if (name)
    free(name);
```

void
docexplain(constvol, type, cast, name)━━━━━━━━━━━━━

char	*constvol,*
	type,
	cast,
	name;

```
if (strcmp(type, "void") == 0)
    if (prev == 'a')
        unsupp("array of type void", "array of type pointer to void");
    else if (prev == 'r')
        unsupp("reference to type void", "pointer to void");
(void) printf("cast %s into %s", name, cast);
if (strlen(constvol) > 0)
    (void) printf("%s ", constvol);
(void) printf("%s\n", type);
```

✂ ---

Figure 3.18: *Function definitions with the rule beside the function name.*

In this figure we put the rule "beside" the declarator and formal parameter list. The irregularity of the length of the ruled line introduces a distraction into the page design. The presence of the rule is significant; its length is usually irrelevant, because it indicates an insignificant artifact of the design of the program.

print out a cast

```
void
docast(name, left, right, type)
    char                                    *name,
                                            *left,
                                            *right,
                                            *type;
    int                                     lenl = strlen(left),
                                            lenr = strlen(right);

    if (prev == 'f')
        unsupp("Cast into function", "cast into pointer to function");
    else if (prev == 'A' || prev == 'a')
        unsupp("Cast into array", "cast into pointer");
    (void) printf("(%s%*s%s)%s\n", type, lenl + lenr ? lenl + 1 : 0, left, right,
        name ? name : "expression");
    free(left);
    free(right);
    free(type);
    if (name)
        free(name);



void
docexplain(constvol, type, cast, name)
    char                                    *constvol,
                                            *type,
                                            *cast,
                                            *name;
    if (strcmp(type, "void") == 0)
        if (prev == 'a')
            unsupp("array of type void", "array of type pointer to void");
        else if (prev == 'r')
            unsupp("reference to type void", "pointer to void");
    (void) printf("cast %s into %s", name, cast);
    if (strlen(constvol) > 0)
        (void) printf("%s ", constvol);
    (void) printf("%s\n", type);
```

✂ -

Figure 3.19: *Function definitions with all the rules removed.*

Here we remove all the rules. The page is cleaner, but essential substructure is no longer distinctive. Visual parsing of the function definition becomes more difficult.

```
print out a cast
```

void
docast(name, left, right, type)

char	*name, *left, *right, *type;
int	lenl = strlen(left), lenr = strlen(right);

```
if (prev == 'f')
    unsupp("Cast into function", "cast into pointer to function");
else if (prev == 'A' || prev == 'a')
    unsupp("Cast into array", "cast into pointer");
(void) printf("(%s%*s%s)%s\n", type, lenl + lenr ? lenl + 1 : 0, left, right,
    name ? name : "expression");
free(left);
free(right);
free(type);
if (name)
    free(name);
```

void
docexplain(constvol, type, cast, name)

char	*constvol, *type, *cast, *name;

```
if (strcmp(type, "void") == 0)
    if (prev == 'a')
        unsupp("array of type void", "array of type pointer to void");
    else if (prev == 'r')
        unsupp("reference to type void", "pointer to void");
(void) printf("cast %s into %s", name, cast);
if (strlen(constvol) > 0)
    (void) printf("%s ", constvol);
(void) printf("%s\n", type);
```

✄ ---

Figure 3.20: *Function definitions followed by a rule.*

Adding a rule at the end of a function definition has the advantage of making it explicitly clear at the bottom of a page whether or not the function definition is complete. On the other hand, this information can be deduced from the absence of an ellipsis (see Figure 3.22) indicating that the function is continued and signifying the nesting level of the first line of the continuation on the next page. Another argument against adding this rule is that it introduces further "busyness"; in other words, it violates the principle of Simplicity.

```
print out a cast
```

```
void
docast(name, left, right, type)
```

char	*name, *left, *right, *type;
int	lenl = strlen(left), lenr = strlen(right);

```
if  (prev == 'f')
        unsupp("Cast into function", "cast into pointer to function");
else if  (prev == 'A' || prev == 'a')
        unsupp("Cast into array", "cast into pointer");
(void) printf("(%s%*s%s)%s\n", type, lenl + lenr ? lenl + 1 : 0, left, right,
    name ? name : "expression");
free(left);
free(right);
free(type);
if  (name)
        free(name);
```

```
void
docexplain(constvol, type, cast, name)
```

char	*constvol, *type, *cast, *name;

```
if  (strcmp(type, "void") == 0)
    if  (prev == 'a')
            unsupp("array of type void", "array of type pointer to void");
    else if  (prev == 'r')
            unsupp("reference to type void", "pointer to void");
(void) printf("cast %s into %s", name, cast);
if  (strlen(constvol) > 0)
        (void) printf("%s ", constvol);
(void) printf("%s\n", type);
```

✄ -

Figure 3.21: *Function definitions with the function name headline removed.*

In this case we no longer use a title (headline) to represent the declarator. This is inferior because it does not provide sufficient emphasis to the essential program structure represented by the constituent functions.

print out a cast

void
docast(name, left, right, type)

char	*name, *left, *right, *type;
int	lenl = strlen(left), lenr = strlen(right);

```
if (prev == 'f')
    unsupp("Cast into function", "cast into pointer to function");
else if (prev == 'A' || prev == 'a')
    unsupp("Cast into array", "cast into pointer");
(void) printf("(%s%*s%s)%s\n", type, lenl + lenr ? lenl + 1 : 0, left, right,
    name ? name : "expression");
free(left);
free(right);
free(type);
if (name)
    free(name);
```

void
docexplain(constvol, type, cast, name)

char	*constvol, *type, *cast, *name;

```
if (strcmp(type, "void") == 0)
    if (prev == 'a')
        unsupp("array of type void", "array of type pointer to void");
    else if (prev == 'r')
        unsupp("reference to type void", "pointer to void");
(void) printf("cast %s into %s", name, cast);
if (strlen(constvol) > 0)
    (void) printf("%s ", constvol);
    • • •
```

Figure 3.22: *Function definitions in the recommended format.*

On a busy page of code and comments, the headline and the heavy underline
rule draw the eye to the most essential feature, the function name. Readability
of the function declarator and formal parameter list is enhanced by the underline rule. The heavy rule, the light rule, and the half-line skip separate each
function definition into four parts: the function declarator and formal parameter
list, the declarations of formal parameters, the declarations of local variables,
and the function body. An ellipsis at the bottom of a page signifies that the
function is continued on the next page; the position of the ellipsis indicates
where the first line of the continuation appears.

The Presentation of Declarations

The definition of new functions adds to the language's *imperative* capabilities, yielding new constructs that transform existing data to produce new data. However, much of a program's intractability often occurs in the *declarative* aspects, i.e., the declaration of variables as instances of particular data types and the initialization specifying values for certain variables. Thus the effective display of declarations is an area that is critical to the success of a C program visualizer.

We believe that the most important factor in achieving display effectiveness is the extent to which the *declarator* portion of the declaration, that listing the identifier being declared, can be found quickly, both when the declarations are read one after the other and when they are scanned looking for a particular identifier. We must therefore provide an appropriate separation between the *storage class specifier* and *type specifier* portions of the declaration, and the *declarator* portion. We must also establish proper tab stops that define implicit vertical rules with respect to which the declarators are aligned. This facilitates scanning, because one always knows where to scan.

Although the basic idea is simple, its realization becomes complex when one begins to deal with the declaration of structures and nested structures, and with lengthy sections of initialization code. We therefore experimented with various methods of using rules and tabular typesetting to enhance the legibility and readability of complex C data declarations, type definitions, and data initialization.

Typesetting

We worked on the tabular typesetting of sequences of declarations of variables (Figures 3.23–3.28). Included in this series of variations is a very radical one (Figure 3.28), for it deals with the intrinsically poor readability of C declarations by rearranging the text, in effect changing the language. The reader should consider whether or not such an innovation, which is likely impossible given the entrenched state of the syntax of C, would in fact increase readability as we suggest it would.

Symbolism

We developed new diagrammatic representations to enhance the constituent structure of declarations of C structures and types (Figures 3.29 and 3.30).

Typesetting

We also experimented with the multi-column setting of lengthy initialization text (Figures 3.31 and 3.32). As with page breaking, introduction of white space, and comment formatting, the system must in this case pay attention to user instructions conveying layout intentions. The reason is that there are subtle interactions between the lexical and syntactic structure of the initializers (which can be deduced by the visualizer), the semantics of the initializers (in other words, the meaning, which cannot be deduced), and the optimal composition of the text. SEE therefore pays attention to the spaces, tabs, and line breaks that appear in the initialization text, assumes they are statements of intent, and obeys them. Examples of why this is desirable appear in Figures 3.31 and 3.32.

Happily Ever After Program

```
#define            No              0
    extern  unsigned int  Newlywed;
    extern  unsigned int  Single;
    int  weddings,
      divorces;
```

really a union!

```
    typedef  struct marital {
        struct human {
```

secs past millenium
m/f/n yes/no
Canadian dollars!
alive, dead, decaying

```
            int age;
            int sex;
            int income;
            int health;
            int status;
```

the main squeeze
your younger sibling

```
            struct human *mate;
            struct human *sibling;
        } husband;
        struct human wife;
```

a queue

```
        struct human *rug_rats;
        int status;
    } MARRIAGE;
```

in the beginning

```
    struct human  adam;
```

```
MARRIAGE *
courtship(him, her)
```

```
        struct human him;
        struct human her;
```

```
    MARRIAGE *m;

    if ( !compat(him, her) || him . status != Single
     || her . status != Single)
```

The marriage is off!

```
        return ((MARRIAGE *) No);

    if (attracted(him, her))
        while (still_talking(him, her))
            if (asks(him) && accepts(her))
                tell_parents();
```

✂ --

Figure 3.23: *No tab stops in declarations.*

This figure uses no tabs in the declaration of structures; identifiers follow immediately after their type specifiers. Because the constituent structure of declarations is obscured, this variation is unacceptable.

Happily Ever After Program

```
#define            No              0
        extern  unsigned int  Newlywed;
        extern  unsigned int  Single;
        int    weddings,
               divorces;
```

really a union!
```
        typedef struct marital {
               struct human {
```
secs past millenium
m/f/n yes/no
Canadian dollars!
alive, dead, decaying
```
                      int    age;
                      int    sex;
                      int    income;
                      int    health;
                      int    status;
```
the main squeeze
your younger sibling
```
                      struct human    *mate;
                      struct human    *sibling;
               }    husband;
               struct human   wife;
```
a queue
```
               struct human   *rug_rats;
               int   status;
        }    MARRIAGE;
```
in the beginning
```
        struct human    adam;
```

```
MARRIAGE *
courtship(him, her)
        struct human   him;
        struct human   her;

        MARRIAGE *m;
        if ( !compat(him, her) || him.status != Single
           || her.status != Single)
```
The marriage is off!
```
               return ((MARRIAGE *) No);

        if (attracted(him, her))
               while (still_talking(him, her))
                      if (asks(him) && accepts(her))
                             tell_parents();
```

✂ --

Figure 3.24: *Variable tab stops in declarations.*

Now multiple tab stops (spaced every 2 picas from the left edge of the main code column) are used, and identifiers are tabbed to the next available position. The result appears busy and cluttered, and the structure is still obscure, since the horizontal position of identifiers is the accidental result of the lengths of the type specifiers.

Happily Ever After Program

```
#define                No                    0
      extern  unsigned int                   Newlywed;
      extern  unsigned int                   Single;
      int                                    weddings,
                                             divorces;
```

really a union!
```
      typedef struct marital {
             struct human {
```
secs past millenium
```
                    int               age;
```
m/f/n yes/no
```
                    int               sex;
```
Canadian dollars!
```
                    int               income;
```
alive, dead, decaying
```
                    int               health;
                    int               status;
```
the main squeeze
```
                    struct human      *mate;
```
your younger sibling
```
                    struct human      *sibling;
             }                        husband;
             struct human             wife;
```
a queue
```
             struct human             *rug_rats;
             int                      status;
      }                                       MARRIAGE;
```
in the beginning
```
      struct human                            adam;
```


```
      MARRIAGE *
      courtship(him, her)
```
```
             struct human                    him;
             struct human                    her;
```
```
             MARRIAGE                        *m;

      if ( !compat(him, her) || him . status != Single
         || her . status != Single)
```
The marriage is off!
```
             return ((MARRIAGE *) No);

      if (attracted(him, her))
             while (still_talking(him, her))
                    if (asks(him) && accepts(her))
                           tell_parents();
```

✄ ---

Figure 3.25: *Alignment to two fixed tab stops within declarations.*

A third variation tabs all identifiers to the 16-pica tab stop and all component declarators (structure member names) to the 12-pica stop. All identifiers being declared are now clearly visible and can be found by scanning down the column at their tab stop. However, the proper constituents within the nested structure declarations do not yet clearly emerge.

Happily Ever After Program

```
# define                NO                0
        extern  unsigned int              Newlywed;
        extern  unsigned int              Single;
        int                               weddings,
                                          divorces;
```

really a union!
```
        typedef struct marital {
            struct human {
```
secs past millenium
m/f/n yes/no
Canadian dollars!
alive, dead, decaying

```
                int             age;
                int             sex;
                int             income;
                int             health;
                int             status;
```
the main squeeze
your younger sibling
```
                struct human    *mate;
                struct human    *sibling;
            }                       husband;
            struct human            wife;
```
a queue
```
            struct human            *rug_rats;
            int                     status;
        }                                   MARRIAGE;
```
in the beginning
```
        struct human                        adam;
```

```
MARRIAGE *
courtship(him, her)
```

struct human	him;
struct human	her;

```
        MARRIAGE            *m;
        if ( !compat(him, her) || him.status != Single
           || her.status != Single)
```
The marriage is off!
```
                return ((MARRIAGE *) NO);

        if (attracted(him, her))
            while (still_talking(him, her))
                if (asks(him) && accepts(her))
                    tell_parents();
```

Figure 3.26: *Alignment to multiple fixed tab stops within declarations.*

The tab style we recommend is shown in this figure. Tab stop 16 is used for identifiers. Tab stop 10 is used for structure member names if there are no structure declarations embedded within the top-level structure declaration. If there is embedding, then all structure member names are pushed 2 picas to the right for each level of embedding.

Happily Ever After Program

```
# define              No              0
       extern  unsigned int_____Newlywed;
       extern  unsigned int_____Single;
       int_____weddings,
                                                    divorces;
```

really a union!
```
       typedef struct marital {
              struct human {
```
secs past millenium
m/f/n yes/no
Canadian dollars!
alive, dead, decaying
```
                     int_____age;
                     int_____sex;
                     int_____income;
                     int_____health;
                     int_____status;
```
the main squeeze
your younger sibling
```
                     struct human____*mate;
                     struct human____*sibling;
              }_____husband;
              struct human_____wife;
```
a queue
```
              struct human_____*rug_rats;
              int_____status;
       }_____MARRIAGE;
```
in the beginning
```
       struct human_____adam;
```

```
MARRIAGE *
courtship(him, her)
```

| struct human | him; |
struct human	her;
MARRIAGE	*m;

```
       if ( !compat(him, her) || him.status != Single
       || her.status != Single)
```
The marriage is off!
```
           return ((MARRIAGE *) No);

       if (attracted(him, her))
           while (still_talking(him, her))
               if (asks(him) && accepts(her))
                   tell_parents();
```

✂ --

Figure 3.27: *Effective use of leader lines in declarations.*

There is still a weakness in the solution presented in the previous figure. Large areas of white space are sometimes introduced between the declarators and their type specifiers. They can be linked together visually through a mechanism such as the leader lines shown here. (The reader may wonder why we didn't align the ''mate'' in ''*mate'' with ''status'' in this entire series of illustrations. The reason is that the technique leads to unattractive results when applied to declarations such as ''int (*f)();''.)

> ### Some standard C declarations
>
> | | |
> |---|---|
> | *int* | **vec**[10]; |
> | *struct vehicle* | ***car**,
 truck; |
> | *struct vehicle* | ***cars**[10]; |
> | *struct vehicle* | (***fleet**)[10]; |
> | *int* | (***oldsig**)(); |
> | *struct cons* { | |

```
struct cons {
    struct cons        *left;
    struct cons        *right;
}                      cell;
```

✂ --

> ### The equivalent declarations in a Pascal-like form
>
> **vec**:   *array* [10] *of int;*
>
> **car**:   *pointer to struct vehicle;*
>
> **truck**:   *struct vehicle;*
>
> **cars**:   *array* [10] *of pointer to struct vehicle;*
>
> **fleet**:   *pointer to array* [10] *of struct vehicle;*
>
> **oldsig**:   *pointer to function returning int;*
>
> **cell**:   *struct const {*
>
>   *left:*   *pointer to struct cons;*
>
>   *right:* ,   *pointer to struct cons;*
>
>   *};*

✂ --

Figure 3.28: *Rearrangement of declarations to enhance readability.*

The syntax of C declarations makes them very hard to read, despite any improvements we may make by applying better typography and layout. Declarators in C are identifiers that may be surrounded by prefix and postfix addressing operators. The result is that identifiers do not line up at a margin, and can sometime get lost in the clutter. If more than one identifier is declared in a single declaration, for example, "car" and "truck" above, reading their individual types can be confusing. Finally, declarators must be read "inside out." Thus, "int *i;" declares a pointer, not an integer.

We can imagine a series of transformations of C declarations as follows:

```
int   *p[];              /* C style */
int*  p[];               /* C++ style */
p:    int *[];           /* Half Pascal style */
p:    array of pointer to int;   /* Pascal style */
```

Shown above is a set of C declarations and their equivalent in a Pascal-like form. The result is to turn the declarators inside out, making clear how they are to be parsed, and therefore improving their readability.

Happily Ever After Program

```
#define              No              0
extern  unsigned int                 Newlywed;
extern  unsigned int                 Single;
int                                  weddings,
                                     divorces;
```

really a union!
```
typedef struct marital
        struct human
            int             age;
```
secs past millenium
```
            int             sex;
```
m/f/n yes/no
```
            int             income;
```
Canadian dollars!
```
            int             health;
```
alive, dead, decaying
```
            int             status;
```
the main squeeze
```
            struct human    *mate;
```
your younger sibling
```
            struct human    *sibling;
                            husband;
        struct human        wife;
```
a queue
```
        struct human        *rug_rats;
        int                 status;
                                MARRIAGE;
```
in the beginning
```
struct human                 adam;
```

```
MARRIAGE *
courtship(him, her)
```

struct human	him;
struct human	her;

```
    MARRIAGE                    *m;

    if ( !compat(him, her) || him . status != Single
        || her . status != Single)
```
The marriage is off!
```
            return ((MARRIAGE *) No);

    if (attracted(him, her))
        while (still_talking(him, her))
            if (asks(him) && accepts(her))
                tell_parents();
```

✂ --

Figure 3.29: *Large rectangular brackets to enhance structure definitions.*

In this and the following figures, we try some variations that are graphically more imaginative: we remove the curly braces in structure definitions and replace them with various kinds of brackets. The large brackets shown here are a little too strong,

Happily Ever After Program

```
# define              No                0
    extern  unsigned int                Newlywed;
    extern  unsigned int                Single;
    int                                 weddings,
                                        divorces;
```

really a union!   `typedef struct marital`
                           `⌈   struct human`
secs past millenium   `    ⌈   int          age;`
m/f/n yes/no   `        int          sex;`
Canadian dollars!   `        int          income;`
alive, dead, decaying   `        int          health;`
                           `        int          status;`
the main squeeze   `        struct human *mate;`
your younger sibling   `    ⌊   struct human *sibling;`
                           `                     husband;`
                           `        struct human wife;`
a queue   `        struct human *rug_rats;`
                           `⌊   int              status;`
                           `                     MARRIAGE;`

in the beginning   `    struct human                 adam;`


```
MARRIAGE *
courtship(him, her)
```
_____
```
    struct human                 him;
    struct human                 her;
```
_____
```
    MARRIAGE                     *m;

    if ( !compat(him, her) || him.status != Single
       || her.status != Single)
```
The marriage is off!
```
           return ((MARRIAGE *) No);

    if (attracted(him, her))
            while (still_talking(him, her))
                    if (asks(him) && accepts(her))
                            tell_parents();
```

✂ ---

Figure 3.30: *Small rectangular brackets to enhance structure definitions.*

Compared to the larger brackets, these communicate as well and are more economical. Compared to the usual curly braces, the brackets are stronger, visually more distinctive, and cleaner in delimiting structure and substructures. We therefore believe that this convention should be considered for adoption in the recommended standard.

Initializers with spaces as delimiters

```
char                                          *vocab[] = {
        "cat",  "dog",  "cow",  "platypus"
```
(a)   };

%‑‑

Initializers with tabs as delimiters

```
int                                           primes[] = {
        607,    947,    1109,   1511,
        1913,   2393,   2707,   3121,
        3529,   3911,   4363,   4721,
        5167,   5521,   5939,   6311,
        6719,   7121,   7541,   0
```
(b)   };

%‑‑

Initializers with line breaks as delimiters

```
char                                          *warnings[] = {
        "enum member hides previous use of name",
        "anonymous bit-field in a union",
        "unpadded size of aligned struct is odd",
        "tag already appeared in this scope",
        "tag %s redefined in inner scope",
        "storage class specifier after type specifier",
        "CONST or VOLATILE senseless with VOID",
        "implied INT type",
        "array parameter promoted to pointer",
        "parameter of type function promoted to pointer",
        "tag declared in prototype",
        "CONST or VOLATILE senseless for function result",
        "tag declared with formal parameters",
        "parameter \"%s\" implicitly declared int",
        "useless storage class",
        "useless qualifier",
```
(c)   };

%‑‑

Figure 3.31: *The display of initializers.*

Shown above is a set of simple initializers formatted according to programmer intentions. The first employs spaces as delimiters, the second tabs (with tab stops set at every 2 picas), and the third line breaks. Formatting this well automatically would be very difficult.

Two-dimensional display of a matrix

```
int                                    times[10][10] = {
    0, 0, 0, 0, 0, 0, 0, 0, 0, 0,
    0, 1, 2, 3, 4, 5, 6, 7, 8, 9,
    0, 2, 4, 6, 8, 10, 12, 14, 16, 18,
    0, 3, 6, 9, 12, 15, 18, 21, 24, 27,
    0, 4, 8, 12, 16, 20, 24, 28, 32, 36,
    0, 5, 10, 15, 20, 25, 30, 35, 40, 45,
    0, 6, 12, 18, 24, 30, 36, 42, 48, 54,
    0, 7, 14, 21, 28, 35, 42, 49, 56, 63,
    0, 8, 16, 24, 32, 40, 48, 56, 64, 72,
    0, 9, 18, 27, 36, 45, 54, 63, 72, 81,
};
```

(a)

✂ -

A complex initializer display

```
struct PersonalComputer {
    char                    *manufacturer;
    char                    *model;
    char                    *microprocessor;
    int                     DataWidth;
    int                     AddrWidth;
    int                     kilobytes;
    int                     year;
};
struct PersonalComputer         holdings[] = {
    "MITS",        "Altair 8800",    "INTEL 8080A", 8, 16, 4, 1982,
    "NLS",         "Kaypro 2",       "Zilog Z80",   8, 16, 64, 1982,
    "Nabu",        "Nabu 1600",      "NEC V30",     16, 20, 1024, 1984,
    "Atari",       "Atari 600XL",    "6502",        8, 16, 64, 1985,
    "Atari",       "Atari 1040ST",   "MC68000",     16, 24, 1024, 1986,
    "Sun Micro",   "Sun 3/60",       "MC68020",     32, 32, 4096, 1987,
};
```

(b)

✂ -

Figure 3.32: *The display of more complex initializers.*

More complex initializers are shown above. The multiplication table is formatted with spaces and line breaks in accordance with the two-dimensional structure of the array. The personal computer holdings example is particularly interesting, in that it shows how the ability to mix spaces, tabs, and line breaks as delimiters allows the programmer, with very little effort, to request an appearance which is likely optimal given the specific contents of the initializer. No algorithm could do as well.

On the other hand, we have drawn a very hard line in terms of user control. The personal computer holdings example would look even better if the user could request right justified fields for the numerical entries. Equally compelling arguments for additional features emerge out of other examples. To avoid opening the Pandora's box of typesetting features, and eventually throwing the user into a full typesetting language (as WEB does with T$_E$X), we allow only space, tab, and line break.

The Presentation of Preprocessor Commands

The lexical structure of C encodes all preprocessor commands with a prepended "#". In addition, a standard (although not universal) convention for C programming is the use of all capitalized letters to differentiate preprocessor identifiers (such as manifest constants) from all other tokens. A C program visualizer must assist in achieving a strong visual separation of preprocessor commands from ordinary C declarations and statements. Thus we have experimented with methods for further differentiation.

Page Composition and Layout

One method is the use of a positional encoding such as exdenting all preprocessor commands so that the "#" appears in the margin (Figure 3.33).

Color and Texture

We also tried highlighting and separating the preprocessor statement from the remainder of the code with a convention such as gray tone (Figure 3.34).

Typesetting

Our recommended standard (Figure 1.3) uses the typographic attribute of boldface to highlight preprocessor commands, and uses small caps after the initial capital letter in identifiers so that they do not receive undue emphasis.

Advanced Uses of the Preprocessor

We considered but do not recommend showing the macro call in relationship to the text into which it expands. This could be a very effective option in an interactive environment, where one might like to check one's interpretation of the macro expansion. For the "publication version," it seems appropriate to show only the way the program has been expressed, i.e., the macro call.

Our approach is suitable for common uses of the preprocessor. It handles **#include**'s occurring at the outermost level of a file that references files of syntactically well-formed C. It handles object-like **#define**'s which give symbolic names to "magic numbers" in programs, and function-like **#define**'s which create in-line code comprised of syntactically valid C constructs.

On the other hand, there are serious difficulties which arise in principle when one attempts to produce enhanced presentations of C source text containing arbitrary preprocessor sequences. These stem from either of two sources. Advanced uses of **#define** employ fragments of text that are not necessarily syntactically valid C code but become so when expanded and inserted into their destination (Figure 3.35). The visualizer thus *cannot* know whether or not to use roman, italic, or boldface, or how to perform suitable indentation. There are also advanced uses of **#ifdef** and **#include** which employ fragments of text that do not necessarily consist of whole lines and that would be indented differently depending upon which state of conditional compilation is in effect (Figure 3.36). Again the visualizer is incapable of making the "right" choice. The situation becomes even worse when these two phenomena are combined. The only solution in such cases is to adopt a WEB-like approach (Knuth, 1984), allowing the user to escape to a typesetting language in which the desired appearance can be created.

phone.c – Prints all potential words corresponding to a given phone number.

Only words containing vowels are printed.
Acceptable phone numbers range from 1 to 10 digits.

```
#include            <string.h>
#include            <stdio.h>

typedef int                             bool;
#define             FALSE               0
#define             TRUE                1
```

labels on each digit of dial

```
char                                    *label[] = {
    "0",
    "1",        "abc",      "def",
    "ghi",      "jkl",      "mno",
    "prs",      "tuv",      "wxy"
};
```

max digits in phone number

```
#define             PNMAX               10
```

actual number of digits

```
int                                     digits;
```

phone number

```
int                                     pn[PNMAX];
```

current position in label, per digit

```
char                                    *label_ptr[PNMAX];
```

```
main(argc, argv)
```

```
    int                                 argc;
    char                                *argv[];
```

```
    register int                        i;
    bool                                foundvowel = FALSE;
```

For each phone argument ...

```
    while (*++argv != NULL)
        if ( !getpn(*argv))
            fprintf(stderr, "PhoneName:  %s is not a phone number\n", *argv);
        else
```

✂ --

Figure 3.33: *Aligning the preprocessor command lines flush left.*

This figure shows an inferior variation in which the "#" in the preprocessor commands is not exdented, but is aligned flush left with the code. This makes it somewhat harder to separate the preprocessor statements from the code.

---

phone.c – Prints all potential words corresponding to a given phone number.

Only words containing vowels are printed.
Acceptable phone numbers range from 1 to 10 digits.

```
# include          <string.h>
# include          <stdio.h>
```

```
typedef int                              bool;
```

```
# define  0        FALSE
# define  1        TRUE
```

labels on each digit of dial

```
char                                    *label[] = {
    "0",
    "1",      "abc",     "def",
    "ghi",    "jkl",     "mno",
    "prs",    "tuv",     "wxy"
};
```

max digits in phone number

```
# define  10       PNMAX
```

actual number of digits
phone number
current position in label, per digit

```
int                                     digits;
int                                     pn[PNMAX];
char                                    *label_ptr[PNMAX];
```

```
main(argc, argv)
```

```
    int                                  argc;
    char                                 *argv[];
```

```
    register int                         i;
    bool                                 foundvowel = FALSE;
```

For each phone argument ...

```
    while (*++argv != NULL)
        if ( !getpn(*argv))
            fprintf(stderr, "PhoneName:  %s is not a phone number\n", *argv);
        else
```

✂ ---

Figure 3.34: *Gray tone to highlight preprocessor commands.*

Here the preprocessor commands are highlighted by the use of gray tone. In order to do this, we have returned to using boxes and brackets for comments. The achievement of visual separation is very effective.

```
#define            loop            for (;;)
```

```
void
skip()
```
```
    loop
        int                        c = getchar();
        if (c != ' ')
            break;
    ungetc(c, stdin);
```

✂ ---

```
#define            IF              if (
#define            THEN            ) {
#define            ELSE            ; } else {
#define            FI              ; }
```

```
    int                            CurChar;
```

```
void
ShiftChar()
```
```
    IF  CurChar == EOF   THEN
        abort()
    ELSE
        CurChar = getchar()
    FI
```

✂ ---

Figure 3.35: *Difficulties that arise with advanced macro definitions.*

In the first example, a programmer introduces a distinct notation for an unconditional loop. The second example provides a simulation of ALGOL-68's if-statement, in which the macros support semicolon-as-separator (not as terminator).

Both examples have been typeset "by hand," that is, using TROFF rather than SEE. SEE cannot know what to do, since the right hand side of the **#define** can be an arbitrary sequence of characters, and not necessarily a valid C construct.

```
#ifdef        __STDC__
#define              proto(x)              x
#else
#define              proto(x)              ()
#endif

    char                                    *main proto((int argc,  char *argv[]));
```

✂ --

```
#ifdef        __STDC__

    extern  int
    main(                                                                      )
```

| int | argc, |
| char | *argv[] |

```
#else

    extern  int
    main(argc,  argv)
```

| int | argc; |
| char | *argv[]; |

```
#endif
    return  atoi(argv[argc − 1]);
```

✂ --

Figure 3.36: *Difficulties that arise with advanced conditional compilations.*

In the first example, the proto macro allows programs to use function prototypes in declarations (not definitions) when the compiler supports them, and suppresses the prototypes when the compiler does not support them. The second example illustrates how preprocessor conditionals can cut across the structure of the underlying C program. This causes a clash; which structure should be reflected in the presentation?

Both examples have been typeset "by hand," that is, using TROFF rather than SEE. SEE cannot know what to do, because the appearance of the source code should depend upon the state of the conditional compilation.

The Visual Parsing of Statements

Another key aspect of any program is the syntactic structure of program statements. Statements within a C program may nest arbitrarily deeply. At any level, statements such as the *if*, *do...while*, and *switch* contain several component expressions or statements that must be parsed and understood in order that the statement as a whole may be understood. The resulting configuration of separate and nested statements presents a challenge to effective spatial structuring.

Thus the display of program statements and their control structure is one of the most significant areas in which a program visualizer can enhance the legibility and readability of code. It is also the area that is closest to conventional "prettyprinting," for all such systems indent programs according to the control structure. All such programs also adopt one of the many possible styles for formatting curly braces, styles which are often embraced and defended with religious fervor by programmers.[†]

We therefore considered or experimented with various methods of applying visible language attributes to enhance a reader's ability to parse complex C statements.

Typesetting: Indentation

One can vary the amount of indentation used in visually encoding the nesting of phrases within statements, for example, 1, 2, or 3 picas for each level of indentation. We quickly settled on 2 picas per level, which is sufficient for good visual separation, not terribly wasteful of space, and consistent with some published empirical results (Miara, et al., 1983).[††]

Symbolism: Braces

We thought about the adoption of a standard "brace style" (Figure 3.37). This involves making a decision with respect to four issues: (1) The horizontal position of a left brace, e.g., all the way to the left, hierarchically aligned with the text on the current line, at the end of the text on the previous line, and all the way to the right. (2) The vertical position of the left brace, e.g., the previous line, between the previous line and the current line, or the current line. (3) The horizontal position of a right brace, e.g., all the way to the left, at the end of the text on the current line, and all the way to the right. (4) The vertical position of the right brace, e.g., the current line, between the current line and the next line, or the next line.

Instead of adopting a standard "brace style," we have chosen the controversial path of dropping curly braces from C statement control structures (Figure 1.3) and using in its stead systematic, consistent indentation to encode visual hierarchy. We have to be careful in implementing this solution for two reasons. One is the problem of following the nesting level across page boundaries (see Figures 3.20 and 3.22). The other reason is that there is one case where curly braces cannot be dropped (Figure 3.38).

[†]   For example, the original idea behind the style used in Kernighan and Ritchie (1978) was that the structure was to be shown by indentation, with the braces just a concession to the compiler, so that they should be put where they would get in the way the least (Ritchie, 1989). Kernighan and Ritchie (1978, p. 10) write: "The position of braces is less important; we have chosen one of several popular styles. Pick a style that suits you, then use it consistently." Yet, despite the caution shown by the authors, this style has become known in the UNIX community as the "One True Brace Style!"

[††] We considered but discarded the use of some more complex schemes to deal with keeping track of the large numbers of levels in heavily nested code. If there were more than three or four levels of indentation, these schemes would cluster three or four adjacent levels into groups, distinguishing the groups by larger indentations such as four picas, rules, leader lines, gray screen tints, or other visual devices.

Alternatively, we can replace braces with a new diagrammatic notation using arrows, pointing symbols, nested brackets, parallel vertical lines, or channels of varying gray value. We rejected these new conventions based on the principles of Simplicity and Consistency, since any gains that could be achieved would likely be negated by the clash with the established and familiar use of the curly brace.

**Typesetting:
Short Lines**

It is possible to suppress line breaks normally introduced where statements are very short. The advantage of this technique is that it saves space. The disadvantage is that it makes it hard to scan for assignment statements, since sequences of short statements are often assignments. We rejected this idea as unsuitable for automation, because of the subtleties involved in invoking it appropriately, and as unsuitable for manual control, because the benefit was not worth the additional complexity.

**Typesetting:
Long Lines**

A severe problem arises in dealing with long lines of code. The problem can be seen in Figure 3.39. One solution is to allow the code to be set in a smaller type size (Figure 3.40). Another option not illustrated is the use of the entire width of the page for code, at the cost of the loss of the marginalia column and the risk that comments will be lost in the code as they often are in current program listings (see Figures 1.1, 1.2, and 3.3).

We can also vary the amount of indentation used after a line break, in various increments finer than the amount of indentation (2 picas) used to encode new levels. The obvious choice is 1 pica. Another option is to vary the amount of linespacing used between segments of a broken line, starting with the standard linespacing and decreasing it slightly by one or two points. Both these possibilities are illustrated in Figures 3.41 and 3.42.

**Symbolism:
Long Lines**

Two other ways of denoting broken lines are the use of various diagrammatic notations to indicate continuity with segments of a broken line, such as arrows, ellipses, or regions of gray value (Figures 3.41 and 3.42), and the "tab zone shift" for dealing with very heavily nested long lines (Figure 3.43).

**Typesetting:
Line Breaks**

The issue of where a line break should occur is much more difficult than how it is handled. Figures 3.44 and 3.45 deal with the cases of lines that need to be broken. We can place line breaks according to various rules and heuristics, for example, before or after an operator of low precedence such as "||" or ",". As with white space introduction, comment composition, and initializer formatting, we need to adopt a solution that pays attention to user preferences.

**Symbolism:
Semicolons**

Figure 3.46 illustrates another radical variation, one in which semicolons are omitted at the end of statements.

**Symbolism:
Control Flow**

Finally, we can employ various diagrammatic notations such as pointers and arrows to indicate "unusual" control constructs (Figure 3.47). A UNIX utility such as LINT (Johnson, 1978) could automatically annotate a listing with warnings about certain error-prone or suspicious statements.

For each combination of characters ...

```
do {
    for (i = 0;  i < digits;  ++i) {
        if (strchr("aeiou", *label_ptr[i]) != NULL)
            foundvowel = TRUE;
    }
    if (foundvowel) {
        for (i = 0;  i != digits;  i++)
            printf("%c", *label_ptr[i]);
        printf("\n");
    }
    foundvowel = FALSE;
}
↑while  (incr());
```

Only print things with vowels!

Encode phone number as a vector of digits, without punctuation.
Returns number of digits in phone number, or FALSE to indicate failure.

```
static bool
getpn(str)

    char                              *str;

{
    int                               i = 0;

    while  (*str != '\0') {
        if  (i >= PNMAX)
            return  FALSE;

        Set pn to the digits ignoring spaces and dashes

        if  (*str != ' '  &&  *str != '-') {
            if  ('0' <= *str  &&  *str <= '9') {
                pn[i++] = *str - '0';
            }
```

Figure 3.37: *Reintroduction of curly braces into statements.*

Here we reintroduce the curly braces, showing one reasonable style with which this may be done. Notice how much space is wasted. Curly braces are a very uneconomical way to encode the nesting of statements.

```
int
main(argc, argv, envp)
```

int	argc;
char	**argv;
char	**envp;

```
int                                  argbytes = 0,
                                     envbytes = 0;

if  (argc < 2)
    char                             fmt[] = "usage: %s arg ...\n";

    fprintf(stderr, fmt, argv[0]);
    exit(1);
{
    register char                    **p;

    for (p = argv + 1;  *p != NULL;  p++)
        argbytes += strlen(*p);
}
{
    register char                    **p;

    for (p = envp;  *p != NULL;  p++)
        envbytes += strlen(*p);
}
printf("%d arg characters; %d environment characters\n", argbytes,
    envbytes);
return  0;
```

✂ ---

Figure 3.38: *One place where curly braces should remain.*

Curly braces should not be removed in *compound statements*, or *blocks*, which
exist solely to define a new scope for declarations. Most blocks, such as the
first one in the figure, have a visible introducer, such as an *if* or a *do*. Because of
the absence of such an introducer in a "just-for-scope" block, we preserve the
curly braces to serve as an introducer. Two instances of this appear in the
figure.

An example of very deep nesting and long expressions. It's all
nonsense, so don't become anxious that you don't understand it.

```
while (a)
    if (bellow)
        while (carp)
            while (flange)
                if (aubergine)
                    for (rangoon = aubergine;
                         rangoon < bellow / carp;  rangoon += 2)
                        switch (a)
                        case 1:
                            while (aubergine / (rangoon + (carp *
                                flange)))
                                if ((flange + (aubergine - bellow)) /
                                    rangoon)
                                    aubergine = ((a == flange) ?
                                        (-1) : (1));
                                if (a)
                                    if (bellow)
                                        if (flange > a + bellow +
                                            carp / a - bellow)
                                            flange = 1;
                                        else
                                            flange = 2;
                                    else
                                        flange = 3;
                                else
                                    flange = 4;
                            break;
                        default :
                            flange = 10;
                            break;
                else
                    flange = 5;
        else
            flange = 6;

switch (a)
case '1':
    if (bellow == flange)
        if (flange == bellow)
```

Figure 3.39: *A program with many broken lines.*

When lines of code are very long and/or very deeply nested, the result is likely
to be many broken lines. Such code can be very hard to read, as this example
illustrates.

An example of very deep nesting and long expressions. It's all nonsense, so don't become anxious that you don't understand it.

```
while (a)
    if (bellow)
        while (carp)
            while (flange)
                if (aubergine)
                    for (rangoon = aubergine;  rangoon < bellow / carp;  rangoon += 2)
                        switch (a)
                        case 1:
                            while (aubergine / (rangoon + (carp * flange)))
                                if ((flange + (aubergine − bellow)) / rangoon)
                                    aubergine = ((a == flange) ? (−1) : (1));
                                if (a)
                                    if (bellow)
                                        if (flange  >  a + bellow + carp / a − bellow)
                                            flange = 1;
                                        else
                                            flange = 2;
                                    else
                                        flange = 3;
                                else
                                    flange = 4;
                            break;
                        default :
                            flange = 10;
                            break;
                        else
                            flange = 5;
                else
                    flange = 6;
    switch (a)
    case '1':
        if (bellow == flange)
            if (flange == bellow)
```

we want to be confident

```
                rangoon = bellow;
    original_sin:
        do
            flange = bellow;
        ↑while (bellow != flange);
```

fall through

```
    case '2':
        for (a = 1;  a < flange;  a += carp)
            while (bellow)
                if (aubergine)
                    switch (rangoon)
                    case 123:
                        exit(1);
                        break;
```

Figure 3.40: *A smaller point size to deal with long lines of code.*

Here we show one solution to the problem that arises when a program contains many long lines and, as a result, is typeset with numerous lines that are broken and wrapped to the following lines. We reduce the size of the code to 8 points (with a leading of 9 points), and the size of the indent to 1 pica. Although individual lines become less legible and readable, there are two advantages: fewer broken lines and more code on a page.

```
for (rangoon = aubergine;
     rangoon < a − bellow / carp;
     rangoon += 2)
   switch (a)
   case 1:
       while (aubergine / (rangoon + (carp *
           flange)))
```

(a)

✂ --

```
for (rangoon = aubergine;
     rangoon < a − bellow / carp;
     rangoon += 2)
   switch (a)
   case 1:
       while (aubergine / (rangoon + (carp *
           flange)))
```

(b)

✂ --

```
for (rangoon = aubergine;
   rangoon < a − bellow / carp;
   rangoon += 2)
     switch (a)
     case 1:
         while (aubergine / (rangoon + (carp *
             flange)))
```

(c)

✂ --

```
for (rangoon = aubergine;
   rangoon < a − bellow / carp;
   rangoon += 2)
     switch (a)
     case 1:
         while (aubergine / (rangoon + (carp *
             flange)))
```

(d)

✂ --

Figure 3.41: *Highlighting broken lines of code through the use of spacing.*

We illustrate some options in the display of broken lines: (a) Use of a one tab stop (2 pica) indent leads to confusion between indentation due to statement nesting and indentation due to line breaking. (b) Alternatively, we attempt to link the line and its continuation visually by reducing the leading by two points. Although the linkage works, the effect is a very uneven and unattractive look to the page. (c) A half tab stop (1 pica) indent allows us to distinguish between indentation for statement nesting and indentation for line continuation. (d) Combining the 1 pica indent with the reduced leading is still unattractive.

```
(a)
        for (rangoon = aubergine; ↓
        → rangoon  <  a − bellow / carp; ↓
        → rangoon += 2)
            switch (a)
            case 1:
                while (aubergine / (rangoon + (carp* ↓
                → flange)))
```

✂ --

```
(b)
        for (rangoon = aubergine;
        ✔ rangoon  <  a − bellow / carp;
        ✔ rangoon += 2)
            switch (a)
            case 1:
                while (aubergine / (rangoon + (carp *
                ✔ flange)))
```

✂ --

```
(c)
        for (rangoon = aubergine; ...
          rangoon  <  a − bellow / carp; ...
          rangoon += 2)
            switch (a)
            case 1:
                while (aubergine / (rangoon + (carp * ...
                  flange)))
```

✂ --

```
(d)
        for (rangoon = aubergine; ...
        ... rangoon  <  a − bellow / carp; ...
        ... rangoon += 2)
            switch (a)
            case 1:
                while (aubergine / (rangoon + (carp * ...
                ... flange)))
```

✂ --

Figure 3.42: *Highlighting broken lines of code through the use of symbolism.*

Symbolism may also be employed to facilitate the reading of broken lines. (a) One solution is to use arrows to link the two parts of the broken line. The result is busy and somewhat gimmicky. (b) A single arrow is somewhat cleaner. (c) We now try adding an ellipsis at the end of the first line to show that there is a continuation. (d) Finally, we use two ellipses, one at the end of the first line, the other at the beginning of the second line. These latter two techniques are economical and forceful methods of visually reinforcing an important condition. (Strictly speaking, we are stretching the meaning of the ellipsis symbol in using it to signal statements that are broken across line boundaries and functions that are broken across page boundaries, since, conventionally, the ellipsis denotes something that has been omitted rather than something located elsewhere. Nonetheless, we believe the ellipses are effective.)

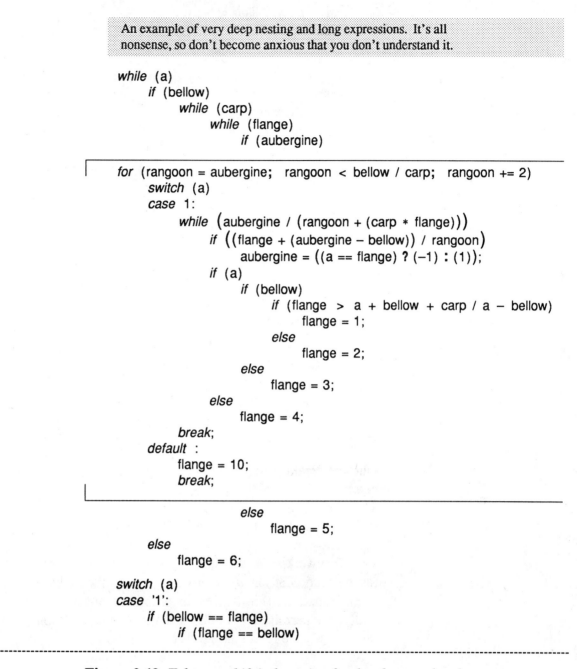

> An example of very deep nesting and long expressions. It's all
> nonsense, so don't become anxious that you don't understand it.

```
while (a)
    if (bellow)
        while (carp)
            while (flange)
                if (aubergine)
```

```
for (rangoon = aubergine;  rangoon < bellow / carp;  rangoon += 2)
    switch (a)
    case 1:
        while (aubergine / (rangoon + (carp * flange)))
            if ((flange + (aubergine - bellow)) / rangoon)
                aubergine = ((a == flange) ? (-1) : (1));
            if (a)
                if (bellow)
                    if (flange > a + bellow + carp / a - bellow)
                        flange = 1;
                    else
                        flange = 2;
                else
                    flange = 3;
            else
                flange = 4;
        break;
    default :
        flange = 10;
        break;
```

```
            else
                flange = 5;
    else
        flange = 6;
switch (a)
case '1':
    if (bellow == flange)
        if (flange == bellow)
```

Figure 3.43: *Tab zone shift indentation for deeply nested code.*

Here is another solution to deal with very deeply nested code and the resulting
line breaks, a technique we call the "tab zone shift." This scheme means that
after the nth level of indentation (we have chosen $n = 9$) the source code shifts
flush left to tab stop zero (0) of the primary text column. Accompanying this
shift is a diagrammatic indicator defining its extent and enclosing the shifted
code in a visually distinctive way.

(a)
```
div400  =  (d→year % 100) == 0
        && ((d→Kyear * 10 + d→year / 100) % 4 == 0);
```

✂ ---

(b)
```
fscanf(dbfile, "%d %d %d %d %d %d", &(db[dbcount].id), &(db[dbcount].min),
        &(db[dbcount].hour), &(db[dbcount].day), &(db[dbcount].month),
        &(db[dbcount].year));
```

✂ ---

(c)
```
if (this)
    if (that)
        if (them)
            fscanf(dbfile, "%d %d %d %d %d %d", &(db[dbcount].id),
                &(db[dbcount].min), &(db[dbcount].hour),
                &(db[dbcount].day), &(db[dbcount].month),
                &(db[dbcount].year));
```

✂ ---

(d)
```
julian  =
    146097L * (year / 100) / 4 + (1461L * year % 100) / 4 + (153L * month
    + 2) / 5 + day + 1721119L;
```

✂ ---

(e)
```
julian  =  146097L * (year / 100) / 4 + (1461L * year % 100) / 4 +
    (153L * month + 2) / 5 + day + 1721119L;
```

✂ ---

Figure 3.44: *Simple line breaking cases.*

Our line breaking algorithm works by associating a "permission to break" with certain operators of low precedence (for example, ";", ",", "=", "||", and "&&"). The user can also give permission by entering a carriage return (newline). If the line is too long, the text formatter module of SEE breaks the line at the last permission point.

This works fine with examples (a), (b), and (c), although we can see in (c) (as in Figure 3.39) how the problem is exacerbated by indentation and long lines. Example (d) illustrates the problem that arises when there is no operator with break permission. In this case the manual addition of a newline to the input allows the reasonable solution shown in (e).

```
    for (thisclass = classes;  thisclass != NULL &&  !STREQ(thisclass→cname,
        class);   thisclass = thisclass→cnext)
(a)
            ;
```

✄ --

```
    for (thisclass = classes;  thisclass != NULL &&
        !STREQ(thisclass→cname, class);  thisclass = thisclass→cnext)
(b)
            ;
```

✄ --

```
    for (thisclass = classes;  thisclass != NULL
        && !STREQ(thisclass→cname, class);  thisclass = thisclass→cnext)
(c)
            ;
```

✄ --

```
    for (thisclass = classes;  thisclass != NULL
        && !STREQ(thisclass→cname, class);   thisclass = thisclass→cnext)
(d)
            ;
```

✄ --

```
    for (thisclass = classes;
        thisclass != NULL &&  !STREQ(thisclass→cname, class);
        thisclass = thisclass→cnext)
(e)
            ;
```

✄ --

Figure 3.45: *A complex line breaking case.*

Lines containing no operators with break permission do not represent the only
problem. We have difficulties (as does any formatter) with very long tokens or
strings. Finally, our algorithm is not very subtle. The break shown in (a) above
is fair but is clearly inferior to that shown in (b), in which we choose an earlier
point with break permission. This break also raises the issue of where the
operator should be placed. Two alternatives appear in (c) and (d); each has the
advantage over (b) in that it emphasizes at the beginning of the continuation
that the second line is a continuation. (Recall also the use of ellipses in Figure
3.42.) Even more interesting is (e), in which the use of two break points leads to
a clearer portrayal. Although this particular operator (the *for*) can be handled
with a special-case solution, it illustrates the need for a more sophisticated
approach which includes look-ahead or backtracking (see Section 6.4).

class.c – provide the class mechanism, for specifying "classes" of words
for pattern–matching.

```
# include              <stdio.h>
# include              "eliza.h"

struct class {
        struct class              *cnext;
```
Class name.   `char                      *cname;`
Words.   `struct text               *members;`
```
}
```
List of all classes.   `static struct class              *classes = NULL`

```
extern char                       *enstring(),
                                  *emalloc()
extern void                       err()
extern void                       append()
```

addtoclass – add a word to a word class, creating the class if necessary.

```
void
addtoclass(word, class)
```

char	*word
char	*class

```
register struct class             *thisclass
```

Find class.

```
for (thisclass = classes;  thisclass != NULL &&  !STREQ(thisclass→cname,
    class);  thisclass = thisclass→cnext)
```

NULLBODY

```
if (thisclass == NULL)
```

Create class.

```
thisclass = (struct class *) emalloc(sizeof(struct class))
thisclass→cnext = classes
classes = thisclass
```

✂ -

Figure 3.46: *Omitting the semicolons at the end of statements.*

Above is another radical appearance; to further reduce needless clutter, we
throw out the semicolons at the end of statements. This could work as long as
there is a clear indication of line continuations. The example shown above
should be compared to page 198 (page E42 of the Eliza program book), the
conventional treatment, which includes the semicolons. We prefer the useful
redundancy achieved by keeping the semicolons.

f()

```
        int                          c;
        int                          i = 0;
    for  (;;)
        c = getchar();
→   reswitch:
        switch  (c)
        case  '–':
            i  =  –i;
↑           continue;
        case  '.':
            c = getchar();
            if  (c  !=  '0'  &&  c  !=  '1')
⇆               goto  reswitch;
        case  '0':
        case  '1':
            i  =  i * 2  +  (c – '0');
↑           continue;
        case  EOF:
↓           return;
↓       break;
    putchar(c + i);
```

✂ --

Figure 3.47: *Flagging suspicious control constructs.*

A definition of the concept of a "suspicious" control construct in C might be:
(1) any label; (2) any *case* that may fall through to the next *case*; (3) any *goto*
statement; (4) any *continue* statement; (5) any *break* statement not at the end of
a *case*; and, (6) any *return* statement not at the end of a function definition.
(Programmers sometimes use comments as warnings about these and similar
constructs, for example, the use of "NULLBODY" on page 183, which is page
E27 of the Eliza program book.)

One method of highlighting suspicious occurrences is shown above. Cases
(1) and (2) are signalled with arrows that point to the right, since they represent
places where control may enter. Case (3) is signalled with an arrow pointing to
the left, since control passes elsewhere in the program. Case (4) is signalled
with an arrow pointing upward, since control flows back to the beginning of a
loop. Cases (5) and (6) are signalled with arrows pointing downward, since
code that follows will be skipped.

Another method of dealing with this problem appears in Figure 3.55.

The Visual Parsing of Expressions

One of the most difficult aspects of the detailed reading of a computer program occurs in the attempt to parse a complex (arithmetic, logical, or string) expression. This is particularly true in the programming language C, where 46 different operators occur at 16 levels of precedence, some associating left to right, others associating right to left (Harbison and Steele, 1984). Current methods of program visualization provide little help to the reader trying to decipher an expression other than the explicit indication of nesting and grouping through the inclusion of parentheses. The resulting visual clutter and masking of what is essential is readily apparent in languages such as LISP. Conversely, we feel that attention to fine detail in the presentation of expressions, especially the choice of wordspacing and the use of parentheses, can enhance the legibility and readability of computer programs.

We considered or experimented with various methods of using typographic attributes to enhance the legibility and readability of complex C expressions.

Typographic Vocabulary

One such method is the substitution of a variable-width typeface in place of the standard fixed-width typeface (Figure 3.48). Another is the use of ligatures, kerning, and other controls over letterspacing to bind tokens and multi-character operators together more tightly. (See the following section entitled "The Typography of Punctuation," and also Figure 3.61.)

We also tried varying the point size and weight of operators in order to facilitate the parsing of expressions, but found the resulting pages too uneven and too busy. Varying the point size of parentheses, however, looked fine and seemed to significantly enhance readability (Figure 3.49, bottom).

Typesetting

We considered the positions of operators in expressions. We first experimented with variations in the vertical placement of *unary* operators, deciding in the end to differentiate them from *binary* operators by encoding the former as superscripts (Figure 3.49, top).

We then began to introduce extra space around binary operators with low precedence that bind less tightly to aid the reader in parsing the expression properly. Some of our insights into this technique are reported in Figures 3.50–3.53.

Symbolism

We also considered including in the expressions light square under-brackets or other diagrammatic notations, somewhat like those one might construct by hand. The implementation seemed too complex to deal with for the moment.

Even more intriguing is the notion that expressions should be typeset with the same techniques and conventions as are used in mathematics. This suggests the introduction of new kinds of braces and brackets, the careful control of the horizontal and vertical placement of phrases, and the explicit introduction of line breaks. What we propose (Figures 3.50–3.53) is a solution that is perhaps 50 percent along the way to typesetting programs as mathematics: we carefully control horizontal and vertical position of operators and allow three sizes of parentheses, but we preserve the essentially linear form of an expression as it conventionally appears in a program.

(a) Fixed width typeface

```
a = 1;
a = b + c;
a = b + c * d + k;
a = (b + c) * (d + k);
a = b + c * d + k == b + d * k;
a = ((b + c) * (d + k)) == ((b + d) * k);

apple = 1;
apple = banana + candy;
apple = banana + candy * dessert + kiwi;
apple = (banana + candy) * (dessert + kiwi);
apple = banana + candy * dessert + kiwi == banana + dessert
  * kiwi;
apple = ((banana + candy) * (dessert + kiwi)) == ((banana +
  dessert) * kiwi);
```

(b) Variable width typeface

```
a = 1;
a = b + c;
a = b + c * d + k;
a = (b + c) * (d + k);
a = b + c * d + k == b + d * k;
a = ((b + c) * (d + k)) == ((b + d) * k);

apple = 1;
apple = banana + candy;
apple = banana + candy * dessert + kiwi;
apple = (banana + candy) * (dessert + kiwi);
apple = banana + candy * dessert + kiwi == banana + dessert * kiwi;
apple = ((banana + candy) * (dessert + kiwi)) == ((banana + dessert) * kiwi);
```

Figure 3.48: *Choice of typeface for expressions.*

Appearing at the top of the figure (phase a) is a conventional form of presenting expressions, with a fixed-width typeface, no raised unary operators, no kerning, wordspacing determined by the programmer, and a single size of parenthesis.

A similar treatment (phase b) appears at the bottom of the figure, only now a Helvetica typeface is used. The readability of simple, short identifiers is not aided by the variable-width typeface; the payoff comes as identifiers become longer, as expressions appear in more substantial bodies of text (e.g., complete programs), and as we apply successive typographic refinements of the kind to be explored in the following five figures.

	(c) Unary Operators
Fixed width Courier typeface	`a = ++d->e * *p++;`
Distinguish pointer from multiply	`a = ++d->e * *p++;`
Helvetica typeface	a = ++d→e * *p++;
Change size	a = ++d→e * *p++;
Raise unary operators	a = $^{++}$d→e * *p^{++};
Adjust spacing in '++'	a = $^{++}$d→e * *p^{++};
Recommended format	a = $^{++}$d→e * *p^{++};

✂ --

	(d) Variable Size of Parenthesis
Fixed width Courier typeface	`a = f + x * (e + x * (d + x * (c + x * b)));`
Helvetica typeface	a = f + x * (e + x * (d + x * (c + x * b)));
Change sizes of parentheses	a = f + x * (e + x * (d + x * (c + x * b)));
Recommended format	a = f + x * (e + x * (d + x * (c + x * b)));

✂ --

Figure 3.49: *Expressions with unary operators superscripts and three parenthesis sizes.*

Next we introduce (phase c, at the top of the figure) the use of superscripts for unary operators, a convention that will likely look strange to experienced C programmers and may therefore be controversial. Because it provides an additional visual clue to the nature of each operator, we propose this convention and suggest that it will look "natural" once used for a little while.

Inspired by the appearance of standard mathematics typography, we would like to vary the size and shape of parentheses. Varying the shape is difficult in C, since square and curly braces already have distinguished meanings (but see Figure 3.63). However, we can introduce (phase d, at the bottom of the figure) a number (3) of different sizes of parenthesis. Already, at this stage, the constituent structure of an expression is becoming more evident.

(e) Variable Word Spacing

Fixed width Courier typeface	`a = b + c * d;`
Constant word spacing	a = b + c * d;
Variable word spacing, exaggerated	a = b + c * d;
Variable word spacing, recommended	a = b + c * d;

✂ --

(f) Absolute vs. Relative Precedence Based

Fixed width Courier typeface	`a = b;` `a = b + c * d || e;`
Absolute precedence based, exaggerated	a = b; a = b + c * d || e;
Relative precedence based, exaggerated	a = b; a = b + c * d || e;
Relative precedence based, recommended	a = b; a = b + c * d || e;

```
                =
               / \
              a   ||
                 / \
                +   e
               / \
              b   *
                 / \
                c   d
```

Figure 3.50: *Variations in wordspacing in expressions.*

This and the next three figures assume kerned binary operators, raised unary operators, and three sizes of parenthesis, and illustrate variations in wordspacing. At the top of the figure (phase e), we show the difference between constant wordspacing, exaggerated variable wordspacing, and reasonable variable wordspacing. The tighter the wordspacing, the greater the binding; thus visual clues guide us in parsing the expression.

At the bottom of the figure (phase f), we contrast a technique in which all operators are given fixed spacings determined by their *absolute* precedence and independent of the syntax of the expressions in which they appear, with a technique using spacing based on the *relative* precedence of operators, where we add spacing based on the syntax of each expression tree, adding less and less spacing as one progresses lower and lower in the tree.

(g) N–ary Compression

Fixed width Courier typeface	`if (p || q || r || s)`
Precedence based spacing, exaggerated	if (p || q || r || s)
N–ary operator spacing, exaggerated	if (p || q || r || s)
N–ary operator spacing, recommended	*if* (p || q || r || s)

```
        ||
       / \
      ||   s
     / \
    ||   r
   / \
  p   q
```

✂ -

(h) Parentheses Reset

Fixed width Courier typeface	`a = b * (c + d);`
Parentheses don't reset, exaggerated	a = b * (c + d);
Parentheses reset, exaggerated	a = b * (c + d);
Parentheses reset, recommended	a = b * (c + d);

```
         =
        / \
       a   *
          / \
         b   ()
              |
              +
             / \
            c   d
```

✂ -

Figure 3.51: *Variations in wordspacing in expressions.*

The technique shown in Figure 3.50 can be improved in several ways. One problem occurs when we have sequences of operators of identical precedence, such as shown above as phase g, at the top of the figure. Since this is better viewed as a single "*n*-ary" operator, we collapse the sequence and use identical spacing around each component operator.

Parentheses present another opportunity, for they provide visual clues to guide the parsing of the expression. It is therefore better (as shown as phase h, at the bottom of the figure) to reset the spacing to be added whenever the algorithm enters a parenthesized sub-expression, and thus to add extra space only when really needed.

(i) Top Down vs Bottom Up

Fixed width Courier typeface

```
if (a + b < c || c <= d)
```

Spacing determined top down,
exaggerated (1 2 3 2)

if (a + b < c || c <= d)

Spacing determined bottom up,
exaggerated (1 2 3 1)

if (a + b < c || c <= d)

Spacing determined bottom up,
recommended

if (a + b < c || c <= d)

```
                ||
               /  \
              <    <=
             / \  / \
            +   c c   d
           / \
          a   b
```

✂--

Figure 3.52: *Variations in wordspacing in expressions.*

Another subtlety is illustrated in this figure (phase i). Applying our algorithm
top-down results in adding more spacing than we need where trees are unbal-
anced, as we add space in inverse proportion to the distance of a node from the
root of the tree. It is better to scan the tree in a bottom-up fashion, adding space
based on the height of the largest subtree under each node, because we then no
longer introduce needless extra space.

The difference between these two algorithms can be seen in the above
example. The top-down approach adds the largest spacing (3, in rank order)
around the "||", intermediate spacing (2, in rank order) around the "<" and "<=",
and the smallest spacing (1, in rank order) around the "+". The bottom-up algorithm only adds the smallest spacing around the "<=".

Fixed width Courier typeface

```
k = n |= a << 2 & 07 ^ 04 | 01;
```

Overflow - discard top
distinctions, exaggerated
(4 4 1 2 3 4)

k   =   n |=   a ≪ 2 & 07   ^   04 | 01;

Underflow - discard bottom
distinctions, exaggerated
(4 3 1 1 1 2)

k   =   n |=   a ≪ 2 & 07 ^ 04 | 01;

Allow many dynamic
distinctions, exaggerated
(6 5 1 2 3 4)

k   =   n |=   a ≪ 2 & 07   ^   04 | 01;

Many dynamic distinctions,
recommended

k   =   n |=   a ≪ 2 & 07 ^ 04 | 01;

```
            =
           / \
          k   |=
             / \
            n   |
               / \
              ^   01
             / \
            &  04
           / \
          << 07
         / \
        a   2
```

✂--

Figure 3.53: *Variations in wordspacing in expressions.*

Finally (phase j), we consider the situation where the tree is so deep that it
requires too many different spacings for the reader to perceive the magnitude of
each level. We can collapse distinctions at the top of the tree, at the bottom of
the tree, or nonetheless use as many distinctions as there are levels in the tree,
even if these are finer, perhaps imperceptible. This last approach is simpler and
seems acceptable, so it is the one that we recommend.

Typographic Encodings of Token Attributes

Current attempts at program visualization often employ crude mechanisms for distinguishing typographically one kind of token from another. Reserved words are often shown in boldface; manifest constants are often named using capital letters only. These attempts, typical of many prettyprinting programs, represent but a small fraction of the wealth of the purely typographic possibilities for enhancing the legibility and readability of programs. The optimum encoding is a complex synthesis of the reader's needs for clarity, when scanning the text with a variety of search motives, and when examining the text slowly and in detail. Unfortunately, extensive data on programmers' reading patterns are not yet available in the literature of computer science or visible language.

We have experimented with mappings from C token attributes to typographic attributes. After organizing C tokens into a hierarchy (Section 3.3), we then considered or experimented with the appearance of token attributes in an attempt to achieve optimum legibility and readability.

Typographic Vocabulary

Typographic attributes used in the encodings included the following:
- Choice of typeface, for example, Helvetica, Times Roman, or Courier.
- Choice of weight, for example, medium or bold.
- Choice of proportion, for example, condensed, normal, or extended.
- Choice of slant, for example, roman or italic.
- Choice of point size, for example, 8, 9, 10, 11, 12, or 14 point.
- Choice of capitalization, for example, all capitals, all lowercase, initial capitals, small capitals, embedded capitals, and standard prefixes (such as "#").

There are countless interesting variations (some of which appear in Figures 3.54–3.58) in the mapping of typographic attributes onto token attributes. Because of the variety of reading and scanning tasks that programmers undertake, there is no single optimal choice. Yet the "most visible" tokens should always be the "most important" or the "most noteworthy." One must also be careful to avoid overloading the reader by including too many different visual elements within a single page. Thus it is inappropriate to use large numbers of combinations of font, slant, weight, and point size.

One of the most effective methods of encoding is the use of color. Examples appear on the inside front and back covers and are discussed in Section 6.7.

```
static STATUS
keyrespond(key)
```

struct keyword	*key;

For stepping through pattern list.
Eventual return value.

```
register struct pattern              *pat;
register STATUS                      ret;

for  (pat = key→pats; pat != NULL; pat = pat→pnext)
     ret = patrespond(pat);
     if (ret == S_DONE || ret == S_NEXT)
          return (ret);
if (debug)
     printf("---no match\n");
return (S_FAIL);
```

✀ --

```
static STATUS
keyrespond(key)
```

struct keyword	*key;

For stepping through pattern list.
Eventual return value.

```
register struct pattern              *pat;
register STATUS                      ret;

for  (pat = key→pats; pat != NULL; pat = pat→pnext)
     ret = patrespond(pat);
     if  (ret == S_DONE || ret == S_NEXT)
          return (ret);
if (debug)
     printf("---no match\n");
return (S_FAIL);
```

✀ --

Figure 3.54: *Too few and too many distinctions among token classes.*

We begin with a variation (at the top of the figure) that uses only roman type. Function names in their definitions are set as headlines in 14-point type, a convention we adopt throughout this entire series (see also Figures 3.15-3.22). Although appealing in its simplicity, using only roman type seems to miss the potential of the medium to aid the recognition of token classes through reasonable typographic encoding.

At the bottom of the figure, we show how typography can be overused. We apply bold for reserved words, italic for non-global variables, operators, and function names in use, bold italic for global variables and function names in their definitions, and roman for everything else except strings, which appear in a fixed-width typeface. The result is too busy, hence unattractive and ineffective.

```
static STATUS
keyrespond(key)
```

struct keyword	*key;

For stepping through pattern list.
Eventual return value.

```
register struct pattern              *pat;
register STATUS                      ret;

for (pat = key→pats; pat != NULL; pat = pat→pnext)
    ret = patrespond(pat);
    if (ret == S_DONE || ret == S_NEXT)
        return (ret);
if (debug)
    printf("---no match\n");
return (S_FAIL);
```

✂ --

```
static STATUS
keyrespond(key)
```

struct keyword	*key;

For stepping through pattern list.
Eventual return value.

```
register struct pattern              *pat;
register STATUS                      ret;

for (pat = key→pats; pat != NULL; pat = pat→pnext)
    ret = patrespond(pat);
    if (ret == S_DONE || ret == S_NEXT)
        return (ret);
if (debug)
    printf("---no match\n");
return (S_FAIL);
```

✂ --

Figure 3.55: *Uses for boldface in the typographic encoding of token classes.*

We show (at the top of the figure) a variation of the recommended attributes that is suggested by the typography used in the presentation of ALGOL, i.e., all reserved words are shown in boldface. This use of bold for reserved words is inappropriate, for it highlights too many elements, most of them not needing highlighting.

Another important token class is that of the control-flow altering reserved words (*return, continue, break,* and *goto*). We call attention (at the bottom of the figure) to instances of these constructs that alter normal control flow (we termed these "suspicious" in Figure 3.47) by emboldening them. We also use boldface to highlight function names in their definitions. (We shall continue this convention throughout the remainder of this series.) Both these uses are very effective.

```
static STATUS
keyrespond(key)
```

struct keyword	*key;

For stepping through pattern list.
Eventual return value.

```
register struct pattern          *pat;
register STATUS                  ret;

for  (pat  =  key → pats; pat  != NULL; pat  =  pat → pnext)
      ret =  patrespond(pat);
      if  (ret ==  S_DONE  ||  ret ==  S_NEXT)
            return  (ret);
if  (debug)
      printf("---no  match\n");
return  (S_FAIL);
```

✂ --

```
static STATUS
keyrespond(key)
```

struct keyword	*key;

For stepping through pattern list.
Eventual return value.

```
register struct pattern          *pat;
register STATUS                  ret;

for  (pat  =  key → pats; pat  != NULL; pat  =  pat → pnext)
      ret =  patrespond(pat);
      if  (ret ==  S_DONE  ||  ret ==  S_NEXT)
            return  (ret);
if  (debug)
      printf("---no  match\n");
return  (S_FAIL);
```

✂ --

Figure 3.56: *Other uses of boldface for typographic token encoding.*

Another role for boldface is to highlight the constituent structure of the code in the sense of calling attention to how certain functions are defined in terms of certain other functions. We do this by typesetting all such function names in boldface (at the top of the figure). This technique assists in the task of browsing and navigating through the code.

A restrained and effective use of boldface is the use for denoting global variables, as is shown at the bottom of the figure. In doing so, we highlight a small number of tokens, those in which the program violates the "regular" use of parameter passing as the vehicle of communication between various functions. Our eyes are thereby drawn to places in the code where local actions can result in non-local effects.

```
static STATUS
keyrespond(key)
```

struct keyword	*key;

For stepping through pattern list.
Eventual return value.

```
register struct pattern          *pat;
register STATUS                  ret;

for (pat = key→pats; pat != NULL; pat = pat→pnext)
    ret = patrespond(pat);
    if (ret == S_DONE || ret == S_NEXT)
        return (ret);
if (debug)
    printf("---no match\n");
return (S_FAIL);
```

```
static STATUS
keyrespond(key)
```

struct *keyword*	**key*;

For stepping through pattern list.
Eventual return value.

```
register struct pattern          *pat;
register STATUS                  ret;

for (pat = key→pats; pat != NULL; pat = pat→pnext)
    ret = patrespond(pat);
    if (ret == S_DONE || ret == S_NEXT)
        return (ret);
if (debug)
    printf("---no match\n");
return (S_FAIL);
```

Figure 3.57: *Uses for italics in the typographic encoding of token classes.*

Our recommended standard uses italics to distinguish reserved words from identifiers. We can see (at the top of the figure) that the result is quite restrained and very effective.

At the bottom of the figure, we reverse the use of roman and italic type. Thus identifiers appear in italic, reserved words in roman. Although the effect is interesting, italic is overused, and the result is less readable than the presentation at the top.

```
static STATUS
keyrespond(key)
```

struct keyword	*key;

For stepping through pattern list.
Eventual return value.

```
register struct pattern              *pat;
register STATUS                      ret;

for (pat = key→pats; pat != NULL; pat = pat→pnext)
    ret = patrespond(pat);
    if (ret == S_DONE || ret == S_NEXT)
        return (ret);
if (debug)
    printf("---no match\n");
return (S_FAIL);
```

✂ --

```
static STATUS
keyrespond(key)
```

struct keyword	*key;

For stepping through pattern list.
Eventual return value.

```
register struct pattern              *pat;
register STATUS                      ret;

for (pat = key→pats; pat != NULL; pat = pat→pnext)
    ret = patrespond(pat);
    if (ret == S_DONE || ret == S_NEXT)
        return (ret);
if (debug)
    printf("---no match\n");
return (S_FAIL);
```

✂ --

Figure 3.58: *Our recommendation for the typographic encoding of tokens.*

We have proposed, in Figures 3.55 and 3.56, a number of useful roles for boldface, namely, highlighting suspicious control flow, function names in their definitions, embedded function calls, and global variable occurrences. We have also shown, earlier in the book, another good use, that is, for preprocessor command names. The combination of all of these (at the top of the figure) overloads boldface. In an interactive environment, one can choose the most appropriate use, depending upon the task at hand; one can also very effectively employ color (see the inside front and back covers and Section 6.7).

At the bottom of the figure, we show our single recommended default mode of presentation of C programs on paper. Boldface is used for function names in their definitions and for global variables. Italic is used for reserved words, structure tags, and defined types. We substitute 8-point fixed-width Courier for the normal 10-point Helvetica regular roman for character string constants. The use of the lighter fixed-width font helps to separate character strings visually from the surrounding code and makes it easier to see and count the spaces in a string where the precise number is important.

The Typography of Punctuation

Attention to fine detail in the choice of fonts and in the design of their characters, in interletter spacing, and in interword spacing is essential to enhancing the legibility and readability of computer programs.

The punctuation marks of computer programs consist of separators such as ";" and ",", containment symbols such as "(" and "}", and operators such as ".", "!", and "!=". The legibility of punctuation marks in program text is a critical component affecting the comprehensibility of a program, much more so than the legibility of English language punctuation affects the comprehensibility of a passage in English. This is true both because punctuation marks occur more frequently in programs than in English, and also because errors in reading punctuation are far more serious with programs than with English.

Unfortunately, no typeface currently exists that has been optimized for use in representing computer programs (Figure 3.59). The bold is often slightly too heavy; the regular weight is sometimes too easily overlooked if the original has been poorly displayed with badly adjusted equipment or if it has been degraded through photocopying. In addition, idiosyncratic size and positioning changes for particular characters in particular fonts are often desirable.

We have therefore considered or experimented with various methods of enhancing the legibility of program punctuation.

Typographic Vocabulary

These methods have included:
- Emboldening and/or enlarging punctuation marks (Figures 3.60 and 3.61).
- Reducing the letterspacing within compound (multicharacter) operators (Figures 3.60 and 3.61). Roughly speaking, we are kerning the operators to form ligatures.
- Substituting symbols that are more meaningful and not as overloaded as the existing C symbol set. In the presentation of C source text appearing in this book, we have generally preserved the C character set and resisted the temptation to change it. Although changing the C symbol set would be traumatic to experienced C readers, it could result in enhanced legibility and readability. We illustrate this with a series of examples (Figures 3.62 and 3.63) showing in each case a conventional presentation in a fixed-width font, our recommended presentation style, and a more radical variant.

Fixed width typeface

```
i != j | !11;
j |= i || 11;
```

Times Roman typeface

```
i != j | ! 11;
j |= i || 11 ;
```

Helvetica typeface

```
i != j | ! 1l;
j |= i || l1 ;
```

Figure 3.59: *Weaknesses of Helvetica for representing programs.*

The program shown above illustrates some weaknesses of Helvetica for representing programs. Particularly awkward are "i," "j," "l," "1," "!," and "|" (as we can see at the bottom of the figure), although they are not significantly better in a traditional fixed-width font such as Courier (shown at the top of the figure), or in a traditional serif font such as Times Roman (shown at the middle of the figure). Notice that the token just to the left of the semicolon in the first statement is the long constant represented by a one followed by an ell, whereas the token just to the left of the semicolon in the second statement is the variable identified by an ell followed by a one.

The research reported in this book has restricted itself to Postscript™ fonts, because of their wide availability. We wanted a sans-serif typeface for code and a serif face for comments. This restricted us to Helvetica and Avant Garde for code. The latter has no advantages in dealing with the letter confusion problems illustrated above, so we chose Helvetica, which is better known and more widely used.

More research needs to be done on the design of appropriate typefaces for representing program source text. Lucida® (Bigelow and Holmes, 1986) should be examined carefully, as it does have the advantages of screen and laser printer consistency as well as having unified serif, sans-serif, and fixed-width fonts.

```
void
fiddlesticks()
{
    int eight = 5;
    int five = 7;
    struct pattern {
        struct pattern *pat;
        int        this,
                   that;
    } rec[5];

    rec[1].pat = &rec[0];
    for (rec[2].this = 0; !rec[1].that; rec[2].this++, bit <<= 1) {
        rec[1].that *= (((bit | flag2) ^ ~3) == OPT3);
        rec[2].pat->this += rec[3].that ? 3 * 4 : ('a' & 15);
    }

both: if (eight && five)
        eight >>= five++;
    if (--eight || five && five * 2 != 10 || eight <= 8)
        eight %= (five &= 127);
    }
```

✂ --

```
void
fiddlesticks()
{
    int eight = 5;
    int five = 7;
    struct pattern {
        struct pattern    *pat;
        int        this,
                   that;
    } rec[5];

    rec[1].pat = &rec[0];
    for (rec[2].this = 0; !rec[1].that; rec[2].this++, bit <<= 1) {
        rec[1].that *= (((bit | flag2) ^ ~3) == OPT3);
        rec[2].pat->this += rec[3].that ? 3 * 4 : ('a' & 15);
    }

both:   if (eight && five)
        eight >>= five++;
    if (--eight || five && five * 2 != 10 || eight <= 8)
        eight %= (five &= 127);
    }
```

✂ --

Figure 3.60: *Controlling the weight, size, and position of punctuation marks and operators.*

Figures 3.60 and 3.61 show how the appearance of source text may be improved if certain punctuation marks and operators are emboldened, and enlarged or reduced, and if the constituent characters in certain multi-character operators are moved closer together. The top of this figure shows, in a fixed-width font, a complex series of declarations and statements that together include most of the punctuation marks and operators of C. The bottom of this figure shows the same code displayed in Helvetica.

void
fiddlesticks()

```
        int                             eight = 5;
        int                             five = 7;
        struct pattern {
                struct pattern      *pat;
                int                 this,
                                    that;
        }                               rec[5];

        rec[1].pat = &rec[0];
        for (rec[2].this = 0;  !rec[1].that;  rec[2].this++  , bit <<= 1)
            rec[1].that *= (((bit | flag2) ^ ~3) == OPT3);
            rec[2].pat→this  += rec[3].that ? 3 * 4 : ('a' & 15);

both:
        if (eight && five)
            eight >>= five++;
        if (--eight || five && five * 2 != 10 || eight <= 8)
            eight %= (five &= 127);
```

✀ --

Figure 3.61: *Controlling the weight, size, and position of punctuation marks and operators.*

This figure shows the recommended appearance of the complex series of declarations and statements introduced in Figure 3.60. The legibility of individual punctuation marks such as the ",", "*", "!", "?", ";", and ":" has been enhanced by emboldening them, by enlarging or reducing them, by repositioning them, and in some cases by substituting more meaningful symbols (see also Figures 3.62 and 3.63). The appearance of multi-character C operators has been enhanced by moving the constituent symbols closer together; the goal has been to ensure that each pair or triple of ASCII characters will be rapidly and reliably recognized as a single operator. Details of all the transformations applied appear in Section D.9 of Appendix D.

Assignment and comparison operators

Courier	`a  +=  b<=c?  b-c  :  0;` `a  =  b==c  ||  b!=c;`
standard SEE output	a += b <= c ? b − c : 0; a = b == c ǁ b != c;
enhanced SEE output	a $\xleftarrow{+}$ b ≤ c ? b − c : 0; a ← b ≡ c ǁ b ≠ c;

✂ --

Unary and binary operators

Courier	`*p--  =  -c  *  d  -  e;`
standard SEE output	*p⁻⁻ = −c ∗ d − e;

✂ --

Figure 3.62: *A set of substitutions for some symbols of C.*

We begin this series of variations by illustrating (at the top of the figure) the appearance of a program presented with symbol substitutions made where conventional C symbolism is not the most appropriate or meaningful. (Symbol substitutions not currently implemented in SEE appear in the rows labelled "enhanced SEE output.") This is particularly true with the simple assignment operator, where we substitute a left-pointing arrow; with the variants of the assignment statement; and with the comparison operators, where, for example, we substitute a mathematical "less than or equal to" in place of "<=", and a mathematical "not equals" sign in place of "!=". (In these cases, we have used a "≡" instead of the conventional "=", because the latter is a legal symbol, the assignment operator, in standard C.)

Other symbol substitutions are made to help distinguish unary from binary operators, as for example with the indirection and multiply operators. The use of symbol substitutions as well as superscripting is illustrated at the bottom of the figure.

Dot and comma operators

Courier
```
for (i=0,j=0; f(i,j)<(i+j); i++,j++)
    s[i].x = 1.0;
```

standard SEE output

for (i = 0 , j = 0; f(i, j) < (i + j); i++ , j++)
    s[i].x = 1.0;

✂ ---

Parentheses

Courier
```
if (malloc((size_t)  (i+j))  !=  (char  *)  NULL)
    fatal("malloc(i+j)");
```

standard SEE output

if (malloc((*size_t*)(i + j)) != (*char* *) NULL)
    fatal("malloc(i+j)");

enhanced SEE output

if (malloc⌈⌊*size_t*⌋ (i + j)⌉ != ⌊*char* *⌋ NULL)
    fatal⌈"malloc(i+j)"⌉;

✂ ---

Token substitution

Courier
```
do  {
    ptr = ptr->next;
} while (ptr != 0);
```

standard SEE output

do
    ptr = ptr→next;
↑*while* (ptr != 0);

enhanced SEE output

do
    ptr = ptr→next;
↑*while* (ptr ≠ ∅);

✂ ---

Figure 3.63: *More substitutions for symbols of C.*

Another class of symbol substitutions are suggested by C's tendency to over-load the use of certain symbols, that is, to use them for multiple purposes. We can avoid overloading and achieve more meaningful distinctions by employing new symbolism for the dot and comma operators, such as that illustrated at the top of the figure, and for the many kinds of parentheses, such as that illustrated at the middle of the figure. We distinguish between the use of the dot in a floating point number and its use as a selection operator; between the use of the comma as a separator of function arguments and its use in sequential expressions; and among the uses of parentheses in expressions and in certain control structures such as the *for* and the *if*, its use surrounding function arguments (represented by top brackets), and its use as the cast operator (represented by bottom brackets).

Yet another kind of symbol substitution operates upon reserved words and tokens rather than punctuation or operators. Examples illustrated at the bottom of the figure include distinguishing the two kinds of *while* and introducing a special symbol for NULL.

Finally, we recall that a major kind of symbol substitution is the clutter reduction through the elimination of most occurrences of curly braces recommended in this book, and the suggestion (Figure 3.46) that we could also do away with semi-colons.

The Presentation of Program Metadata

A full understanding of a program rarely comes from reading only the code. Comprehension requires a knowledge of numerous items of metadata describing the context in which the program was created and is used. Unlike comments, which usually describe a piece of a program, these metadata refer to the entire program. A partial list of program metadata follows:

- Title of program
- Author(s)
- Further developer(s)
- Maintainer(s)
- Owner(s)
- Publisher(s)
- User(s)
- In addition to names for all of the above individuals, their faces, affiliations, postal and network addresses, and telephone and facsimile transmission numbers
- Location of source code, i.e., machine, directory, file(s)
- Version, revision number
- Date and time of this version or revision
- Date and time that the current listing was created

Related to but distinct from the metadata are longer texts that describe the program, such as an abstract, statement of purpose, and history. These texts are described in Chapter 5.

Metadata describing the context in which the program has been created and the state in which it currently exists appear in the program on the title page(s), table(s) of contents, and indices, and in the headers of individual program pages. Exactly what is displayed in each of the ten fields of the header or in a modified header (see Figure 3.64) will clearly be varied by the individual company, site, or programmer using a program visualizer.

Dynamic Graphics Project
Computer Systems Research Inst.
University of Toronto

main()   Phone Name   Printed 14 Apr 17:18

PROPRIETARY AND CONFIDENTIAL

Chapter 1   # phone.c

phone.c – Prints all potential words corresponding to a given phone number.

Only words containing vowels are printed.
Acceptable phone numbers range from 1 to 10 digits.

```
#include            <string.h>
#include            <stdio.h>

typedef int                             bool;
#define             FALSE               0
#define             TRUE                1
```

labels on each digit of dial

```
char                                    *label[] = {
    "0",
    "1",        "abc",      "def",
    "ghi",      "jkl",      "mno",
    "prs",      "tuv",      "wxy"
};
```

max digits in phone number

```
#define             PNMAX               10
```

actual number of digits

phone number

current position in label, per digit

```
int                                     digits;
int                                     pn[PNMAX];
char                                    *label_ptr[PNMAX];
```

```
main(argc, argv)

    int                                 argc;
    char                                *argv[];

    register int                        i;
    bool                                foundvowel = FALSE;
```

For each phone argument ...

```
    while (*++argv != NULL)
        if ( !getpn(*argv))
            fprintf(stderr, "PhoneName:  %s is not a phone number\n", *argv);
        else
```

✂ --

Figure 3.64: *A proprietary and confidential program page.*

This figure illustrates the imposition of a piece of metadata, a ''Proprietary and Confidential'' Notice, within the field of the header space on the program page. The company clearly considers it important for this to be dominant on each page.

Chapter 4

A Graphic Design Manual for the C Programming Language

"To design is
to plan and to organize, to order, to relate and to control.
In short it embraces
all means opposing disorder and accident.
Therefore it signifies
a human need
and qualifies man's
thinking and doing."

Josef Albers, as cited by Francois Bucher (1961), *Josef Albers: Despite Straight Lines*, New Haven: Yale University Press. Reprinted with permission of the Josef Albers Foundation Inc.

Once you get the hang of these designed environments, they're really OK.

Section 4.1   Graphic Design Manuals

At this point it is appropriate to document systematically our new approach to the presentation of computer programs and their documentation. Because so many features can be changed, it is helpful to organize a preferred visual differentiation of appearances in a graphic design manual.

A graphic design manual is a reference tool specifying the visual representation of the structure and component parts of a system or process that is being designed, for example, a computer program. The manual consists of guidelines and detailed specifications for the appearance of and a reader's interaction with the visible language of that system or process.

Goals

Our primary goal is to provide an organized set of well-designed conventions for the appearance of C programs and documentation that the C programming community can readily adopt. The manual's specifications are based on thoughtful analysis of the previously described variations, as well as careful consideration of the limits and capabilities of software, hardware, program writers, and program readers.

A secondary goal is to acquaint the computer science, software engineering, and programming communities with the importance and complexity of researching, developing, writing, and designing instructions and specifications for the visual appearance of a computer programming language, in effect establishing a visible language schema.

Users

The primary users of a graphic design manual for a programming language are computer scientists, software engineers, programmers, and their managers. We believe that all programming language definitions should be accompanied by specifications for functional and attractive appearance and that all programming language processors should be accompanied by visible language processors that can automate the production of this appearance.

The secondary group of users are documentation specialists: technical writers, editors, and graphic designers. Until now, these professionals have not been concerned with the level of documentation that includes computer program source code because they could not readily manipulate it. Given the existence of this graphic design manual and suitable software to support it, documentation specialists could help programmers meet the visual requirements of good programming "literature" without taking too much of their time away from program development.

Other potential users are identified in the Preface to this book.

Contents and Usage

This graphic design manual addresses the presentation of programs in the C programming language. Section 4.2 discusses principles for effective visual communication with typeset text, then applies these recommendations to develop guidelines for the presentation of C programs. This section is organized according to the visible language taxonomy, in other words, in terms of visual appearance. Section 4.3 and Appendix D detail complete and precise specifications for all aspects of C program appearance. These sections are organized according to the C language taxonomy, in other words, in terms of C language constructs. Together, Chapter 4 and Appendix D constitute the graphic design manual for C.

Assumptions

The manual's typographic specifications are intended primarily for medium-resolution display devices (for example, 300-dots-per-inch laser printers) and secondarily for high-resolution display devices (for example, 1200-dots-per-inch phototypesetters) that produce hardcopy on paper. These conventions could easily be adapted to low-resolution devices (for example, 80-dots-per-inch display screens).

Because loose-leaf program pages occasionally will be photocopied, text legibility and the clarity of all design conventions (such as the use of gray scale tones) must survive through at least two generations of photocopying.

Although our illustrations and our implementation have been with hard copy, our principles and most of our design apply equally well to soft copy, i.e., bit-mapped raster displays. The concept of a *recommended appearance* is still important in such an environment, even though screen appearance may be immediately alterable upon demand. The role of design specifications in such an environment is to serve as the *default appearance*. Other major differences are the lower resolution, which limits the use of small type and symbols, and the ability to view content details interactively, which fundamentally changes spatial layout requirements. We shall return to this topic in Section 6.7.

Section 4.2

Graphic Design Guidelines

Page Characteristics

Since hardcopy program output appears on pages that must be printed and stored, and sometimes distributed and copied, the characteristics of these pages is a primary consideration.

Page Size and Proportion

To assist in conveying a uniform, integral appearance, all pages of the program and its related documents use the same basic format, i.e., the same choice of page size and proportion, orientation, layout grid, and composition within that grid. This manual recommends that the typical program document be laid out in the standard American paper size, 8.5″ x 11″. This paper size is efficient and cost effective, especially in terms of laser printed sheets, xerographic copying, binding, and conventional paper storage on most bookshelves and in most file drawers.[†]

Paper Properties

The selection and use of paper (the largest single cost factor in large-volume commercial publishing) can greatly influence the printability, appearance, and overall quality of print reproduction. Paper characteristics, while seemingly an insignificant factor in laser printer-oriented publishing, can play a noticeable role in the success of publishing a document. For example, using paper with the grain running in the short direction causes pages to curl at the top and bottom of a bound document. This error can be avoided by using the right kind of paper.

[†] The page layout described below can easily be transferred to European paper size with minimal changes.

Special matte-finish coated and/or colored papers can dramatically enhance the legibility of text and fine-line or fine-texture images. Special paper stocks can impart a more finished, professional look to a document or can denote the temporary, unfinished, undebugged, or unique status of certain sections of code, comments, or commentary. Some manufacturers, e.g., Hammermill and Letraset, are currently providing special-purpose laser printer papers. More variety can be expected in the future as desktop and electronic publishers become a significant market for these products.

Binding and Orientation

Three-ring vertically oriented notebooks are probably the most widely available, easily used, and efficiently updated format. Perfect or sidestitched binding should be used for most archival publications. Velobinding™ (plastic laminate strip) may be used when restricted budgets demand it, and when it is not objectionable that the publications do not lie flat. If the publications must lie flat, then three-ring or plastic spiral binding should be used.

Page Composition and Layout

Grid

The most important tool utilized by the designer and publication production specialist is the grid. The grid is an invisible framework that provides organization and consistency within a program page as well as throughout a program document. By ensuring consistent spatial locations, the grid provides design efficiency and visual coherence. The primary grid for the recommended layout of C source code (see Figure 4.1) is based on a 12-point square unit (10-point type with 2-point leading).

Layout

The page design is arranged in two columns (see Figure 4.1), a primary text column and a secondary marginalia column, plus areas at the top of the page for a header and at the bottom of the page for footnotes. The division of space between the primary and secondary columns considers the typical nesting and length of code lines, and the typical length of marginalia comments, attempting to reduce the frequency that either code or marginalia comments will be broken and will need to be folded to the following line. Line breaks in code are considered more serious than those in marginalia comments. Allocating 31.5 picas for the width of the primary text column means that there is space for roughly 75 characters of 10-point Helvetica type. This leaves 11 picas for the marginalia column, 1 pica for a separation between the two columns, and 3.75 picas for the left and right outside margins, sufficient to three-hole-punch either edge. For simplicity and consistency, the layout for a left-hand page is identical to that shown in the figure for a right-hand page.

Header Area

A typical C program is laid out with a header that contains global program metadata at the top of the page (see Figures 1.3 and 4.1).

Footnote Area

The footnote area appears under a hairline rule that is a minimum of 3.5 picas above the bottom of the page. The footnotes contain references to items defined and used elsewhere in the code.

Primary Text Column

Directly below the header begins the program text (or, on the first page of every file, the file name shown as a chapter title). Program text appearing in this column is the C source code as well as three kinds of comments: prologue, internal, and external comments. The primary text column can be divided into two 15-pica-wide columns or four 7-pica-wide columns to accommodate tabular material.

Marginalia Column

The narrower left-hand marginalia column is 11 picas wide and contains the marginalia comments, each of which is typically associated with a line of C source code.

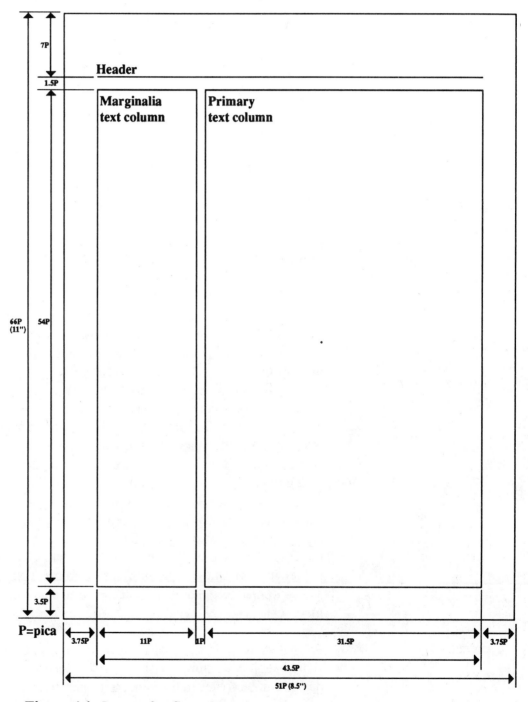

Figure 4.1: *Layout for C program pages.*

Typographic Vocabulary

Typography concerns the character set, typeface name (sometimes called font style), weight, slant, proportion, size, and other attributes of alphanumeric characters and regular punctuation symbols. Additionally, typography deals with the sizing and location of letters, words, lines, and blocks of text, topics we consider below under the heading "Typesetting."

The specifications for program code are among the most complex typographic conventions ever created because of the need for a wide variety of differentiations. We have therefore used the following typographic variables:

- three styles: variable-width serif, variable-width sans-serif, and fixed-width
- two weights: regular and bold
- two slants: roman and italic
- one proportion
- seven sizes

Currently, no typeface exists that has been designed specifically to meet the special requirements of programming languages. The ratio of alphanumeric characters to punctuation is very different for code than it is for normal prose text. Code requires many emphasized punctuation marks; however, normal type fonts developed for prose text tend to de-emphasize the size and weight of punctuation in favor of alphanumeric characters. In order to optimize legibility and readability, code requires a typeface with emphasized punctuation marks. In our specifications we have tried to overcome the limitations of normal type design as best we could by careful choice of typesetting parameters (see Figures 3.59 through 3.63, and Appendix D).

Character Set of Font

A *font* is a complete set of all characters and symbols for a given typeface, size, weight, proportion, and slant. The choice of character set is primarily determined by C and consists of standard alphanumerics and punctuation symbols included in the ASCII character set. We additionally employ a number of *pi symbols* available in standard laser printer font families. (See Figures B.6 and B.33 in Appendix B.)

By convention, macros and defined types in C are usually written with all capital letters. To improve the appearance of such constructs, we typeset them with an initial capital letter and subsequent "small caps," in other words, letters sitting on the same character baseline but with the size reduced by 2 points.

Generally, all source code punctuation should be set in 10-point Helvetica Regular, roman. Specific exceptions are described in the specification in Appendix D (see also Figures 3.60 and 3.61). For example, parentheses increase in size from 10 points to 12 points to 14 points as they go outward in expressions with nested parentheses. Comment punctuation should be set in Times Roman Regular, roman, at the point size identical to that of the comment text.

Typeface

A *typeface* is a collection of fonts of varying size, weight, proportion, and slant that all have similar visual form. Consistency and organization of page design can be achieved through the proper selection of typefaces (see Figure 4.2). Because of their simplicity, widespread availability, and proven performance, the use of the typefaces Helvetica and Times Roman are recommended in two weights, regular and bold, as well as two slants, roman and italic. To represent ASCII character string input and output, we also recommend a fixed-width font, Courier.

Size

Characters in the chosen typeface styles should be confined to the following point sizes: 8, 9, 10, 12, 14, 18, and 24.

Helvetica Regular, roman (HR):

> ABCDEFGHIJKLMNOPQRSTUVWXYZ0123456789
> abcdefghijklmnopqrstuvwxyz.,:;"!?@#&+-()[]{}

Helvetica Bold, roman (HB):

> **ABCDEFGHIJKLMNOPQRSTUVWXYZ0123456789**
> **abcdefghijklmnopqrstuvwxyz.,:;"!?@#&+-();]{}**

Helvetica Regular, italic (HI):

> *ABCDEFGHIJKLMNOPQRSTUVWXYZ0123456789*
> *abcdefghijklmnopqrstuvwxyz.,:;"!?@#&+-();]{}*

Helvetica Bold, italic (HBI):

> ***ABCDEFGHIJKLMNOPQRSTUVWXYZ0123456789***
> ***abcdefghijklmnopqrstuvwxyz.,:;"!?@#&+-();]{}***

Times Roman Regular, roman (TR):

> ABCDEFGHIJKLMNOPQRSTUVWXYZ0123456789
> abcdefghijklmnopqrstuvwxyz.,:;''!?@#&+-();]{}

Times Roman Bold, roman (TB):

> **ABCDEFGHIJKLMNOPQRSTUVWXYZ0123456789**
> **abcdefghijklmnopqrstuvwxyz.,:;''!?@#&+-();]{}**

Times Roman Regular, italic (TI):

> *ABCDEFGHIJKLMNOPQRSTUVWXYZ0123456789*
> *abcdefghijklmnopqrstuvwxyz.,:;''!?@#&+-();]{}*

Times Roman Bold, italic (TBI):

> ***ABCDEFGHIJKLMNOPQRSTUVWXYZ0123456789***
> ***abcdefghijklmnopqrstuvwxyz.,:;''!?@#&+-();]{}***

```
Courier Regular, roman (CR):†

    ABCDEFGHIJKLMNOPQRSTUVWXYZ0123456789
    abcdefghijklmnopqrstuvwxyz.,:;`'!?@#&+-();]{}
```

Figure 4.2: *Typeface system for C program visualization.*

---

†   The use of Courier is intended to mimic the fixed-width font capability currently in use, so we do not currently specify Courier in bold or italic or bold italic.

Weight

Limiting the text to two distinctly different weights, regular and bold, is essential. Because of the complexity in the appearance of a program page, the human eye could not easily discern differences among more than two weights. In addition, if laser printing and xerographic reproduction were not precisely controlled, the differences would be significantly diminished.

Bold typefaces reduce legibility when set in large blocks, and their emphatic quality is diluted relative to quantity of usage, so boldface should never be used for large amounts of text. Bold type can be used effectively **to emphasize individual words or phrases,** so it should be used as a means of emphasizing key elements in a program such as function definitions, global variables, and warning comments.

Proportion

In general, to optimize readability, regular-proportion fonts should be used rather than extremely condensed or extended fonts. However, slightly condensed fonts such as Helvetica Narrow offer a viable alternative to Helvetica regular where horizontal space is at a premium.[†]

Slant

As with boldface type, italics should be used sparingly *for individual words or phrases* such as certain reserved words and comments, because their legibility and emphatic qualities are impaired when set in large blocks.

Typographic Assignments

Minimizing the variables of style, weight, slant, and proportion heightens legibility and readability through familiarity and consistency. With a few different styles, sizes, weights, and slants, the designer can establish a systematic hierarchy for the default setting of C source text. Thus source code in the primary text column has a default setting of 10/12 Helvetica Regular, roman, flush left at each indentation level, ragged right.[††] Exceptions to the regular setting of source code are made to emphasize lexical, syntactic, or semantic differences and are detailed in Figure 4.3.

Internal, external, and prologue comments are set in single and multiple lines as 10/12 Times Roman Regular, roman. Prologue and external comments are contained inside of a light gray area.[†††] Internal comments are highlighted by a similar gray area box, that, along with the comment, is indented in relation to the code to which the comment refers (see Figure 1.3). The marginalia comments are set in 8-point Times Roman Regular, roman. Regular marginalia comments are set in regular weight while warning and other special kinds of annotations (to be defined in the future, see, for example, Figure 5.20) may be set in bold, italic, or bold italic.

The complete list of recommended typographic assignments appears in the table shown as Figure 4.3.

[†]   We do make use of Helvetica Narrow Bold, regular, in one case detailed in Appendix D. The reason is not to save space, but because Helvetica Bold, regular, is too strong, and Helvetica, regular, is too weak, and the Narrow provides an appropriate effect intermediate in strength.

[††]   The notation "10/12" means that the size of the type is 10 points and that the distance from baseline to baseline is 12 points, in other words, the *leading* is 2 points. See the next section on "Typesetting" for a discussion of indentation, hyphenation, and justification.

[†††]   The gray tone needs to be chosen so it is light, survives photocopying, and does not impede the legibility of text. The exact choice will depend on the capabilities of the particular laser printer. A 10% gray area seems to be appropriate.

C Construct	Typeface	Size/Leading
Marginalia comments	TR	8/12
All other comments	TR	10/12
Punctuation marks	HR	10/12[†]
Preprocessor command names	HB	10/12
Macro names	HR	8–10/12[††]
Reserved words	HI	10/12
Structure tags	HI	10/12
Defined types	HI	10/12
Global variables	HB	10/12
Other variables	HR	10/12
Function names in their definitions	HB	14/16
Other instances of functions names	HR	10/12
Other identifiers	HR	10/12
String constants	CR	8/12
Other constants	HR	10/12
File names	HB	18/21
Headers to program pages	TR	8/9
Footnotes to program pages	HR/HB	8/9[†††]

Figure 4.3: *Typographic assignments for C program visualization.*

Typesetting

Typesetting is the organization and placement of typographic characters on a page within the constraints imposed by page layout and typographic parameters and according to the semantic requirements of the text. Appropriate selection of typesetting parameters allows the programmer or program viewer to emphasize or de-emphasize the components of a program according to individual user preferences and task requirements.

Letterspacing

To ensure maximum legibility and readability, the amount of space between characters should be visually consistent. Letterspacing should never vary from standard amounts for well-designed fonts, except to kern pairs of characters in multi-character operators (see Figures 3.60 and 3.61 and Section D.9).

---

†	With some exceptions (see Figures 3.60 and 3.61 and Section D.9).
††	10-point letters with the remainder of the word in "small caps" (8 points).
†††	Global variables are set in Helvetica Bold, roman; file static variables are set in Helvetica Regular, roman.

Superscripts

Unary operators should be displayed as superscripts, in order to make them more distinguishable from binary operators. This approach is particularly useful in long, complex expressions.

Wordspacing

To ensure maximum readability, the amount of space between words should be visually consistent. The default wordspacing is 1/3 of an em for both code and comments. However, the wordspacing within C source code needs to vary for three reasons:

- Some tokens require more space around them to increase their distinctiveness and give them more emphasis.
- Because of the interspersed use of roman and italic and the prevalence of separators and other punctuation, readability can sometimes be enhanced by adding more space between pairs of tokens from certain token classes.
- Extra space should be added to clarify the precedence hierarchy of sub-expressions within expressions.

Our wordspacing model adds the sum of the additional spaces that result from applying these three criteria, each of which is now described in more detail.[†]

The spacing associated with individual tokens is determined by a "strings file" for C tokens that was derived through an iterative design process and is documented in Appendix D.9.

When two symbols are to be placed next to each other, the space between them is adjusted based on an "after" attribute of the first (which affects space after the symbol) and a "before" attribute of the second, according to the following algorithm:

- If the "after rank" of the first is greater than the "before rank" of the second, the "after spacing" of the first is used; otherwise,
- If the "after rank" of the first is less than the "before rank" of the second, the "before spacing" of the second is used; otherwise,
- The longer of the "after spacing" of the first and the "before spacing" of the second is used.

Ranks and spacings for token classes have been derived through an iterative design process, and are documented in Appendix D.8.

Finally, the extra space calculated for individual tokens and augmented by the extra space for adjacent pairs of tokens is increased based on the occurrence of binary operators in C expressions. The algorithm for adding extra space around binary operators works as follows: The lower the precedence of the operator, and the higher it occurs in the parse tree of the expression (i.e., closer to the root), the greater the space that is added. More specifically, space is added around binary operators based on the height of the taller of the left and right subtrees below the operator (Figure 3.52). The occurrence of parentheses in an expression resets the algorithm so that the parenthesized sub-expression acts as a leaf in the parent expression and so that the algorithm begins anew on the sub-expression (Figure 3.51). Sequences of operators of identical precedence are treated as a single "n-ary" operator with identical spacing around each operator (Figure 3.51). Assuming no more than six levels of spacing to be added in an expression, these levels are 0 em, 0.2 em, 0.4 em, 0.6 em, 0.8 em, and 1.0 em (Figure 3.53). If more than six levels are required, which is almost inconceivable for

---

†   The details of the wordspacing model are complex and may be skipped at first reading.

reasonable C given the "parenthesis reset" and "*n*-ary operator" strategies just described, then the levels are scaled so that the largest space is 1.0 em (Figure 3.53).

Justification

All program text should be set flush left at each indentation level (see below), ragged right.

Indentation

Indentations are the primary visual indicators of the hierarchical levels of source code and the associated internal comments. Indentations of 2-pica intervals provide the ideal visual signal to discern one level from another yet provide economy of space. This regularity and consistency eliminates the need for braces (except for the one case documented in Figure 3.38). Note that 2 picas differ from the recommendations of Miara, et. al. (1983), but their research concerns fixed-width characters and does not remove braces. Indentation levels of 2-pica intervals is also consistent with the underlying grid of the source code format in which the main text is sub-divided into 8-pica intervals as indicated by the header components.

Line Length and Line Breaks

Long lines retard reading speed, thus line lengths of more than 60 characters in comments should be avoided. Although the primary column width allows for a maximum of approximately 75 characters of 10-point type in Times Roman Regular, roman, lines will typically have fewer characters. Programmer tabs and line breaks specified by carriage returns (newlines) in comments are preserved so that these may be used for simple formatting and tabulation without requiring the user to go into a special formatting language, as does WEB (Knuth, 1984).

In occurrences of long statement lines or deeply indented source code, line breaks are inevitable. Presently, SEE breaks long lines at a selected set of operators of low precedence, namely, "?", ":", "&&", and "||". Although this algorithm does a reasonable job a great majority of the time, it performs badly in some cases that are detailed in Figures 3.44 and 3.45. The ability to break lines "correctly" is limited in SEE by the lack of good "look ahead" capabilities. Further discussion of the problem appears in Section 6.4.

Each continuation line of a broken line of code is indented 1 pica. The vertical space between a broken line of code and any continuation line should be the same as between two normal statement lines (see below). Otherwise, spatial anomalies may occur as a result of digression from the primary grid unit measurement. Other suggestions for improving the readability of broken lines appear in Figures 3.41 and 3.42.

Linespacing

Leading is the amount of extra spacing introduced between each line of text when lines are set in continuous blocks. Consistent linespacing should be established for all continuous program text as well as in the relationship between title, subtitles, and text. The point size and leading for both program source code and comments is 10-point type with 2 points of leading, with exceptions as noted in Figure 4.3. This leading in each case provides the proper tightness of linespacing so that clear text groupings are formed and readability is enhanced.

Paragraphs

In the case of long prologue, external, and internal comments, paragraphs should be clearly distinguished by inserting blank lines between them.

Code is organized into major sections consisting of sequences of top-level declarations and definitions of functions. To facilitate the scanning and comprehension of code, each such section is automatically separated from the next by two blank lines. Blank lines within sequences of declarations and within function definitions are preserved, allowing the programmer further control over the division of code into logical subsections.

Lists and Tables

Tabular organization facilitates program scanning and reading by locating all text of a particular kind at positions defined by a regular and predictable pattern.

Three particularly critical tab stops are those at 8 picas, 10 picas, and 16 picas to the right of the left margin of the primary text column. The names of macros being defined and files being included are aligned flush left, ragged right along the tab stop at 8 picas. The structure and union member names within their declarations are aligned flush left, ragged right along the tab stop at 10 picas. If structure definitions are embedded within other structure definitions, each additional level beyond the innermost is pushed 2 picas further to the right (see Figure 3.26). The names of all variables being declared and the values of all macros being defined are aligned flush left, ragged right along the tab stop at 16 picas. All of these evenly spaced divisions provide compatibility with other aspects of the program page layout.

Forms

Function definitions are typeset in a stylized form in order to highlight the function names and in order to structure visually the definition's component parts.

The names of functions in their definitions are set as a headline in 14-point Helvetica Bold, roman. Names and formal parameter lists are underscored by a rule that is 2 points wide and 31.5 picas long. Formal parameter declarations in function definitions, if any exist, are underscored by a hairline rule. The rule is indented 2 picas. The hairline rule is placed 4 points down from the baseline of the last declaration statement and extends to the right boundary of the primary text column. The function type specifier is set on a separate line above the function headline.

If a function definition does not terminate on the page on which it begins, an ellipsis (...) is introduced as the last line of code on that page. Its horizontal position indicates the nesting level of the code continuation on the next page. The control constructs in which this code continuation is embedded (the "nesting context") is shown in the header on the second page (see Figure 1.3).

Page Breaking

The judicious organization and breaking of pages is necessary to help orient the reader to meaningful clusters of contents and to provide a smooth, continuous transition when page breaking does occur. Each file begins on a new page. A formfeed character is taken to mean a request for a new page. If possible, SEE avoids breaking a page in the middle of a comment, function header, type definition, or structure definition.

Optimal automatic pagination is very difficult because of the difficulty of inferring proper organization and because SEE does not have sufficient "look ahead" capabilities. (See Section 6.4.)

Symbolism

Symbolism refers to all non-typographic elements appearing with the code, comments, commentary, or other documentation. Symbolism ranges from the abstract, such as typographic rules, enclosure symbols, ideograms, charts, and diagrams, to the representational, such as photographs, illustrations, and pictograms. For all non-verbal graphic elements, one must specify attributes so that they have a clear consistency and appropriateness. Ruled lines, for example, should have only a limited set of variations of length, thickness, and beginning locations.

Rules

The manual suggests using typographic ruled lines as visual separators between file names and function names and the text elements which define them.

Two thick 6-point rules appear below the main titling, that is, below the file name and the chapter number. The thickness is approximately equal to the height of the lower-case "x" of code and prose text. The rules are 11 picas and 31.5 picas in length.

Two-point rules 31.5 picas long appear below function names in their definitions. All other rules are 1/6-point thick (hairline rules). They vary in their length (see the preceding section on "Forms").

Pictograms and Ideograms

The manual recommends the use of regular indentation in place of braces. It also recommends the use of an "up arrow" pictogram to distinguish the *while* in *do...while* from the other kind of *while*. Additional suggestions for pictograms and ideograms to reduce the overloading of C symbols and to enhance presentation clarity may be found in Figure 3.62.

Color and Texture

Color is a three-dimensional attribute that applies to all displayed entities. One way of referring to the three dimensions is to introduce the concepts of hue, value, and chroma. *Hue* concerns the spectral mixture of wavelengths identifying the color, to which one usually refers when naming colors such as red, orange, and blue. *Value* concerns the position of the color on a gray-scale range from black to white. *Chroma*, sometimes called *saturation*, concerns the purity of the color, i.e., the amount of gray present in it.

Value

In this manual, color occurs in the context of black-and-white laser printer or digital typesetter output. The only dimension of concern is value, i.e., the hierarchy of varying areas of gray tone created by the relative percentage of the overall areas of black typography on a white page and the gray halftone textured areas used for comments. The highest order of hierarchy is the chapter title, which is the densest black area due to boldness of the typography and the ruled line underscore. As the reader moves down through the typographic hierarchy the text diminishes in size and weight, and the ruled lines disappear altogether.

Contrast

The key factor in the relationship of color is contrast. In terms of paper output, all text, gray patterns, and accompanying typographic elements such as rules and punctuation should be printed black on a white paper surface. As mentioned previously, the gray screens and rules have been selected to maintain adequate contrast for legibility and readability of text, even after two generations of photocopying.

All elements of a presentation should be considered to have possible highlighted, lowlighted, and neutral states. Highlighting primarily occurs in program text through type size and weight changes in the case of titles, and through emboldening and italicization of reserved words and certain comments. Lowlighting primarily occurs in program text through the use of gray dot screens placed over prologue, external, and internal comments, and through diminished size, e.g., for marginalia comments and footnotes.

Section 4.3

Graphic Design Specifications for C: An Introduction

Section 4.1 explained the rationale behind a graphic design manual for program visualization. Section 4.2 presented guidelines for the general appearance of C program hardcopy in printer resolutions equal to or greater than 300 dots per inch.

We must now define the detailed appearance of the C programming language and its numerous elements. The constructs of C have been organized in a systematic manner and then analyzed syntactically, semantically, and pragmatically. This taxonomy was used to guide the definition of a natural mapping of the program constructs onto visible language elements identified in Appendix B, so that the resulting programs are more legible and readable.

The following are the basic program elements that the specification addresses:
- Program structure
- Comments
- Function definitions
- Declarations of identifiers
- Preprocessor directives
- Statements
- Expressions
- Tokens (words)
- Punctuation tokens
- Program environment

The overall specification is divided into specifications for each distinct type of C program element according to our taxonomy. Each specification has several parts:
- Definition
- Universe
- Format
- Specification
- Notes
- Example and depiction

A typical specification for a single C program element looks like the following:

Name of C Program Element

Definition	A brief description of the C program element from the programmer's point of view.
Universe	A description of the exact parts of C to which this specification applies.
Format	A syntactic representation of this C program element and its immediate environment. Since our presentation of C does not require a complete syntactic description of every detail of the language, we include here only references to sections of Harbison and Steele (1984), which contains a complete description.
Specification	A description of the recommended typography of the C program element.
Notes	Commentary concerning exceptions to the specifications, alternative approaches to the specifications, and other helpful information.
Example and Depiction	Given more space in this book, we would first show a traditional representation of an example of this C program element and its immediate environment using "line printer" typography with a single font, a single type size, no variations of weight or slant, and fixed width characters. We would then show the exact typeset representation (the depiction) of this C program element and its immediate visual environment as it is produced by the SEE program visualizer.
	Because of space limitations, we include only a reference to a figure that contains an example of the typeset representation.

Section 4.4

Graphic Design Specifications for C: Details

The detailed specifications may be found in Appendix D.

Chapter 5

Programs as Publications

"I believe that the time is ripe for significantly better documentation of programs, and that we can best achieve this by considering programs to be *works of literature*. Hence, my title: 'Literate Programming.'

"Let us change our traditional attitude to the construction of programs: Instead of imagining that our main task is to instruct a *computer* what to do, let us concentrate rather on explaining to *human beings* what we want a computer to do.

"The practitioner of literate programming can be regarded as an essayist, whose main concern is with exposition and excellence of style. Such an author, with thesaurus in hand, chooses the names of variables carefully and explains what each variable means. He or she strives for a program that is comprehensible because its concepts have been introduced in an order that is best for human understanding, using a mixture of formal and informal methods that nicely reinforce each other."

Donald E. Knuth (1984), "Literate Programming," *The Computer Journal* 27(2), p. 97. Reprinted with permission.

| Section 5.1 | # The Approach |

Programs are publications, a form of literature. Just as English prose can range in scope from a note scribbled on a pad to a historical treatise appearing in multiple volumes and representing a lifetime of work, so do we find a variety of programs ranging from a two-line *shell* script created whenever needed to an edition of the collected program works of a laboratory, as is the case, for example, with the UNIX™ operating system.[†] The line printer listing, which represents the output of conventional program publishing technology, is woefully inadequate for documenting an encyclopedic collection of code such as the UNIX system, or even for such lesser program treatises as compilers, graphics subroutine packages, and database management systems.

The problem is that computer program code and the accompanying comments do not by themselves have sufficient communicative depth. A program is a large document, an information narrative in which the components should be arranged in a logical, easy-to-find, easy-to-read, and easy-to-remember sequence. The reader should be able quickly to find a table of contents to the document, to determine its parts, to identify desired sections, and to find their locations quickly. Within the program source text of code and comments, the overall structure and appearance of the page should furnish clues regarding the nature of the contents. The page headers and footnotes should also serve to reinforce the structure and sequencing of the document.

Other document elements that aid and orient the reader are needed. For example, a published program requires an *abstract*, a summary of the function, significance, and capabilities of the program. It should have several kinds of *overview* and *index* pages, all providing the reader with summaries of other facets of the program's function, structure, and processing. The program should also be augmented by a variety of kinds of documentation, some for its users and some for its programmers and maintainers.

Program Publications

More formally, we define a *program publication* as a document (either paper or electronic) consisting of program *text* and *metatext*. The text is the program proper, its source code and comments. The metatext is the body of supporting texts and illustrations that augment, describe, clarify, and explain the text.

Another view of a program publication can be formulated in terms of the concepts of *primary text*, *secondary text*, and *tertiary text*:

- Primary text includes what typically appears in a program listing: the program's source code and comments.
- Secondary text is metatext that augments the primary text directly on the program listing pages. Examples of secondary text are headers, footnotes, and annotations. These typically are *metadata* describing the context in which the program is used, and short *commentaries* (some mechanically produced) pointing out salient features of the program.
- Tertiary text is metatext appearing on pages that supplement the program pages. Tertiary text is the source of additional information about the program, how it was built, and how it is to be used. Examples of tertiary text include the overview and index pages described above, as well as the

---

[†]   See Lions (1977) for an early example of this idea applied to the UNIX kernel.

longer descriptions and explanations of the program that typically are called documentation.

In our research (Marcus and Baecker, 1982; Baecker and Marcus, 1983, 1986; Baecker, et al., 1985; Baecker, 1988, under review; Baecker, et al., in preparation), we have applied the tools of modern computer graphics technology and the visible language skills of graphic design, guided by the metaphors and precedents of literature, printing, and publishing, to suggest and demonstrate in prototype form that enduring programs should and can be made more accessible and more usable.

Program Views

More specifically, we have invented and systematized a set of *program views*, abstractions that enrich the documentation of program source text and thereby aid the design, construction, debugging, maintenance, and understanding of the program's function, structure, and method of processing.

Each new method encapsulates essential aspects of the program's function, structure, or behavior and provides an answer to a question about the program that could reasonably and frequently be asked by an experienced programmer. (See Section 5.7.) Thus each technique adds a level of richness that can aid in communicating the meaning of a program to its readers and users and can help the programmer in carrying out required tasks.

A Prototype Program Publication

To illustrate these concepts, we include as Section 5.4 a prototype of a program publication.[†] The example is based on a new implementation of the famous Eliza program originally devised by Joseph Weizenbaum (1969). The version we are publishing was written in C by Henry Spencer of the University of Toronto Department of Zoology, and has been modified by Alan Rosenthal of the Dynamic Graphics Project. The SEE program visualizer has been used to produce listings of the source text of Eliza, which have been modified only in terms of better pagination and the adding of nesting information and footnotes, features not yet handled automatically be SEE.

These listings have then been combined with metadata, commentaries, indices, overviews, user documentation, system documentation, and other program views to form the program book. Most of the program views have not been produced totally automatically. Generally, relevant data about our sample program or about its execution has been produced automatically using a variety of existing or new UNIX tools and utilities. These have then been processed using other tools and utilities into an appropriate TROFF or Postscript form suitable for printing. It would not be terribly difficult to automate these processes.[††]

Related Work

Others have thought about systems of program documentation (see, for example, Horowitz and Williamson, 1986a, 1986b), but their focus has generally been on the semantics of program specifications and program description, and their approach has generally employed only text, not graphics.

Knuth (1984)[†††] has developed a novel technique of program development in which the writing of code and the writing of documentation are interleaved and then processed by the WEB system into a Pascal program and into

---

†   A shorter exposition on a different example may be found in Baecker (under review).

††   Exceptions to this statement are discussed in Section 5.5.

†††   See also Knuth (1986a,b), Bentley (1986a,b), Thimbleby (1986), Brown (1988), and Reenskaug and Skaar (1989).

a T_EX document incorporating both the source listing and the documentation (see Figure 5.1). Use of WEB requires significant changes in the processes of problem solving and programming from the way they are done conventionally today. Because use of the system encourages a thoughtful and structured exposition of a problem and an algorithm for its solution, the expression of the algorithm (in Pascal), and the documentation of both the solution and the process of solution development (in T_EX), Knuth believes that it will lead to what he calls "literate programming."

Other relevant work will be cited in context throughout the remainder of this chapter.

Section 5.2

Graphic Design Principles

As with the design of individual program pages, the design of program publications, in both their content and their form, is guided by the application of some fundamental principles of document organization and design. The intent of these principles is to produce documents that are as easy as possible to scan, read, comprehend, use, and remember. For program publications, several additional design principles are relevant, in addition to Principles 1 through 17 listed in Section 3.4: [†]

- Principle 18 – *Multiple Views*: Provide a multiplicity of views and perspectives on the program.
- Principle 19 – *Simultaneous Views*: Provide the ability to view simultaneously a major "focus" plus additional information on a single page.
- Principle 20 – *Access Facilitation*: Provide links and cross references among these views, and facilitate navigation through the document using these mechanisms.
- Principle 21 – *Clutter Minimization*: Despite these goals of relatively dense information display, minimize clutter so that key information does not become lost.
- Principle 22 – *Regularity and Similarity*: Maximize the similarity of major types of program metatext, for example, manuals, guides, and quick indices. Maximize the regularity of the location and appearance of individual items of metatext.

These additional principles are in a sense broader than those used in the design of individual program pages, in that they suggest content as well as form, new elements of a taxonomy of program views, the topic to which we shall now turn.

Section 5.3

Program Views

Program views are presentations of program source text or representations computed from program source text or program execution that enrich a program document and thereby aid the reader in comprehending and using the program. We shall illustrate some of the methods with paper examples typical of those that could appear in a paper program publication.

[†]   In their application to program publications, Principles 1 through 17 are clarified by replacing occurrences of the word "visualization" by the word "publication."

---

201   *PART 28: CONDITIONAL PROCESSING*

498. A condition is started when the *expand* procedure encounters an *if_test* command; in that case *expand* reduces to *conditional*, which is a recursive procedure.

procedure *conditional*;
  label *exit*, *common_ending*;
  var *b*: *boolean*;   { is the condition true? }
    r: `"<" .. ">"`;   { relation to be evaluated }
    m, n: *integer*;   { to be tested against the second operand }
    p, q: *pointer*;   { for traversing token lists in \ifx tests }
    save_scanner_status: *small_number*;   { *scanner_status* upon entry }
    save_cond_ptr: *pointer*;   { *cond_ptr* corresponding to this conditional }
    this_if: *small_number*;   { type of this conditional }
  begin ⟨ Push the condition stack 495 ⟩; *save_cond_ptr* ← *cond_ptr*; *this_if* ← *cur_chr*;
  ⟨ Either process \ifcase or set *b* to the value of a boolean condition 501 ⟩;
  if *tracing_commands* > 1 **then** ⟨ Display the value of *b* 502 ⟩;
  if *b* **then**
    begin *change_if_limit*(*else_code*, *save_cond_ptr*); **return**;   { wait for \else or \fi }
    end;
  ⟨ Skip to \else or \fi, then **goto** *common_ending* 500 ⟩;
common_ending: **if** *cur_chr* = *fi_code* **then** ⟨ Pop the condition stack 496 ⟩
  else *if_limit* ← *fi_code*;   { wait for \fi }
exit: **end**;

499. In a construction like '\if\iftrue abc\else d\fi', the first \else that we come to after learning that the \if is false is not the \else we're looking for. Hence the following curious logic is needed.

500. ⟨ Skip to \else or \fi, then **goto** *common_ending* 500 ⟩ ≡
  loop begin *pass_text*;
    if *cond_ptr* = *save_cond_ptr* **then**
      begin if *cur_chr* ≠ *or_code* **then goto** *common_ending*;
      print_err(`"Extra "`); *print_esc*(`"or"`);
      help1(`"I'm ignoring this; it doesn't match any \if."`); *error*;
      end
    else if *cur_chr* = *fi_code* **then** ⟨ Pop the condition stack 496 ⟩;
    end

This code is used in section 498.

---

common_ending = 50, §15.	*get_node*: **function**, §125.	*or_code* = 4, §489.
cond_ptr: *pointer*, §489.	*help1* = macro, §79.	*p*: *pointer*, §366.
confusion: **procedure**, §95.	*if_code* = 1, §489.	*pass_text*: **procedure**, §494.
cur_chr: *halfword*, §297.	*if_limit*: 0 .. 4, §489.	*pointer* = macro, §115.
cur_if: *small_number*, §489.	*if_line*: *integer*, §489.	*print_err* = macro, §73.
else_code = 3, §489.	*if_line_field* = macro, §489.	*print_esc*: **procedure**, §63.
error: **procedure**, §82.	*if_node_size* = 2, §489.	*scanner_status*: 0 .. 5, §305.
exit = 10, §15.	*if_test* = 104, §210.	*small_number* = 0 .. 63, §101.
expand: **procedure**, §366.	*line*: *integer*, §304.	*subtype* = macro, §133.
fi_code = 2, §489.	*link* = macro, §118.	*tracing_commands* = macro, §236.
free_node: **procedure**, §130.	*null* = macro, §115.	*type* = macro, §133.

Figure 5.1: *An example of a right-hand page from a WEB program book.*

This right-hand page from a WEB program book contains sections 498–500 of the document. Each section may contain commentary, Pascal code, comments, and macros. Sections may be abbreviated through references to other sections, as is the case with §498 and §500. Comments appear in curly braces. Reserved words are mostly in boldface; identifiers are in italics. A mini-index appearing at the bottom of every right-hand page lists the names, types, and locations of all definitions of all identifiers referenced on either of the two facing pages.

Donald E. Knuth, *T_EX: The Program*, Copyright © 1986, Addison-Wesley Publishing Company Inc., Reading, MA., p. 201. Reprinted with permission of the publisher.

The reader should keep in mind that an electronic program publication, such as an *electronic book*, will have significant advantages over a paper document. Although we resist strenuously the notion advanced by some computer enthusiasts that paper is now obsolete and all information should be read and manipulated in electronic form, we will see numerous instances in what follows of information presentation that should be computed and generated (and perhaps printed) upon demand, based on requests and specifications from the user. The paper examples that follow, however inadequate, still serve to illustrate the concepts.

We consider twelve kinds of program views:
- Program source text
- Program page metadata
- User documentation
- Programmer documentation
- Program introductions
- Program overviews
- Program indices
- Structured program excerpts
- Program change descriptions
- Program annotations
- Program illustrations
- Program animations

There is some overlap among the concepts, but each one is worth presenting on its own.

Program source text consists of source code, i.e., text expressed within the programming language, and comments, i.e., English (or some other natural language) text embedded within source code and ignored by processors of programs in that programming language.

Program page metadata appear in the headers and footnotes of program pages and clarify the context in which code on a particular page is to be understood.

User documentation is English prose created to help the user understand the purpose, functionality, and use of the program.

Program documentation is English prose created to help the programmer understand the design and construction of the program.

Program introductions are intended to help a reader of a program publication become oriented with respect to the entire series of documents. In books, such introductions are known as "front matter."

Program overviews are concise textual or diagrammatic descriptions or summaries of the program's function, structure, or processing.

Program indices are sorted lists of program elements organized in such a way as to facilitate reference and access to groups of "related" program elements.

Structured program excerpts are presentations of fragments of program source text within the context of "surrounding" or "nearby" text, in which some text has been omitted (elided) in order that the most relevant information be displayed on the page in relative proximity to the program source fragments.

Program change descriptions are presentations of program source text or fragments thereof showing how the program has changed through one or more recent revisions. This component is extremely important for large programs created by teams of people that require version management and control.

Program annotations are superimpositions on pages of program source text of various metatext explaining and clarifying the program's authorship, history, function, structure, processing, problems, or other useful information. Given appropriate technology, these could include commentaries (possibly hand-written) by previous readers and/or maintainers of the software.

Program illustrations are graphic presentations, e.g., charts or diagrams, that explain or clarify some aspects of the program's function, structure, or processing.

Program animations are dynamic program illustrations, i.e., "movies" depicting the program in execution.

Section 5.4   A Prototype Program Book

We now present our prototype program book of the Eliza program.[†] The book is organized as follows:

- The book begins with introductions, or front matter, i.e., tertiary text which may include, for example, a cover page, title page, copyright page, abstract, program history page, authors and personalities page, and table of contents.
- Chapter 1 is tertiary text that comprises the user documentation: a tutorial guide, command summary, and user manual.
- Chapter 2 contains the program overviews, i.e., tertiary text such as a call hierarchy, a function call history, and an execution profile.
- Chapters 3 through 10 constitute the primary text, i.e., the program code and comments. Each file of the eight files in the program appears in a separate chapter. Each program page has useful secondary text included in its header and footnotes.
- Chapter 11 contains the programmer documentation, i.e., tertiary text such as the installation guide and the maintenance guide.
- Chapter 12 contains various indices, e.g., tertiary text in the form of a cross-reference index, caller index, and callee index.

The examples we give in this chapter are meant to be illustrative rather than comprehensive. Numerous other kinds of documentation, such as lists of requirements and system specifications, could also have been included. All program views are shown in their complete form except the function call history and the cross-reference index, where for space reasons we show only excerpts.

Whereas any listing or representation of the program or a section of code will contain primary and secondary text, some of the tertiary texts can and will be omitted in a "quick and dirty" look at a program that is likely to be changed almost immediately, as is the case when one is creating or debugging code. The investment in the production of substantial tertiary text is most easily justified if the program has considerable readership and longevity.

We suggest that the reader now skim through the program book and then, as we explain each concept in Section 5.5, which follows, return to individual pages for a more detailed examination.

---

†   Hugh Redelmeier has noted that Eliza is an example of "shrink-wrapped" software.

Dynamic Graphics Project
University of Toronto
Toronto, Ontario, Canada

Aaron Marcus and Associates
Berkeley, California, USA

Eliza:
The Program

Henry Spencer
Alan Rosenthal
Ronald M. Baecker
Aaron Marcus
Ilona R. Posner
D. Hugh Redelmeier

Dynamic Graphics Project
University of Toronto, with
Aaron Marcus and Associates
Berkeley

Eliza: The Program

Subtitle

A Prototype Program Book of Henry Spencer's Implementation of Joseph Weizenbaum's Eliza Program, including a ''Doctor'' Script

Authors

Henry Spencer, Alan Rosenthal, Ronald M. Baecker,
Aaron Marcus, Ilona R. Posner, and D. Hugh Redelmeier

Publisher

Dynamic Graphics Project
Computer Systems Research Institute
University of Toronto
Toronto, Ontario, Canada

Production and Copyright Information

Typesetting

Dynamic Graphics Project
Computer Systems Research Institute
University of Toronto

Typesetting Technology

Sun 3/280 Computer
Apple LaserWriter IINTX
Sun OS3.5 (derived from AT&T Bell Laboratories UNIX™ Operating System)
SoftQuad Enhanced TROFF Phototypesetting Software
Adobe Postscript™ Fonts
SEE Program Visualizer Package

Design and Specifications

C source text (code and comments) from the Eliza program is set according to formats and specifications documented in the book *Human Factors and Typography for More Readable Programs*, written by Ronald Baecker and Aaron Marcus. The formats were developed by Aaron Marcus and Associates, Berkeley, California, assisted by the Dynamic Graphics Project, University of Toronto, and HCR Corporation, Toronto, Ontario, Canada. Program pages were produced "almost totally automatically" by the SEE Package. Minor electronic fix-ups relating to page breaks, headers, and footnotes were used to produce the final pages which appear in this book.

Trademarks

Many of the designations used by manufacturers and sellers to distinguish their products are claimed as trademarks. When those designations appear in this book, and the Dynamic Graphics Project was aware of a trademark claim, the designations have been printed in initial caps or all caps. In particular, UNIX™ is a trademark of AT&T Bell Laboratories.

Copyright

Dynamic Graphics Project
University of Toronto, with
Aaron Marcus and Associates
Berkeley

Abstract

Eliza is a program that carries on a dialogue with a user and pretends to a very limited extent to understand English language input. Driven by the "Doctor" script, it tries to simulate a Rogerian therapist.

Eliza operates with a very simple keyword and pattern-matching scheme that sometimes enables it to appear to recognize significant phrases. It reuses these phrases in a dialogue, thus sometimes conveying the illusion of comprehension. Extensive or even modest use of Eliza should make apparent to even the most naive of users that one is not communicating with an intelligent entity but merely with a simple-minded and very limited automaton.

Program History

The original implementation of Eliza was done by Joseph Weizenbaum. (See Joseph Weizenbaum, "Eliza – A Computer Program for the Study of Natural Language Communication between Man and Machine," *Communications of the ACM,* Volume 9, Number 1, January 1966, pages 36 to 45.) Eliza had made a name for itself through the grapevine in the early 60's, and Weizenbaum eventually felt compelled to publish this CACM paper to explain just how simplistic it really was. He is reported to have been horrified by how readily people accept a simple imitation of intelligence as the real thing. The original was written in a Fortran-based list handling package. There have been Snobol implementations since then, and some in LISP as well.

Shapiro and Kwasny, at Indiana University, experimented with using radically different Eliza scripts as smart "help" commands. (See Stuart C. Shapiro and Stanley C. Kwasny, "Interactive Consulting via Natural Language," *Communications of the ACM,* Volume 18, Number 8, August 1975, pages 459 to 462. More details can be found in their technical report, Computer Science Technical Report #12, "Interactive Consulting via Natural Language," by Stuart C. Shapiro and Stanley C. Kwasny, Indiana University, Bloomington, June 1974.)

Interest in these notions motivated Henry Spencer to implement a new version of Eliza in C for a UNIX environment. This book presents the implementation and documentation of this version of Eliza, based on the original idea of Joseph Weizenbaum, and with further refinements of Spencer's code made by Alan J Rosenthal.

Authors and Personalities

1   Ron Baecker directed the research that conceived of and produced this program book. Although he has been on sabbatical leave, he may be reached via baecker@dgp.toronto.edu, which will forward his mail electronically.

2   This book was designed by Aaron Marcus and Associates. Send suggestions for design improvements to Aaron Marcus and Associates, 1196 Euclid Avenue, Berkeley, California 94708-1640, or to marcus3@violet.berkeley.edu.

3   Henry Spencer, implementor of this Eliza version. You may reach Henry at (416) xxx-xxxx, or via mail to henry@zoo.toronto.edu.

4   If you have trouble with the Eliza program, call the person in charge of its maintenance, Alan J Rosenthal, at (416) xxx-xxxx, or mail to flaps@dgp.toronto.edu.

5   Joseph Weizenbaum, originator of Eliza and creator of the first implementation.

6, 7, 8, 9, 10   Need help in improving or replacing the "Doctor" script for Eliza? Call Hugh Redelmeier, Ilona Posner, or Cynthia Wong, other members of the project team, at (416) xxx-xxxx (but not before 11 a.m., please!!!), or Greg Galle or Sandra Ragan at (415) xxx-xxxx.

Dynamic Graphics Project   toc   Printed 2 Jun 15:51
University of Toronto, with
Aaron Marcus and Associates
Berkeley

Page **Table of Contents: Program Metatext**

Dynamic Graphics Project
University of Toronto, with
Aaron Marcus and Associates
Berkeley

dtoc   Printed 2 Jun 15:52

Page   # Table of Contents: Program Text

Dynamic Graphics Project
University of Toronto, with
Aaron Marcus and Associates
Berkeley

dtoc   Printed 2 Jun 15:52

Chapter 1   # User Documentation

Dynamic Graphics Project
University of Toronto, with
Aaron Marcus and Associates
Berkeley

Eliza: The Program

Chapter 1:
User Documentation

Section 1.1:
Tutorial Guide

Printed 2 Jun 15:53

| Section 1.1 | # Tutorial Guide |

To use Eliza with its default "Doctor" script, just wait until it asks you about your problem, and type at it. Your input can be only one line, but Eliza generally will pay attention to only one sentence of each input anyway, so this isn't a hardship.

To get out of Eliza, just give it end-of-file (often expressed as control-D) or interrupt it (DEL, RUBOUT, or control-C depending on how your system is set up).

Eliza is easily confused, so don't expect miracles. In particular, this version is probably a bit simplistic compared to the one around which all the folklore has grown up.

No record of your inputs is being kept, so you can be frank with Eliza.

A Sample Dialogue with Eliza

In the following "classic" dialogue, the "Doctor" script makes Eliza look pretty good. Eliza's output is denoted with a ">", the user's input with a "<".

```
> How do you do.  Please tell me your problem.
>
< Men are all alike.
> In what way?
>
< They're always bugging us about something or other.
> Can you think of a specific example?
>
< Well, my boyfriend made me come here.
> Your boyfriend made you come here?
>
< He says I'm depressed much of the time.
> I am sorry to hear you are depressed.
>
< It's true.  I am unhappy.
> Do you think coming here will help you not to be unhappy?
>
< I need some help, that much seems certain.
> What would it mean to you if you got some help?
>
< Perhaps I could learn to get along with my mother.
> Tell me more about your family.
>
< My mother takes care of me.
> Who else in your family takes care of you?
>
< My father.
> Your father?
>
< You are like my father in some ways.
> What resemblance do you see?
>
< You are not very aggressive, but I think you don't want me to notice that.
> What makes you think I am not very aggressive?
>
< You don't argue with me.
> Why do you think I don't argue with you?
>
```

Dynamic Graphics Project
University of Toronto, with
Aaron Marcus and Associates
Berkeley

Eliza: The Program   Chapter 1:   Section 1.1:   Printed 2 Jun 15:53
    User Documentation   Tutorial Guide

```
< You are afraid of me.
> Does it please you to believe I am afraid of you?
>
< My father is afraid of everybody.
> What else comes to mind when you think of your father?
>
< Bullies.
> Does that have anything to do with the fact that your boyfriend made you come here?
>
```

Another Dialogue with Eliza

A slight change of input, on the other hand, produces a dialogue illustrating how stupid Eliza really is.

```
> How do you do.  Please tell me your problem.
>
< Men are all alike.
> In what way?
>
< They're always bugging us about something or other.
> Can you think of a specific example?
>
< Well, my boyfriend made me come here.
> Your boyfriend made you come here?
>
< He says that I am not a happy person.
> How have I helped you to be happy?
>
< Doctor, you don't understand, I said that I am not happy!
> We were discussing you, not me.
>
< I am getting very frustrated!!!
> Is it because you are getting very frustrated that you came to me?
>
```

explorer:/green/flaps/see/pb   user   31 May 16:59   Revision 3.1   Page E4 / 160

Dynamic Graphics Project | Eliza: The Program | Chapter 1: | Section 1.2: | Printed 2 Jun 15:53
University of Toronto, with | | User Documentation | Manual Page and |
Aaron Marcus and Associates | | | Command Summary |
Berkeley

Section 1.2

Manual Page and Command Summary

Name

eliza – Weizenbaum's fake natural-language understander

Synopsis

eliza [–d] [script]

Date

19 December 1988

Description

Eliza is a straightforward implementation of the famous program. The program proper is a simple automaton controlled by a script. The default *script*, named "Doctor," imitates a Rogerian psychiatrist.

Eliza basically just reformats the user's input and spits it back. After simple preprocessing, the input is scanned for *keywords*, words known to Eliza. As they are found, keywords are placed on a linked list, either at front or back depending on their *rank* (a numeric priority). Then the top keyword gets control. The input is matched against one or more *patterns* associated with the keyword; when one matches, one of possibly several *responses* associated with the pattern is chosen and printed. The illusion of reality is enhanced by simple word substitution (for changing personal pronouns appropriately, and for synonyms), the ability to punt to another keyword's patterns or to give up and try the next keyword in the list, incorporation of parts of the user's input into the response, and by an attempt (the *memory*) to remember some user input for re-stimulating the conversation later.

The "–d" option turns on debugging output, which gives a fair indication of how Eliza is processing the user's input, although this appears in a somewhat cryptic form.

Script syntax vaguely resembles that of "make." Lines starting with "#" are comments. First, up until a blank line, is the startup monologue. After that are keywords, each followed by patterns, each followed by responses. Response lines begin with white space; neither keyword lines nor pattern lines do. The pattern/responses groups for a keyword are ended by a blank line.

A keyword line begins with the keyword and may be followed by one or more of:

@number	rank of keyword (default 0)
[class]	keyword is member of this class, for patterns
=word	substitute *word* for keyword
%number	this is the memory keyword; also sets memory size to *number*

Substitution is done *after* the keyword has been placed in the list, for the benefit of reply formatting, *unless* the keyword has no pattern/response groups

Dynamic Graphics Project   Eliza: The Program   Chapter 1:   Section 1.2:   Printed 2 Jun 15:53
University of Toronto, with   User Documentation   Manual Page and
Aaron Marcus and Associates   Command Summary
Berkeley

attached at all, in which case it's just a synonym and substitution occurs before any other processing.

Patterns are ordinary text, with a few metasymbols. An asterisk, "*", matches any number of words, including none. A parenthesized list of comma-separated words (no spaces anywhere) matches any single word in the list. A bracketed class name (no spaces between brackets and name) matches any word in that class.

Responses are ordinary text, with one metasymbol: "#n" (n a single digit) replaced by the text that matched the nth thing in the pattern. The special response, "+", means to abandon this keyword and go to the next one in the list.

Either a pattern or a response can be of the form "> word," which transfers control (*punts*) to that keyword's pattern/response list (without altering the input sentence). If there is a string in double quotes between the ">" and the word, the input sentence is first replaced by the contents of the string, which can contain "#n" metasymbols like those of normal responses.

When the memory keyword (which must be an ordinary keyword as well) gains control, it matches the input against its pattern and saves the resulting response in memory instead of printing it. Then the ordinary-keyword version gets control. There can be only one memory keyword, and only its first pattern is ever used.

If a sentence contains no keywords at all, a saved sentence from the memory will be printed if there is one. Otherwise, the pattern/response group(s) associated with the special keyword "!" will gain control; in the "Doctor" script, this prints a vague response.

See Also

Joseph Weizenbaum, "Eliza: A Computer Program for the Study of Natural Language Communication between Man and Machine," *CACM 9* (1), 36–45.

History

Henry Spencer of the University of Toronto Department of Zoology wrote this program. Alan J Rosenthal of the Dynamic Graphics Project modified it for the purposes of *Human Factors and Typography for More Readable Programs* and the associated human factors experiments. The "Doctor" script is a transliteration of the one in the Weizenbaum paper.

Bugs

The "Doctor" script is known to have bugs. It is pretty simplistic and is probably only a subset of the script(s) that made Eliza famous.

Saved sentences from the memory should be revived only under certain conditions, but Weizenbaum doesn't say what they are.

Dynamic Graphics Project   Eliza: The Program   Chapter 1:   Section 1.3:   Printed 2 Jun 15:53
University of Toronto, with   User Documentation   User Manual
Aaron Marcus and Associates
Berkeley

Section 1.3

User Manual

In lieu of a detailed discussion of how to write Eliza scripts, we present a few hints and the complete listing of the "Doctor" script.

Experiment. Try things out on naive customers; it's too easy not to exercise scripts thoroughly yourself.

Eliza is completely case-insensitive. It is not so completely insensitive to white space, alas; particularly in patterns, things like "[class]" have to be written without space inside.

The debugging output, apart from its initial report on where it's getting its script from, consists of a bunch of things following each user input. Basically this is a trace of what Eliza is doing. First you get the sentence, with substitutions done so you can see what Eliza is using as a basis for its pattern matches and reply assembly. Then you get the keyword list, terminated by a "–", in top-first order. Then you get a running narrative about patterns tried and special actions (if any) performed.

The Default Eliza Script ("Doctor")

Annotations in the left margin indicate features of the script language.

Opening monologue

> How do you do. Please tell me your problem.

First keyword, rank 0
matches any input

> sorry @0
> *

>> Please don't apologize.
>> Apologies are not necessary.
>> What feelings do you have when you apologize?
>> I've told you that apologies are not required.

translate dont to don't

> dont = don't

> cant = can't

> wont = won't

first pattern for "remember"

> remember @5
> * you remember *

>> Do you often think of #4?
>> Does thinking of #4 bring anything else to mind?
>> What else do you remember?
>> Why do you remember #4 just now?
>> What in the present situation reminds you of #4?
>> What is the connection between me and #4?

second pattern for "remember"

> * do I remember *

>> Did you think I would forget #5?
>> Why do you think I should recall #5 now?
>> What about #5?

punt to "what"

>> > what
>> You mentioned #5.

> if @3
> * if *

>> Do you think it's likely that #3?

		Do you wish that #3?
		What do you think about #3?
		Really, #2 #3?
	dreamt @4	
	* you dreamt *	
		Really, #4?
		Have you ever fantasized #4 while you were awake?
		Have you dreamt #4 before?
		> dream
use next keyword match		+
	dreamed = dreamt @4	
dreamed always goes to dreamt	> dreamt	
	dream @3	
	*	
		What does that dream suggest to you?
		Do you dream often?
		What persons appear in your dreams?
		Don't you believe that dream has something to do with your problem?
		+
	dreams = dream @3	
	> dream	
	how	
	> what	
	when	
	> what	
	alike @10	
	> dit	
	same @10	
	> dit	
	certainly	
	> yes	
feel is of class belief	feel [belief]	
	think [belief]	
	believe [belief]	
	wish [belief]	
"my" is the memory keyword	my %10	
	* your *	
		Let's discuss further why your #3.
		Earlier you said your #3.
		But your #3?
		Does that have anything to do with the fact that your #3?
the "dunno" response	!	
	*	
		I am not sure I understand you fully.
		Please go on.
		What does that suggest to you?
		Do you feel strongly about discussing such things?
	perhaps	
	*	
		You don't seem quite certain...
		Why the uncertain tone?
		Can't you be more positive?
		You aren't sure?

>   Don't you know?

maybe
> perhaps

name @15
*
>   I am not interested in names.
>   I've told you before, I don't care about names -- please continue.

deutsch
> xfremd

francais
> xfremd

italiano
> xfremd

espanol
> xfremd

xfremd
*
>   I am sorry, I speak only English.

hello
*
>   How do you do. Please state your problem.

computer @50
*
>   Do computers worry you?
>   Why do you mention computers?
>   What do you think machines have to do with your problem?
>   Don't you think computers can help people?
>   What about machines worries you?
>   What do you think about machines?

machine @50
> computer

machines @50
> computer

computers @50
> computer

am = are
* are you *
>   Do you believe you are #4?
>   Would you want to be #4?
>   You wish I would tell you you are #4?
>   What would it mean if you were #4?
>   > what

*
>   Why do you say 'am'?
>   I don't understand that, I'm afraid.

are
* are I *
>   Why are you interested in whether I am #4 or not?
>   Would you prefer if I weren't #4?
>   Perhaps I am #4 in your fantasies?
>   Do you sometimes think I am #4?
>   > what

* are *
>   Did you think they might not be #3?

explorer:/green/flaps/see/pb   user   31 May 16:59   Revision 3.1   Page E9 / 165

Dynamic Graphics Project   Eliza: The Program   Chapter 1:   Section 1.3:   Printed 2 Jun 15:53
University of Toronto, with   User Documentation   User Manual
Aaron Marcus and Associates
Berkeley

                                           Would you like it if they were not #3?
                                           What if they were not #3?
                                           Possibly they are #3?

your = my
* my *

                                           Why are you concerned over my #3?
                                           What about your own #3?
                                           Are you worried about someone else's #3?
                                           Really, my #3?

was @2
* was you *

                                           What if you were #4?
                                           Do you think you are #4?
                                           Were you #4?
                                           What would it mean if you were #4?
                                           What does '#4' suggest to you?
                                           > what

* you was *

                                           Were you really?
                                           Why do you tell me you were #4 now?
                                           Perhaps I already knew you were #4.

* was I *

                                           Would you like to believe I was #4?
                                           What suggests that I was #4?
                                           What do you think?
                                           Perhaps I was #4.
                                           What if I had been #4?

*

                                           +

were = was
> was

# This is suboptimal, because "tell me about yourself" really should
# punt to the we're-talking-about-you-not-me responses.
me = you

you're = I'm
* I'm *
                                           > "I are #3" you

punt with reformation

I'm = you're
* you're *
                                           > "You are #3" I

myself = yourself

yourself = myself

mother [family]

mom = mother [family]

dad = father [family]

father [family]

sister [family]

brother [family]

wife [family]

children [family]

I = you
* you (want,need) *

explorer:/green/flaps/see/pb   user   31 May 16:59   Revision 3.1   Page E10 / 166

Dynamic Graphics Project   Eliza: The Program   Chapter 1:   Section 1.3:   Printed 2 Jun 15:53
University of Toronto, with   User Documentation   User Manual
Aaron Marcus and Associates
Berkeley

What would it mean to you if you got #4?
Why do you want #4?
Suppose you got #4 soon...
What if you never got #4?
What would getting #4 mean to you?
What does wanting #4 have to do with this discussion?

use of alternation in patterns

`* you are * (sad,unhappy,depressed,sick) *`

I am sorry to hear you are #5.
Do you think coming here will help you not to be #5?
I'm sure it's not pleasant to be #5.
Can you explain what made you #5?

`* you are * (happy,elated,glad,better) *`

How have I helped you to be #5?
Has your treatment made you #5?
What makes you #5 just now?
Can you explain why you are suddenly #5?

`* you was *`

> was

use of class mechanism in patterns

`* you [belief] you *`

Do you really think so?
But you are not sure you #5?
Do you really doubt you #5?

`* you * [belief] * I *`

> you

`* you are *`

Is it because you are #4 that you came to me?
How long have you been #4?
Do you believe it normal to be #4?
Do you enjoy being #4?

`* you (can't,cannot) *`

How do you know you can't #4?
Have you tried?
Perhaps you could #4 now?
Do you really want to be able to #4?

`* you don't *`

Don't you really #4?
Why don't you #4?
Do you wish to be able to #4?
Does that trouble you?

`* you feel *`

Tell me more about such feelings...
Do you often feel #4?
Do you enjoy feeling #4?
Of what does feeling #4 remind you?

`* you * I *`

Perhaps in your fantasy we #3 each other?
Do you wish to #3 me?
You seem to need to #3 me.
Do you #3 anyone else?

`*`

You say #1?
Can you elaborate on that?
Do you say #1 for some special reason?
That's quite interesting; do go on.

`you = I`
`* I remind you of *`

> dit

`* I are *`

What makes you think I am #4?
Does it please you to believe I am #4?
Do you sometimes wish you were #4?
Perhaps you would like to be #4?

`* I * you`

Dynamic Graphics Project
University of Toronto, with
Aaron Marcus and Associates
Berkeley

Eliza: The Program   Chapter 1:   Section 1.3:   Printed 2 Jun 15:53
                            User Documentation   User Manual

                             Why do you think I #3 you?
                             You like to think I #3 you -- don't you?
                             What makes you think I #3 you?
                             Really, I #3 you?
                             Do you wish to believe I #3 you?
                             Suppose I did #3 you -- what would that mean to you?
                             Does someone else believe I #3 you?

* I *

                             We were discussing you, not me.
                             Oh, I #3?
                             You're not really talking about me, are you?
                             What are your feelings now?

yes
*

                             I see.
                             I understand.
                             You seem quite positive...
                             You are sure?

no
*

                             Are you saying 'no' just to be negative?
                             You are being a bit negative.
                             Why not?
                             Why 'no'?

my = your @2
* your * [family] *

                             Tell me more about your family.
                             Who else in your family #5?
                             Your #4?
                             What else comes to mind when you think of your #4?

* your *

                             Your #3?
                             Why do you say your #3?
                             Does that suggest anything else which belongs to you?
                             Is it important to you that #2 #3?

can
* can I *

                             You believe I can #4, don't you?
                             > what
                             You want me to be able to #4?
                             Perhaps you would like to be able to #4 yourself?

* can you *

                             Whether or not you can #4 depends on you more than on me.
                             Do you want to be able to #4?
                             Perhaps you don't want to #4?
                             > what

what
*

                             Why do you ask?
                             Does that question interest you?
                             What is it you really want to know?
                             Are such questions much on your mind?
                             What answer would please you most?
                             What do you think?
                             What comes to your mind when you ask that?
                             Have you asked such questions before?
                             Have you asked anyone else?

because
*

                             Is that the real reason?

Dynamic Graphics Project
University of Toronto, with
Aaron Marcus and Associates
Berkeley

Eliza: The Program   Chapter 1:   Section 1.3:   Printed 2 Jun 15:53
                      User Documentation   User Manual

Don't any other reasons come to mind?
Does that reason seem to explain anything else?
What other reasons might there be?

why
* why don't I *

Do you believe I don't #5?
Perhaps I will #5, in good time.
Should you #5 yourself?
You want me to #5?
> what

* why can't you *

Do you think you should be able to #5?
Do you want to be able to #5?
Do you believe this will help you to #5?
Have you any idea why you can't #5?
> what

> what

everyone @2
* (everyone,everybody,nobody,noone) *

Really, #2?
Surely not #2.
Can you think of anyone in particular?
Who, for example?
You are thinking of a very special person, aren't you?
Who, may I ask?
Someone special perhaps?
You have a particular person in mind, don't you?
Who do you think of in particular?

everybody @2
> everyone

nobody @2
> everyone

noone @2
> everyone

always @1
*

Can you think of a specific example?
When?
What incident are you thinking of?
Really, always?

like @10
* (am,is,are,was) * like *

> dit

*

+

dit
*

In what way?
What resemblance do you see?
What does that similarity suggest to you?
What other connections do you see?
What do you suppose that resemblance means?
What is the connection, do you suppose?
Could there really be some connection?
How?

Dynamic Graphics Project   Eliza: The Program   Chapter 2:   Printed 2 Jun 15:55
University of Toronto, with   Overviews
Aaron Marcus and Associates
Berkeley

Chapter 2

Overviews

explorer:/green/flaps/see/map   mapheader1.t   5 Jul 12:44   Revision 3.1   Page E14 / 170

Dynamic Graphics Project
University of Toronto, with
Aaron Marcus and Associates
Berkeley

Eliza: The Program   Chapter 2: Overviews   Section 2.1: Program Map   Printed 6 Jul 11:48

Section 2.1

Program Map

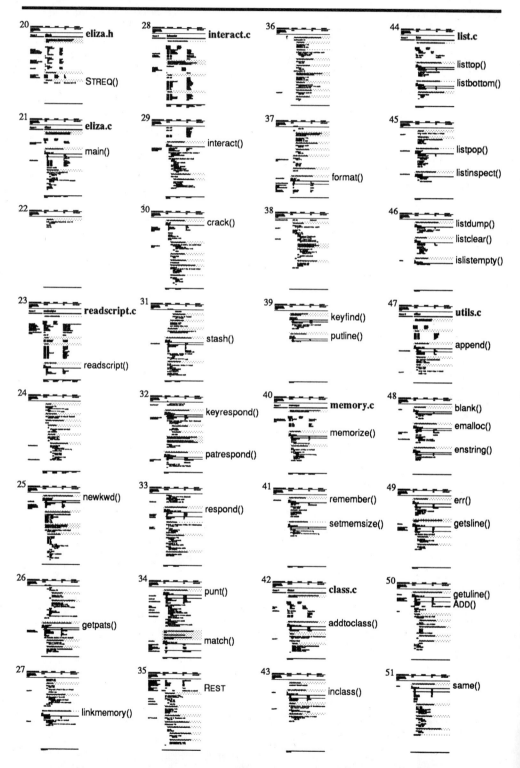

Section 2.2   Item   **Call Hierarchy**

main()...

```
main()
    STREQ()
    readscript()
        err()
        getsline()
        blank()
1       append()
2           emalloc()
                err()
3           enstring()
                emalloc() [item 7]
        STREQ()
        getpats()
            getsline()
            blank()
            err()
            emalloc() [item 2]
            enstring() [item 3]
            append() [item 1]
        newkwd()
            emalloc() [item 2]
            enstring() [item 3]
            addtoclass()
                STREQ()
                emalloc() [item 2]
                enstring() [item 3]
                append() [item 1]
        STREQ()
        err()
        setmemsize()
            err()
    linkmemory()
4       keyfind()
            same()
        err()
```

```
interact()
    putline()
    getuline()
        ADD()
    crack()
        listclear()
        islistempty()
        keyfind() [item 4]
5       listtop()
            emalloc() [item 2]
        listbottom()
            listtop() [item 5]
            emalloc() [item 2]
    listdump()
    listinspect()
    stash()
        STREQ()
        err()
6       match()
            STREQ()
            REST
                match() [recursive, item 6]
            same()
            err()
            inclass()
                STREQ()
                err()
7       respond()
            STREQ()
8           punt()
9               format()
                    err()
                    STREQ()
                keyfind() [item 4]
                err()
10              keyrespond()
11                  patrespond()
                        punt() [recursive, item 8]
                        match() [item 6]
                        respond() [recursive, item 7]
                memorize()
                    append() [item 1]
                format() [item 9]
                putline()
    listpop()
    keyrespond() [item 10]
    remember()
    patrespond() [item 11]
    err()
```

explorer:/green/flaps/see/pb   re   30 May 12:36   Revision 3.1   Page E16 / 172

Dynamic Graphics Project   Eliza: The Program   Chapter 2:   Section 2.3:   Printed 2 Jun 16:58
University of Toronto, with   Overviews   Regular Expression
Aaron Marcus and Associates   Control Diagram
Berkeley

Section 2.3

Regular Expression Control Diagram

eliza.c

main: { STREQ } [fprintf ∧] readscript linkmemory time { rand } interact ∧

readscript.c

readscript: fopen [err] [printf] { getsline blank append } { { getsline [∧] blank } strtok STREQ
               [getpats | newkwd [err] getpats] } ∧

newkwd: emalloc enstring { strtok [strtok] [enstring | atoi | strchr [strchr addtoclass | addtoclass
             strtok STREQ [err]] | atoi setmemsize | err] } ∧

getpats: { getsline blank [err] emalloc enstring { getc ungetc getsline [err] strspn append } ungetc }
          ∧

linkmemory: { keyfind [err] } ∧

interact.c

interact: { putline } putline { getuline crack [printf listdump] listinspect [stash] { listpop keyrespond }
         [remember [putline | patrespond [err]]] putline } ∧

crack: listclear strcpy strtok { { strchr islistempty [strcpy strtok | ∧] } keyfind [keyfind] [[listtop |
       listbottom]] strcat strcat strtok } strlen [strlen] ∧

stash: { STREQ } [err] rand strcpy match [err] respond ∧

keyrespond: { patrespond [∧] [∧] } [printf] ∧

patrespond: [punt ∧] [printf] strcpy match [∧] respond ∧

respond: STREQ [[printf] ∧] [punt ∧] [format memorize ∧] format putline ∧

punt: strspn [strcspn strcpy strncat format strcpy [printf] strspn] [printf] keyfind [err]
       keyrespond ∧

match: strspn strspn [[∧ | ∧]] strcspn strcpy strncat STREQ [∧] STREQ [{ REST [∧] strspn
       strcspn } | strcspn strcpy strncat { strtok strtok same } [∧] REST [∧] | strcspn strcpy
       strncat strlen [err] strlen inclass [∧] REST [∧] | strcspn strcpy strncat same [∧] REST
       [∧]] ∧

format: strcpy { [isascii isdigit [err] [err] STREQ [strlen | strcat] | strcspn strncat] } ∧

keyfind: { same [∧] } ∧

putline: printf ∧

memory.c

memorize: [printf] { [printf] free } append ∧

remember: [∧] strcpy free ∧

setmemsize: [err] [err] ∧

class.c

addtoclass: { STREQ } [emalloc enstring] append ∧

inclass: { STREQ } [err] { STREQ [∧] } ∧

list.c

listtop: emalloc ∧

listbottom: [listtop ∧] emalloc ∧

listpop: [∧] free ∧

listinspect: [∧ | ∧]

listdump: { printf } printf ∧

listclear: { free } ∧

islistempty: ∧

utils.c

append: emalloc enstring ∧

blank: strspn strlen [∧ | ∧]

emalloc: malloc [sprintf err] ∧

enstring: strlen emalloc strcpy ∧

err: [fprintf] fprintf fprintf exit

getsline: { fgets strlen [∧] } ∧

getuline: printf { getc isascii [ADD | strchr [ADD ADD ADD | strchr [ADD]]] } { ∧ | ∧]

same: { isascii isupper [tolower] isascii isupper [tolower] [∧ | ∧ | ∧] [∧] }

Dynamic Graphics Project
University of Toronto, with
Aaron Marcus and Associates
Berkeley

Eliza: The Program   Chapter 2:   Section 2.4:   Printed 2 Jun 16:59
Overviews   Function Call History of
interact.c (Partial)

Section 2.4   Function Call History of interact.c (Partial)

```
                    keyfind()
                    interact()
                            putline()
> How do you do.  Please tell me your problem.

>                           putline()
< Men are all alike.

                        crack()
                            keyfind()
                            keyfind()
                            ... and 2 more times
                        keyrespond()
                            patrespond()
                            punt()
                                    keyfind()
                            keyrespond()
                                patrespond()
                                        match()
                                            match()
                                            match()
                                            ... and 3 more times
                                    respond()
                                        format()
                                        putline()
> In what way?
                            putline()
>
< They're always bugging us about something or other.
                        crack()
                            keyfind()
                            keyfind()
                            ... and 6 more times
                        keyrespond()
                            patrespond()
                                    match()
                                        match()
                                        match()
                                        ... and 7 more times
                                respond()
                                    format()
                                    putline()
> Can you think of a specific example?
                    putline()
>
< Well, my boyfriend made me come here.

                        crack()
                            keyfind()
                            keyfind()
                            ... and 6 more times
                        stash()
                            match()
                                match()
                                    match()
                                        match()
                                        match()
                                        ... and 4 more times
                            respond()
                                    format()
                        keyrespond()
                            patrespond()
                                match()
                                    match()
                                        match()
                                            match()
                                            match()
                                            ... and 5 more times
```

Dynamic Graphics Project
University of Toronto, with
Aaron Marcus and Associates
Berkeley

Eliza: The Program   Chapter 2:
Overviews

Section 2.4:
Function Call History of
interact.c (Partial)

Printed 2 Jun 16:59

```
                                        match()
                                        match()
                                        ... and 5 more times
                        patrespond()
                                match()
                                        match()
                                                match()
                                                        match()
                                                        match()
                                                        ... and 4 more times
                        respond()
                                format()
                                putline()
```

> Your boyfriend made you come here?

```
                putline()
```

\>

< He says I'm depressed much of the time.

```
                crack()
                        keyfind()
                        keyfind()
                        ... and 6 more times
                keyrespond()
                        patrespond()
                                match()
                                        match()
                                        match()
                                        match()
                                                match()
                                                match()
                                                ... and 4 more times
                        respond()
                        punt()
                                format()
                                keyfind()
                        keyrespond()
                                patrespond()
                                        match()
                                                match()
                                                        match()
                                                match()
                                                match()
                                                ... and 5 more times
                                patrespond()
                                        match()
                                                match()
                                                        match()
                                                                match()
                                                                        match()
                                                                                match()
                                                                                match()
                                                                                ... and 3 more times
                                respond()
                                        format()
                                        putline()
```

> I am sorry to hear you are depressed.

```
                putline()
```

\>

< It's true. I am unhappy.

```
                crack()
                        keyfind()
                        keyfind()
                        ... and 3 more times
                keyrespond()
                        patrespond()
                                match()
                                        match()
                                                match()
                                        match()
                                        • • •
```

Dynamic Graphics Project   Eliza: The Program   Chapter 2:
Overviews

Section 2.4:
Function Call History of
interact.c (Partial)

Printed 2 Jun 16:59

explorer:/green/flaps/see/prof   profmock.t   2 Jun 12:05   Revision 3.1   Page E19 / 175

Dynamic Graphics Project   Eliza: The Program   Chapter 2:   Section 2.5:   Printed 2 Jun 17:01
University of Toronto, with   Overviews   Program Execution Profile
Aaron Marcus and Associates
Berkeley

Section 2.5

Program Execution Profile

Global profile (top-down, cumulative)

Function	Cumulative % (% time for self plus descendants)	Seconds for self plus descendants	Seconds for self	Number of calls (includes recursive calls)
main	100.0	0.36	0.00	1
interact	67.2	0.24	0.00	1
readscript	32.6	0.12	0.00	1
crack	24.0	0.09	0.00	15
match	23.4	0.08	0.04	262
same	22.2	0.08	0.08	5413
keyfind	21.8	0.08	0.00	92
getpats	21.6	0.08	0.00	68
patrespond	19.2	0.07	0.00	24
getuline	17.7	0.06	0.04	16
emalloc	16.6	0.06	0.00	811
stash	9.9	0.04	0.00	5
append	9.7	0.04	0.00	236
getsline	8.7	0.03	0.00	432
enstring	8.1	0.03	0.00	398
newkwd	6.8	0.02	0.00	67
respond	1.2	0.00	0.00	21
inclass	0.9	0.00	0.00	9
blank	0.8	0.00	0.00	212
punt	0.8	0.00	0.00	3
addtoclass	0.7	0.00	0.00	12
format	0.7	0.00	0.00	20
listbottom	0.5	0.00	0.00	25
listtop	0.3	0.00	0.00	17
linkmemory	0.2	0.00	0.00	1
memorize	0.2	0.00	0.00	5
putline	0.0	0.00	0.00	32
islistempty	0.0	0.00	0.00	17
keyrespond	0.0	0.00	0.00	17
⋮	⋮			

Local profile (flat, non-cumulative)

Function	% time for self	Seconds for self	Seconds per call for self	Number of calls (doesn't include recursive calls)
same	18.2	0.08	0.00002	5413
match	9.1	0.04	0.00143	28
getuline	9.1	0.04	0.00250	16
emalloc	0.0	0.00	0.00000	811
getsline	0.0	0.00	0.00000	432
enstring	0.0	0.00	0.00000	398
⋮	⋮			

Dynamic Graphics Project
University of Toronto, with
Aaron Marcus and Associates
Berkeley

Eliza   Printed 2 Jun 12:08

Chapter 3

eliza.h

Basic script data structures. Since responses are stored as just plain
character strings, we define a general "text" structure for lists of
strings.

```
struct keyword {
        struct keyword          *knext;
```

The keyword.
Substitution word, if any.
Rank for keyword list building.
Is this a "memory" keyword?

```
        char                    *word;
        char                    *subst;
        int                     rank;
        int                     ismem;
        struct pattern          *pats;
};

struct pattern {
        struct pattern          *pnext;
```

The pattern itself.
Next response to use (0–origin).
The list of responses.

```
        char                    *pat;
        int                     nextresp;
        struct text             *resps;
};

struct text {
        struct text             *tnext;
```

The text itself.

```
        char                    *chars;
};
```

And a couple of maxima.

Max words in pattern.
Longest word.
Miscellaneous buffer size.

```
# define        MAXPAT          5
# define        MAXWORD         50
# define        LINESIZE        200
```

Odds and ends.

```
# define        STREQ(a, b)     (strcmp((a), (b)) == 0)
```

explorer:/green/flaps/see/neliza/book | eliza.c (1 of 2) | 23 Jan 16:33 | Revision 3.1 | Page E21 / 177

Dynamic Graphics Project
University of Toronto, with
Aaron Marcus and Associates
Berkeley

main()

Eliza

Printed 2 Jun 12:08

Chapter 4

eliza.c

Eliza — Weizenbaum's fake natural-language understander —
a new implementation in the C language by Henry Spencer.

```
#include        <stdio.h>
#include        "eliza.h"
int                             debug = 0;
char                            *progname;
```

For error reporting; exported to whoever wants it.

main – parse arguments and handle options.

```
int
main(argc, argv)
```

```
int                     argc;
char                    **argv;
```

```
int                     errorflag = 0;
int                     i;
extern  char            *script;
extern  void            readscript();
extern  void            linkmemory();
extern  long            time();
extern  void            interact();

progname = argv[0];
```

defined in readscript.c

General option parsing loop.

```
while (--argc > 0  &&  (*++argv)[0] == '-')
    if (STREQ(*argv, "-d"))
            debug = 1;
    else
            errorflag = 1;
if (errorflag || argc > 1)
    fprintf(stderr, "usage: %s [-d] [script]\n", progname);
    return (1);

if (argc)
        script = *argv;

readscript();
linkmemory();
...
```

Dynamic Graphics Project
University of Toronto, with
Aaron Marcus and Associates
Berkeley

main()   Eliza   Printed 2 Jun 12:08

Stir rand() a bit.

```
for (i  =  (int) time((long *) NULL)  %  19;  i > 0;  i--)
    (void) rand();
interact();
return  (0);
```

Dynamic Graphics Project
University of Toronto, with
Aaron Marcus and Associates
Berkeley

main()   Eliza   Printed 2 Jun 12:08

Chapter 5

readscript.c

readscript.c -- read the script for eliza.

```
#include            <stdio.h>
#include            "eliza.h"
```

default script file
```
#define             DEFSCRIPT       "/green/flaps/see/neliza/book/doctor"
```

The bulk of the script.
```
struct keyword              *kwdtop = NULL;
```
Last node on kwdtop list.
```
static struct keyword       *lastkwd = NULL;
```
Startup monologue.
```
struct text                 *startup = NULL;
```
Unrecognized–stuff handling.
```
struct pattern              *dunno = NULL;
```
Memory keyword(s).
```
struct keyword              *memkwdtop = NULL;
```

Filename, init to default; changed
by eliza.c.
```
char                        *script = DEFSCRIPT;

extern int                  debug;
```

Forwards.

```
static struct keyword       *newkwd();
static struct pattern       *getpats();
```

Externals.

```
extern char                 *enstring();
extern char                 *emalloc();
extern char                 *getsline();
extern void                 err();
extern void                 setmemsize();
extern struct keyword       *keyfind();
extern void                 append();
extern void                 addtoclass();
extern char                 *strchr();
extern char                 *strtok();
```

readscript -- pick up the script.

```
void
readscript()
```

```
        FILE                    *in;
        char                    buf[LINESIZE];
        register char           *word;
        register struct keyword *kwd;
        ...
```

Dynamic Graphics Project
University of Toronto, with
Aaron Marcus and Associates
Berkeley   readscript()   Eliza   Printed 2 Jun 12:08

Open the file.

```
in = fopen(script, "r");
if (in == NULL)
    err("cannot read script file '%s'", script);
if (debug)
    printf("script file '%s'\n", script);
```

Pick up startup monologue.

```
while (getsline(buf, sizeof(buf), in) != NULL && !blank(buf))
    append(buf, &startup);
```

Body of script — one iteration per keyword.

```
for (;;)
```

Swallow blank lines.

```
    do
        if (getsline(buf, sizeof(buf), in) == NULL)
            return;
    ↑while (blank(buf));
```

Pick up keyword.

```
    word = strtok(buf, " \t");
    if (STREQ(word, "!"))
        dunno = getpats(in);
    else
```

(Note newkwd() knows about that strtok().)

Create keyword structure.

```
        kwd = newkwd(word);
        if (kwd → ismem)
            if (memkwdtop != NULL)
                err("multiple memory keywords", "");
            memkwdtop = kwd;
        else
            if (lastkwd == NULL)
                kwdtop = kwd;
            else
                lastkwd → knext = kwd;
            lastkwd = kwd;
```

Pick up patterns and responses.

```
        kwd → pats = getpats(in);
```

newkwd – pick up remainder of keyword line, create keyword structure.

```
static struct keyword *
newkwd(kwdtext)
```

Text of keyword.

```
    char                              *kwdtext;

    register struct keyword           *k;
    register char                     *word;
    char                              startch;
    char                              *arg;
```

Keyword from kwdtext.
First character of keyword.
Argument to startch if it's a
special char.

Allocate a new struct keyword and set up default field values.

```
    k = (struct keyword *) emalloc(sizeof(struct keyword));
    k→knext = NULL;
    k→word = enstring(kwdtext);
    k→subst = NULL;
    k→rank = 0;
    k→ismem = 0;
    k→pats = NULL;
```

Parse the keyword line. This is pretty ad–hoc, might be
nicer with a proper scanner. In particular, white space
is probably not treated uniformly well.

```
    while ((word = strtok((char *) NULL, " \t")) != NULL)
        startch = word[0];
```

Argument, for things that take it.

```
        arg = word + 1;
        switch (startch)
        case '=':
        case '[':
        case '@':
        case '%':
            if (*arg == '\0')
                arg = strtok((char *) NULL, " \t");
                if (arg == NULL)
                    arg = "";
            break;
        switch (startch)
        case '=':
            k→subst = enstring(arg);
            break;
        case '@':
            k→rank = atoi(arg);
            •••
```

Dynamic Graphics Project   newkwd()   Eliza   Printed 2 Jun 12:08
University of Toronto, with
Aaron Marcus and Associates
Berkeley

while...switch...

```
            break;
        case '[':
            if (strchr(arg, ']'))
```

This word contains the ']'.

```
                *strchr(arg, ']') = '\0';
                addtoclass(kwdtext, arg);
            else
```

This word doesn't contain ']', so next word should be it.

```
                addtoclass(kwdtext, arg);
                arg = strtok((char *) NULL, " \t");
                if (arg == NULL || !STREQ(arg, "]"))
                        err("unmatched '[' for word '%s'", kwdtext);
            break;
        case '%':
            k→ismem = 1;
            setmemsize(atoi(arg));
            break;
        default :
            err("something strange on keyword line for '%s'", kwdtext);
    return (k);
```

getpats – pick up patterns and responses for an already–seen keyword.

```
static  struct pattern *
```
getpats(in)

FILE	*in;

Eventual return value.
For stepping through the list.

struct pattern	*result = NULL;
register struct pattern	*p;
register struct pattern	*new;
char	buf[LINESIZE];
register int	c;

```
while (getsline(buf, sizeof(buf), in) != NULL && !blank(buf))
```

Ensure that the script line is not indented.

```
    if (buf[0] == ' ' || buf[0] == '\t')
        err("bad pattern line '%s'", buf);
```

Allocate and fill in a new struct pattern.

```
    new = (struct pattern *) emalloc(sizeof(struct pattern));
    new→pnext = NULL;
    new→pat = enstring(buf);
    •••
```

while...

```
                              new → nextresp = 0;
                              new → resps = NULL;
```

> Add it to the list.

```
                              if (result == NULL)
                                  result = new;
                              else
NULLBODY                          for (p = result;  p → pnext != NULL;  p = p → pnext)
                                      ;
                                  p → pnext = new;
```

> Pick up more text as long as lines are indented.

```
                              while ((c = getc(in)) == ' ' || c == '\t')
                                  ungetc(c, in);
                                  if (getsline(buf, sizeof(buf), in) == NULL)
                                      err("bad read", "");
                                  append(buf + strspn(buf, " \t"), &new → resps);
                              ungetc(c, in);

                          return (result);
```

> linkmemory – link the memory keywords into the regular keyword list.

```
void
linkmemory()
```

```
                              struct keyword                      *m;
                              struct keyword                      *k;

                          for (m = memkwdtop;  m != NULL;  m = m → knext)
                              k = keyfind(m → word);
in interact.c                 if (k == NULL)
                                  err("memory keyword '%s' not regular keyword", m → word);
                              k → ismem = 1;
```

Dynamic Graphics Project
University of Toronto, with
Aaron Marcus and Associates
Berkeley

Eliza   Printed 2 Jun 12:08

Chapter 6

interact.c

interact.c – the main interaction loop for eliza.

```
#include              <stdio.h>
#include              <ctype.h>
#include              "eliza.h"
      extern  struct keyword              *kwdtop;
      extern  struct text                 *startup;
      extern  struct pattern              *dunno;
      extern  struct keyword              *memkwdtop;
```

Memory keyword(s).

```
      static char                         inbuf[LINESIZE];
      static char                         sentence[LINESIZE];

      extern int                          debug;
```

User's input text.
Transformed version.

Return–code conventions used in this file.
These return codes signal to the caller just how much of the work has
been done by the callee — enough, not enough, or none.

```
typedef enum {

                                          S_DONE,
                                          S_NEXTP,
                                          S_NEXTK

      }                                   STATUS;
```

Job completed.
Try next pattern.
This keyword fails; try next
keyword.

Forwards.

```
      static void                         crack(),
                                          stash(),
                                          putline();
      extern struct keyword               *keyfind();
      static STATUS                       keyrespond();
      static STATUS                       patrespond();
      static STATUS                       respond();
      static STATUS                       punt();
      static int                          match();
      static char                         *format();
```

Externals.

```
      extern char                         *getuline();
      extern char                         *remember();
      extern struct keyword               *listpop();
      extern struct keyword               *listinspect();
      extern void                         err();
```

```
extern  void                              setmemsize(),
                                          memorize();
extern  void                              listtop(),
                                          listbottom(),
                                          listdump(),
                                          listclear();
extern  char                              *strchr();
extern  char                              *strtok();
```

interact – engage in interactive dialogue.

void
interact()

To step through startup text.
Text recalled from memory.
Current keyword.

```
register struct text                      *monologue;
register char                             *mem;
register struct keyword                   *k;

for (monologue = startup;  monologue != NULL;  monologue =
        monologue → tnext)
    putline(monologue → chars);
putline("");

while (getuline(inbuf, sizeof(inbuf), stdin) != NULL)
    crack();
    if (debug)
        printf("%s\n", sentence);
        listdump();
    k = listinspect();
    if (k != NULL  &&  k → ismem)
        stash(k → word);
    while ((k = listpop()) != NULL)
        if (keyrespond(k) == S_DONE)
            break;
```

If no patterns matched, use 'dunno' response.

```
    if (k == NULL)
```

Really should invoke memory only sometimes...

```
        mem = remember();
        if (mem != NULL)
            putline(mem);
        else if (patrespond(dunno) != S_DONE)
            err("problem with dunno response", "");
    putline("");
```

Dynamic Graphics Project
University of Toronto, with
Aaron Marcus and Associates
Berkeley

crack()   Eliza   Printed 2 Jun 12:08

---

crack – analyze and transform input string.

static void
crack()

Current scan point.	*int* rank;
Keyword struct if found.	*register char* *word;
Was word a substitution	*struct keyword* *k;
keyword?	*int* wassubst;

```
listclear();

rank = 0;
strcpy(sentence, "");

word = strtok(inbuf, " \t");
for (;;)
```

Handle punctuation in input string.

i.e. if no keywords seen
start over

```
while (word != NULL && strchr(".,;:()[]", word[0]) != NULL)
    if (islistempty())
        strcpy(sentence, "");
        word = strtok((char *) NULL, " \t");
    else
        return;
```

If no more words, we're finished.

```
if (word == NULL)
    break;
```

Else find this word's keyword struct.

```
k = keyfind(word);
```

Do synonym substitutions (substitutions without patterns).

```
wassubst = 0;
if (k != NULL && k→pats == NULL && k→subst != NULL)
    word = k→subst;
    k = keyfind(word);
    wassubst = 1;
```

If it's a keyword, add it to the list.

```
if (k != NULL)
    if (k→rank > rank)
        listtop(k);
        rank = k→rank;
    else
        • • •
```

Dynamic Graphics Project   crack()   Eliza   Printed 2 Jun 12:08
University of Toronto, with
Aaron Marcus and Associates
Berkeley

for...if...else...

```
                    listbottom(k);
```

And substitute if appropriate.

```
            if (k → subst != NULL && !wassubst)
                word = k → subst;
```

Put it into the definitive version.

```
        strcat(sentence, word);
        strcat(sentence, " ");

        word = strtok((char *) NULL, " \t");
```

Trim trailing blank off.

```
    if (sentence[0] && sentence[strlen(sentence) − 1] == ' ')
        sentence[strlen(sentence) − 1] = '\0';
```

stash – compose a response and stash it in the reply memory.

```
static void
stash(word)
```

The recognized keyword.

char	*word;
register struct keyword	*k;
register struct text	*t;
int	len;
int	i;
char	buf[LINESIZE];
char	*parts[MAXPAT + 1];

```
for (k = memkwdtop; k != NULL; k = k → knext)
    if (STREQ(k → word, word))
        break;
if (k == NULL)
    err("bad memory keyword '%s'", word);
```

Randomize choice of response.

```
len = 0;
for (t = k → pats → resps; t != NULL; t = t → tnext)
    len++;
i = rand() % len;
if (i == k → pats → nextresp)
    i = (i + 1) % len;
k → pats → nextresp = i;

strcpy(buf, sentence);
if ( !match(buf, k → pats → pat, parts))
        • • •
```

---

memkwdtop ← 23   sentence ← 28

if...

```
            err("memory match failure", "");
```
1 means "for memory"
```
    (void) respond(k→pats, parts, 1);
```

---

keyrespond – attempt to respond using a given keyword.

static STATUS
keyrespond(key)

struct keyword	*key;
register struct pattern	*thispat;
register STATUS	ret;

For stepping through pattern list.
Eventual return value.

```
    for (thispat = key→pats;  thispat != NULL;  thispat = thispat→pnext)
        ret = patrespond(thispat);
        if (ret == S_DONE)
```

We just responded, so we're finished.

```
            return (ret);
        if (ret == S_NEXTK)
```

Go to next keyword.

```
            return (ret);
```

No patterns matched. Weizenbaum doesn't say what he did about this.
We'll take the lazy way out, and try the next keyword.

This is probably the right thing to do, in retrospect, since it also
handles cases where a keyword exists only to be a member of a class, etc.

```
    if (debug)
        printf("---no match\n");
    return (S_NEXTP);
```

---

patrespond – attempt to respond using a given pattern.

static STATUS
patrespond(thispat)

struct pattern	*thispat;
char	*parts[MAXPAT + 1];
char	buf[LINESIZE];

array in which pieces matched
are placed

```
    if (thispat→pat[0]  ==  '>')
        return (punt(thispat→pat, (char **) NULL));
    ...
```

Dynamic Graphics Project
University of Toronto, with
Aaron Marcus and Associates
Berkeley

patrespond()

Eliza

Printed 2 Jun 12:08

```
        if (debug)
            printf("trying pattern '%s'\n", thispat → pat);
        strcpy(buf, sentence);
        if ( !match(buf, thispat → pat, parts))
            return (S_NEXTP);
        return (respond(thispat, parts, 0));
```

0 for print at once.

respond – handle the response for a matched pattern.

```
static STATUS
respond(thispat, parts, ismem)
```

struct pattern	*thispat;
char	**parts;
int	ismem;

NULL–terminated.
For the memory?

register struct text	*t;
register int	i;

Current response.

Find the "next" response.

```
        for (i = 0  , t = thispat → resps;  t != NULL && i != thispat → nextresp;
            t = t → tnext , i++)
            ;
        if (t == NULL)
            thispat → nextresp = 0;
            t = thispat → resps;
        thispat → nextresp++;
```

NULLBODY
Ran off the end.

Check for go–to–next–keyword response.

```
        if (STREQ(t → chars, "+"))
            if (debug)
                printf("---newkey\n");
            return (S_NEXTK);

        if (t → chars[0]  ==  '>')
            return (punt(t → chars, parts));

        if (ismem)
            memorize(format(t → chars, parts));
            return (S_NEXTK);
```

Not memory, so just format and print the response.

```
        putline(format(t → chars, parts));
        return (S_DONE);
```

Dynamic Graphics Project   punt()   Eliza   Printed 2 Jun 12:08
University of Toronto, with
Aaron Marcus and Associates
Berkeley

> punt – punt to a new keyword, possibly with reforming.

```
static STATUS
punt(where, parts)
```

punt command line

```
    char                              *where;
    char                              **parts;
```

punted–to word

```
    register char                     *nword;
    register struct keyword           *newkey;
```

temp containing reform pattern

```
    char                              reform[LINESIZE];
    register int                      len;

    nword = where + strspn(where, "> \t");
```

Reform.
Skip opening quote.

to allow strncat

replace with reformed version

```
    if (*nword == '"')
        nword++;
        len = strcspn(nword, "\"");
        strcpy(reform, "");
        strncat(reform, nword, len);
        strcpy(sentence, format(reform, parts));
        if (debug)
            printf("---reformed as '%s'\n", sentence);
```

+1 gets past closing quote

```
        nword += len + 1;
        nword += strspn(nword, " \t");

    if (debug)
        printf("---punt to '%s'\n", nword);
    newkey = keyfind(nword);
    if (newkey == NULL)
        err("unable to find punted keyword '%s'", nword);
    return (keyrespond(newkey));
```

> match – match a sentence against a pattern, breaking the sentence into
> pieces.
>
> Is allowed to alter the sentence, but not the pattern.
>
> The basic algorithm is recursive rather than iterative, because this
> makes "*" much easier.

as for predicates

```
static int
match(sent, thispat, parts)
```

processed sentence, will be
destroyed

```
    char                              *sent;
```

pattern to match it against
array in which pieces matched
are placed

```
    char                              *thispat;
    char                              **parts;
```

the current token of the pattern

```
    char                              pword[MAXWORD];
    •••
```

the current token of the sentence	*char*	sword[MAXWORD];
current scan point in pat	*char*	*pp;
current scan point in sent	*register char*	*sp;
length of pattern word for strncat	*register int*	plen;
length of sentence word for strncat	*register int*	slen;
current alternative when processing ()s	*char*	*word;
recurse through remainder	**#define** REST	match(sp + slen, pp, parts + 1)

Advance to next space.

```
sp = sent + strspn(sent, " \t");
pp = thispat + strspn(thispat, " \t");
```

End of pattern.

```
if (*pp == '\0')
    if (*sp == '\0')
```

End of both, in fact.

```
        return (1);
    else
```

Pattern ends prematurely.

```
        return (0);
```

Pick out next word of pattern.

```
plen = strcspn(pp, " \t");
strcpy(pword, "");
strncat(pword, pp, plen);
pp += plen;
```

Deal with an annoying special case.

Only "*" can match null.

```
if (*sp == '\0' && !STREQ(pword, "*"))
    return (0);
```

Break by pattern type, recursing (via REST) as necessary.

```
if (STREQ(pword, "*"))
```

Match the remainder of the sentence recursively first.

```
    slen = 0;
    while (!REST)
```

No, the rest didn't match. If we're at the end, fail.

```
        if (*(sp + slen) == '\0')
            return (0);
```

There's more, so gobble another token for that '*'.

```
        slen += strspn(sp + slen, " \t");
        slen += strcspn(sp + slen, " \t");
    ...
```

If we get to this point, REST has succeeded so we have a match.

else if (pword[0] == '(')

Do an alternation.

```
slen = strcspn(sp, " \t");
strcpy(sword, "");
strncat(sword, sp, slen);
```

Check all alternates.

```
for (word = strtok(pword, "(,)");  word != NULL;  word =
     strtok((char *) NULL, "(,)"))
       if (same(word, sword))
             break;
```

If we didn't find a word, the match fails.

```
if (word == NULL)
     return (0);
```

Otherwise, try to match the rest.

```
if ( !REST)
     return (0);
```

else if (pword[0] == '[')

Split off this word into sword. Use strncat rather than strncpy
because it makes zero–terminated strings.

```
slen = strcspn(sp, " \t");
strcpy(sword, "");
strncat(sword, sp, slen);
```

Kill terminating ']'.

```
if (pword[strlen(pword) − 1] != ']')
     err("unmatched '[' in script: '%s'", pword);
pword[strlen(pword) − 1] = '\0';
```

If the word isn't in the class, we fail.

+1 to skip the '['

```
if ( !inclass(sword, pword + 1))
     return (0);
```

Otherwise, try to match the rest.

```
if ( !REST)
       • • •
```

Dynamic Graphics Project
University of Toronto, with
Aaron Marcus and Associates
Berkeley

match()   Eliza   Printed 2 Jun 12:08

else if...if...

```
            return  (0);

else
```

Simple case – just match a word. First split off this word into
sword. Use strncat rather than strncpy because it makes
zero–terminated strings.

```
    slen = strcspn(sp, " \t");
    strcpy(sword, "");
    strncat(sword, sp, slen);
```

If the word doesn't match the pattern word, we fail.

```
    if  ( !same(pword, sword))
        return  (0);
```

Otherwise, try to match the rest.

```
    if  ( !REST)
        return  (0);
```

Store into parts at current position.

```
if  (slen == 0)
    *parts  =  "";
```

Can't build null string in sentence
easily.

```
else
    *parts  =  sp;
    sp  +=  slen;
    *sp  =  '\0';
```

If we've got to here, we've succeeded so return true.

```
    return  (1);
```


format – do formatting of line with #n entries in it.

Pointer to static buffer.

```
static char *
format(s, parts)
```

char	*s;
char	**parts;

Vector of parts of input sentence.

int	nparts;

Count of how many parts are
available.

int	number;

Substitution number (e.g., 3 for
#3).

register char	*scan;
register int	len;

Current scan point.

Length of fbuf so far.

...

Formatted line, returned to caller.

```
static char                    fbuf[LINESIZE];
```

Count the parts available.

```
if (parts != NULL)
    for (nparts = 0;  parts[nparts] != NULL;  nparts++)
        ;
```

NULLBODY

```
strcpy(fbuf, "");
scan = s;
while (*scan != '\0')
    if (*scan == '#')
        scan++;
        if ( !isascii(*scan) || !isdigit(*scan))
            err("bad # in '%s'", s);
```

−1 for 0−origin

```
        number = *scan − '0' − 1;
        if (parts == NULL || number >= nparts)
            err("invalid # reference in '%s'", s);
```

A part to be substituted in might be null. If
so, simply substituting null would leave one space
too many between the adjoining words.

```
        if (STREQ(parts[number], ""))
            len = strlen(fbuf);
            if (len > 0 &&  fbuf[len − 1] == ' ')
                fbuf[len − 1] = '\0';
        else
            strcat(fbuf, parts[number]);
        scan++;
    else
```

Not a '#' substitution; copy up to the next one.

```
        len = strcspn(scan, "#");
        strncat(fbuf, scan, len);
        scan += len;
return (fbuf);
```

Dynamic Graphics Project
University of Toronto, with
Aaron Marcus and Associates
Berkeley keyfind() Eliza Printed 2 Jun 12:08

keyfind – look up a keyword in the script.
Also used in readscript.c.

struct keyword *
keyfind(word)

char	**word;*

register struct keyword	**scan;*

```
for (scan = kwdtop;  scan != NULL;  scan = scan → knext)
     if (same(word, scan → word))
          return (scan);
return (NULL);
```

putline – all output goes through here.

static void
putline(s)

char	** s;*

```
printf("> %s\n", s);
```

Dynamic Graphics Project
University of Toronto, with
Aaron Marcus and Associates
Berkeley

memorize()   Eliza   Printed 2 Jun 12:08

Chapter 7

memory.c

memory.c – maintain the memory mechanism, for remembering things to re–stimulate conversation with at a later date.

The stashed–replies memory.
Limit on the number of stashed
replies.

```c
#include            <stdio.h>
#include            "eliza.h"
static  struct text                 *memory = NULL;
static  int                         memsize = 5;

extern  int                         debug;
extern  void                        err();
extern  void                        append();
```

memorize – stash a reply.

```c
void
memorize(s)
    char                            *s;

    register struct text            *m;
    register int                    i;

    if (debug)
        printf("---memorizing '%s'\n", s);
```

Cut memory down to size, if necessary.

```c
    i = 0;
    for (m = memory;  m != NULL;  m = m→tnext)
        i++;
    for (;  i >= memsize;  i--)
        if (debug)
            printf("---flushing older memory entry\n");
        m = memory→tnext;
        free((char *) memory);
        memory = m;

    append(s, &memory);
```

Dynamic Graphics Project remember()   Eliza Printed 2 Jun 12:08
University of Toronto, with
Aaron Marcus and Associates
Berkeley

---

remember – pick a reply from memory.

pointer to static area

char *
remember()

```
    register struct text          *m;
    static char                   membuf[LINESIZE];

    if (memory == NULL)
        return (NULL);

    strcpy(membuf, memory → chars);

    m = memory → tnext;
    free((char *) memory);
    memory = m;

    return (membuf);
```

setmemsize – set maximum size of memory.

void
setmemsize(n)

```
    int                           n;

    if (n <= 0)
        err("attempt to set memory size <= 0", "");
    if (memory != NULL)
        err("attempt to size memory while it's occupied", "");

    memsize = n;
```

Dynamic Graphics Project
University of Toronto, with
Aaron Marcus and Associates
Berkeley

addtoclass()

Eliza

Printed 2 Jun 12:08

Chapter 8

class.c

class.c – provide the class mechanism, for specifying "classes" of words for pattern-matching.

```
#include            <stdio.h>
#include            "eliza.h"
struct class {
    struct class            *cnext;
    char                    *cname;
    struct text             *members;
};
static struct class             *classes = NULL;

extern char                     *enstring(),
                                *emalloc();

extern void                     err();
extern void                     append();
```

Class name.
Words.

List of all classes.

---

addtoclass – add a word to a word class, creating the class if necessary.

```
void
addtoclass(word, class)
```

```
    char                    *word;
    char                    *class;
```

```
    register struct class            *thisclass;
```

Find class.

```
for (thisclass = classes;  thisclass != NULL &&  !STREQ(thisclass → cname,
    class);  thisclass = thisclass → cnext)
        ;
if (thisclass == NULL)
```

NULLBODY

Create class.

```
        thisclass = (struct class *) emalloc(sizeof(struct class));
        thisclass → cnext = classes;
        classes = thisclass;
        thisclass → cname  = enstring(class);
        thisclass → members  = NULL;
    •••
```

Dynamic Graphics Project   addtoclass()   Eliza   Printed 2 Jun 12:08
University of Toronto, with
Aaron Marcus and Associates
Berkeley

Finally, add the new word.

```
append(word, &thisclass → members);
```

inclass – test word for membership in class.

Predicate.

```
int
inclass(word, class)
```

char	*word;
char	*class;
register struct class	*thisclass;
register struct text	*t;

Find the class.

NULLBODY

```
for (thisclass = classes; thisclass != NULL && !STREQ(thisclass → cname,
    class); thisclass = thisclass → cnext)
    ;
if (thisclass == NULL)
    err("unknown word class '%s'", class);
```

Find the word within the class.

```
for (t = thisclass → members; t != NULL; t = t → tnext)
    if (STREQ(t → chars, word))
        return (1);

return (0);
```

Dynamic Graphics Project
University of Toronto, with
Aaron Marcus and Associates
Berkeley

listtop()

Eliza

Printed 2 Jun 12:08

Chapter 9

list.c

list.c – maintain the list of keywords found in the current sentence.

```
#include        <stdio.h>
#include        "eliza.h"
struct list {
    struct list              *lnext;
    struct keyword           *key;
};
static struct list               *currentlist = NULL;

extern char                      *emalloc();
```

listtop – add a keyword pointer to the beginning of the list.

void
listtop(k)

```
struct keyword              *k;

register struct list        *s;

s = (struct list *) emalloc(sizeof(struct list));
s→key = k;
s→lnext = currentlist;
currentlist = s;
```

listbottom – add a keyword pointer to the end of the list.

void
listbottom(k)

```
struct keyword              *k;

register struct list        *s;
```

If there's nothing in the current list, this reduces to a listtop().

```
if (currentlist == NULL)
    listtop(k);
    return;
...
```

Dynamic Graphics Project
University of Toronto, with
Aaron Marcus and Associates
Berkeley

listbottom()   Eliza   Printed 2 Jun 12:08

Find the end.

NULLBODY

```
for  (s = currentlist;  s → lnext != NULL;  s = s → lnext)
       ;
```

Add the keyword pointer.

```
s → lnext  =  (struct list *) emalloc(sizeof(struct list));
s  =  s → lnext;
s → key  =  k;
s → lnext  =  NULL;
```

listpop – pick a keyword pointer off the top of the list.

NULL if the list is empty.

struct keyword *
listpop()

```
register struct list              *s;
register struct keyword           *k;

if (currentlist == NULL)
     return (NULL);

s = currentlist;
k = s → key;
currentlist = s → lnext;
free((char *) s);

return (k);
```

listinspect – inspect top of list without popping.

NULL if the list is empty.

struct keyword *
listinspect()

```
if  (currentlist == NULL)
     return (NULL);
else
     return (currentlist → key);
```

Dynamic Graphics Project
University of Toronto, with
Aaron Marcus and Associates
Berkeley

listdump()

Eliza

Printed 2 Jun 12:08

---

listdump – print the contents of the list, for debugging.

void
listdump()

```
register struct list                    *s;

for (s = currentlist;  s != NULL;  s = s→lnext)
    printf("%s,",  s→key→word);
printf("-\n");
```

---

listclear – clear out the list.

void
listclear()

```
register struct list                    *s;
register struct list                    *temp;

s = currentlist;
while  (s != NULL)
    temp  = s→lnext;
    free((char *) s);
    s = temp;
currentlist = NULL;
```

---

islistempty – is the list empty?

Predicate.

int
islistempty()

```
return  (currentlist == NULL);
```

Dynamic Graphics Project
University of Toronto, with
Aaron Marcus and Associates
Berkeley

append()   Eliza   Printed 2 Jun 12:08

Chapter 10

utils.c

utils.c – general utilities, not interrelated.
In alphabetical order by function name.

```
#include         <stdio.h>
#include         <ctype.h>
#include         "eliza.h"
```

Externals.

```
extern  char              *enstring();
extern  char              *emalloc();
extern  char              *strtok();
extern  char              *strchr();
extern  void              err();
```

append – append a string to a text.

```
void
append(str,  txtptr)
```

Pointer to text header pointer.

```
        char                      *str;
        struct text               **txtptr;

        register struct text      *t;
        register struct text      *new;
```

Make new struct text.

```
new  =  (struct text *) emalloc( sizeof( struct text));
new → tnext  =  NULL;
new → chars  =  enstring(str);
```

Append it.

```
if  (*txtptr  ==  NULL)
        *txtptr  =  new;
else
        for (t  =  *txtptr;  t→tnext  != NULL;  t  =  t→tnext)
```

NULLBODY

```
                ;
        t → tnext  =  new;
```

blank – is the string blank?

Predicate.

```
int
blank(s)
```

char	*s;

```
if (strspn(s, " \t") == strlen(s))
    return (1);
else
    return (0);
```

emalloc – malloc with err() called when out of space.

```
char *
emalloc(amount)
```

unsigned int	amount;

register char	*it;

Big enough to sprintf an unsigned.

char	camount[25];

extern char	*malloc();

```
it = malloc(amount);
if (it == NULL)
```

because err() only takes strings

```
    sprintf(camount, "%u", amount);
    err("malloc(%s) failed", camount);

return (it);
```

enstring – dynamically allocate space for a string.

```
char *
enstring(s)
```

char	*s;

register char	*it;

```
it = emalloc((unsigned int) strlen(s) + 1);
strcpy(it, s);
return (it);
```

Dynamic Graphics Project
University of Toronto, with
Aaron Marcus and Associates
Berkeley

err()   Eliza   Printed 2 Jun 12:08

---

err – print error message and exit.

void
err(s1, s2)

| *char* | *s1; |
| *char* | *s2; |

| *extern char* | **progname**; |

```
if (progname != NULL)
    fprintf(stderr, "%s: ", progname);
fprintf(stderr, s1, s2);
fprintf(stderr, "\n");
exit(1);
```

---

getsline – get a script line, stripping the trailing newline and deleting comments.

buf or NULL

*char **
getsline(buf, size, fp)

char	*buf;
unsigned int	size;
FILE	*fp;

where the input should go
size of the buf array
where to get the input from

| *register int* | len; |

```
while (fgets(buf, (int) size, fp) != NULL)
```

Remove trailing newline.

```
    len = strlen(buf);
    if (len > 0 && buf[len − 1] == '\n')
        buf[len − 1] = '\0';
```

If it's not a comment, return it, else loop around.

```
    if (buf[0] != '#')
        return (buf);
return (NULL);
```

getuline – get a user input line, with punctuation as separate "words".

buf or NULL

```
char *
getuline(buf, size, fp)
```

where the input should go
size of the buf array
where to get the input from

```
    char                          *buf;
    unsigned int                  size;
    FILE                          *fp;

    register char                 *bp;
    register char                 *endptr;
    register int                  c;
# define            ADD(c)        ((bp < endptr) ? (*bp++ = (c)) : (c))
    bp = buf;
    endptr = buf + size − 1;
```

prompt
```
    printf("< ");
```

Do scanning.

```
    while ((c = getc(fp)) != EOF && c != '\n')
        if (!isascii(c))
```

Weird character – convert it to a space.

```
            ADD(' ');
        else if (strchr(",.;:()[]", c) != NULL)
```

Keep these punctuation marks, but surround them with spaces.

```
            ADD(' ');
            ADD(c);
            ADD(' ');
        else if (strchr("!?", c) != NULL)
```

Throw away these punctuation marks.

```
        else
```

Not punctuation – just concatenate.

```
            ADD(c);
    *bp = '\0';
    if (c == EOF)
        return (NULL);
    else
        return (buf);
```

Dynamic Graphics Project
University of Toronto, with
Aaron Marcus and Associates
Berkeley

same()   Eliza   Printed 2 Jun 12:08

same – compare strings for equality, case–insensitive.

Predicate.

```
int
same(s1, s2)

    char                    *s1;
    char                    *s2;

    char                    *p1;
    char                    *p2;
    register char           c1;
    register char           c2;

    p1 = s1;
    p2 = s2;

    for (;;)
```

Get characters and translate to lower case.

```
        c1 = *p1++;
        c2 = *p2++;
        if (isascii(c1) && isupper(c1))
            c1 = tolower(c1);
        if (isascii(c2) && isupper(c2))
            c2 = tolower(c2);
```

Check for termination of either string.

```
        if (c1 == '\0')
            if (c2 == '\0')
                return (1);
            else
                return (0);
        else if (c2 == '\0')
            return (0);
```

Otherwise, if unequal return failure, else continue checking.

```
        if (c1 != c2)
            return (0);
```

NOTREACHED

Dynamic Graphics Project
University of Toronto, with
Aaron Marcus and Associates
Berkeley

Chapter 11

Programmer Documentation

Section 11.1

The README File and Installation Guide

This is Weizenbaum's Eliza program, implemented from scratch in C by Henry Spencer at the University of Toronto. "Doctor" is a transliteration of the script in Weizenbaum's CACM paper.

This stuff compiles fine under System V and under the University of Toronto Department of Zoology's slightly hacked V7. 4.2BSD (but not Sun UNIX) is missing some of the standard string functions; they can be found in "string.c," which should be included with this distribution.

You may want to fiddle with compiler options and such in the Makefile to get it right for your compiler and loader. In particular, LFLAGS is rather system-specific.

"w.dialogue" is the dialogue from the CACM paper, which this program can reproduce faithfully except for one random element that comes in on the last line. "make try" will run a regression test using this dialogue.

The program has the directory path for the default script hardcoded in "readscript.c." You will have to modify this to point to the correct place; you may want to modify the manual page (eliza.6) to match.

"maintenance" is some sketchy implementation notes.

explorer:/green/flaps/see/pb   prog   31 May 17:11   Revision 3.1   Page E54 / 210

Dynamic Graphics Project   Eliza: The Program   Chapter 11:   Section 11.2:   Printed 2 Jun 17:03
University of Toronto, with   Programmer   Makefile
Aaron Marcus and Associates   Documentation
Berkeley

Section 11.2

Makefile

```
CFLAGS = −O
LINTFLAGS = −bx
LFLAGS = −s
SRCS = eliza.c readscript.c interact.c memory.c class.c list.c utils.c
OBJS = eliza.o readscript.o interact.o memory.o class.o list.o utils.o

eliza: $(OBJS)
        cc $(LFLAGS) $(OBJS) −o eliza

eliza.o: eliza.c eliza.h
readscript.o: readscript.c eliza.h
interact.o: interact.c eliza.h
memory.o: memory.c eliza.h
class.o: class.c eliza.h
list.o: list.c eliza.h
utils.o: utils.c eliza.h

lint:
        lint $(LINTFLAGS) $(SRCS)

clean:
        rm -f $(OBJS) eliza

try:

        @egrep '^< ' w.dialogue | eliza | sed 's/^< //' >w.out
        @echo 'The last response, line 31, about the boyfriend, may differ.'
        @−egrep '^> ' w.dialogue | diff − w.out
        @rm −f w.out
```

explorer:/green/flaps/see/pb   prog   31 May 17:11   Revision 3.1   Page E55 / 211

Dynamic Graphics Project   Eliza: The Program   Chapter 11:   Section 11.3:   Printed 2 Jun 17:03
University of Toronto, with   Programmer   Maintenance Guide
Aaron Marcus and Associates   Documentation
Berkeley

Section 11.3

Maintenance Guide

"eliza.h" defines the main data structures, used mostly by readscript.c and interact.c, and some other odds and ends that are used in several places.

"eliza.c" contains main().

"readscript.c" reads the script file and sets up keyword and pattern data structures.

"interact.c" contains the guts of the program.

"memory.c" manages the memory mechanism.

"class.c" manages the data structures that keep track of classes (e.g., "mother [family]").

"list.c" maintains the list of keywords in the current sentence.

"utils.c" contains a number of non-interdependent utility routines.

It would be straightforward to fix a few deficiencies of the existing code, notably the only-one restrictions on the memory feature. Making the program significantly smarter about understanding the input is very hard and probably not worthwhile. Much can be done by making the script more intelligent.

This code does not contain one feature of Weizenbaum's original, the metasymbol in patterns that means "any single word." Nothing in the "Doctor" script uses it, so we didn't bother. It wouldn't be hard.

It also gets the order of keyword precedence slightly wrong in that it always adds keywords to the top or bottom of the list even if they should really go somewhere in the middle. This might be harder to fix, as well as less worthwhile.

Be careful when messing with any of the functions with a STATUS return, since they are all mutually recursive and must work together properly. Beware also that "match()" destroys its "sentence" argument.

It may look tempting to make "#" start a comment anywhere in the script (not just at the beginning of the line), but remember that "#" is special in responses.

Dynamic Graphics Project   Eliza: The Program   Chapter 12:   Printed 2 Jun 17:04
University of Toronto, with   Indices
Aaron Marcus and Associates
Berkeley

Chapter 12

Indices

Dynamic Graphics Project	Eliza: The Program	Chapter 12:	Section 12.1:	Printed 2 Jun 17:04
University of Toronto, with		Indices	Cross-Reference Index	
Aaron Marcus and Associates			(Partial)	
Berkeley				

Section 12.1 Cross-Reference Index (Partial)

Declaration/Definition Page	Symbol	File	Function	Used on Page
	.	.	.	.
	.	.	.	.
	.	.	.	.
*32	key	interact.c	keyrespond()	32 32
*44		list.c	–	
		list.c	listbottom()	45
		list.c	listdump()	46
		list.c	listinspect()	45
		list.c	listpop()	45
		list.c	listtop()	44
	keyfind()			
28 *39		interact.c	–	
		interact.c	crack()	30 30
		interact.c	punt()	34
23		readscript.c	–	
		readscript.c	linkmemory()	27
	keyrespond()			
28		interact.c	–	
*32		interact.c	–	
		interact.c	interact()	29
		interact.c	punt()	34
*20	keyword	eliza.h	–	20
		interact.c	–	28 28 28 28 28 39
		interact.c	crack()	30
		interact.c	interact()	29
		interact.c	keyfind()	39
		interact.c	keyrespond()	32
		interact.c	punt()	34
		interact.c	stash()	31
		list.c	–	44
		list.c	listbottom()	44
		list.c	listpop()	45
		list.c	listtop()	44
		readscript.c	–	23 23 23 23 23 25
		readscript.c	linkmemory()	27 27
		readscript.c	newkwd()	25 25
		readscript.c	readscript()	23
*20	knext	eliza.h	–	
		interact.c	keyfind()	39
		interact.c	stash()	31
		readscript.c	linkmemory()	27
		readscript.c	newkwd()	25
		readscript.c	readscript()	24
*23	kwd	readscript.c	readscript()	24 24 24 24 24 24 24
*25	kwdtext	readscript.c	newkwd()	25 25 26 26 26 26
28	kwdtop	interact.c	–	
		interact.c	keyfind()	39
*23		readscript.c	–	
		readscript.c	readscript()	24
*23	lastkwd	readscript.c	–	
		readscript.c	readscript()	24 24 24
*37	len	interact.c	format()	38 38 38 38 38 38
*34		interact.c	punt()	34 34 34
*31		interact.c	stash()	31 31 31 31
*49		utils.c	getsline()	49 49 49
	linkmemory()			
21		eliza.c	main()	21
*27		readscript.c	–	
*44	list	list.c	–	44 44
		list.c	listbottom()	44 45
		list.c	listclear()	46 46
		list.c	listdump()	46
		list.c	listpop()	45

* denotes definition

Dynamic Graphics Project
University of Toronto, with
Aaron Marcus and Associates
Berkeley

Eliza: The Program   Chapter 12:
Indices   Section 12.1:
Cross-Reference Index
(Partial)   Printed 2 Jun 17:04

Dynamic Graphics Project
University of Toronto, with
Aaron Marcus and Associates
Berkeley

Eliza: The Program   Chapter 12:
Indices   Section 12.2:
Caller Index   Printed 2 Jun 17:04

Section 12.2

Caller Index

Caller	File, Page	Callee	File, Page
addtoclass()	class.c, 42	append() emalloc() enstring()	utils.c, 47 utils.c, 48 utils.c, 48
append()	utils.c, 47	emalloc() enstring()	utils.c, 48 utils.c, 48
crack()	interact.c, 30	islistempty() keyfind() listbottom() listclear() listtop()	list.c, 46 interact.c, 39 list.c, 44 list.c, 46 list.c, 44
emalloc()	utils.c, 48	err()	utils.c, 49
enstring()	utils.c, 48	emalloc()	utils.c, 48
format()	interact.c, 37	err()	utils.c, 49
getpats()	readscript.c, 26	append() blank() emalloc() enstring() err() getsline()	utils.c, 47 utils.c, 48 utils.c, 48 utils.c, 48 utils.c, 49 utils.c, 49
inclass()	class.c, 43	err()	utils.c, 49
interact()	interact.c, 29	crack() err() getuline() keyrespond() listdump() listinspect() listpop() patrespond() putline() remember() stash()	interact.c, 30 utils.c, 49 utils.c, 50 interact.c, 32 list.c, 46 list.c, 45 list.c, 45 interact.c, 32 interact.c, 39 memory.c, 41 interact.c, 31
keyfind()	interact.c, 39	same()	utils.c, 51
keyrespond()	interact.c, 32	patrespond()	interact.c, 32
linkmemory()	readscript.c, 27	err() keyfind()	utils.c, 49 interact.c, 39
listbottom()	list.c, 44	emalloc() listtop()	utils.c, 48 list.c, 44
listtop()	list.c, 44	emalloc()	utils.c, 48
main()	eliza.c, 21	interact() linkmemory() readscript()	interact.c, 29 readscript.c, 27 readscript.c, 23
match()	interact.c, 34	err() inclass() match() same()	utils.c, 49 class.c, 43 interact.c, 34 utils.c, 51

Dynamic Graphics Project
University of Toronto, with
Aaron Marcus and Associates
Berkeley

Eliza: The Program   Chapter 12: Indices   Section 12.2: Caller Index   Printed 2 Jun 17:04

memorize()	memory.c, 40	append()	utils.c, 47
newkwd()	readscript.c, 25	addtoclass()	class.c, 42
		emalloc()	utils.c, 48
		enstring()	utils.c, 48
		err()	utils.c, 49
		setmemsize()	memory.c, 41
patrespond()	interact.c, 32	match()	interact.c, 34
		punt()	interact.c, 34
		respond()	interact.c, 33
punt()	interact.c, 34	err()	utils.c, 49
		format()	interact.c, 37
		keyfind()	interact.c, 39
		keyrespond()	interact.c, 32
readscript()	readscript.c, 23	append()	utils.c, 47
		blank()	utils.c, 48
		err()	utils.c, 49
		getpats()	readscript.c, 26
		getsline()	utils.c, 49
		newkwd()	readscript.c, 25
respond()	interact.c, 33	format()	interact.c, 37
		memorize()	memory.c, 40
		punt()	interact.c, 34
		putline()	interact.c, 39
setmemsize()	memory.c, 41	err()	utils.c, 49
stash()	interact.c, 31	err()	utils.c, 49
		match()	interact.c, 34
		respond()	interact.c, 33

Dynamic Graphics Project
University of Toronto, with
Aaron Marcus and Associates
Berkeley

Eliza: The Program   Chapter 12:
Indices   Section 12.3:
Callee Index   Printed 2 Jun 17:04

Section 12.3

Callee Index

Callee	File, Page	Caller	File, Page
addtoclass()	class.c, 42	newkwd()	readscript.c, 25
append()	utils.c, 47	addtoclass() getpats() memorize() readscript()	class.c, 42 readscript.c, 26 memory.c, 40 readscript.c, 23
blank()	utils.c, 48	getpats() readscript()	readscript.c, 26 readscript.c, 23
crack()	interact.c, 30	interact()	interact.c, 29
emalloc()	utils.c, 48	addtoclass() append() enstring() getpats() listbottom() listtop() newkwd()	class.c, 42 utils.c, 47 utils.c, 48 readscript.c, 26 list.c, 44 list.c, 44 readscript.c, 25
enstring()	utils.c, 48	addtoclass() append() getpats() newkwd()	class.c, 42 utils.c, 47 readscript.c, 26 readscript.c, 25
err()	utils.c, 49	emalloc() format() getpats() inclass() interact() linkmemory() match() newkwd() punt() readscript() setmemsize() stash()	utils.c, 48 interact.c, 37 readscript.c, 26 class.c, 43 interact.c, 29 readscript.c, 27 interact.c, 34 readscript.c, 25 interact.c, 34 readscript.c, 23 memory.c, 41 interact.c, 31
format()	interact.c, 37	punt() respond()	interact.c, 34 interact.c, 33
getpats()	readscript.c, 26	readscript()	readscript.c, 23
getsline()	utils.c, 49	getpats() readscript()	readscript.c, 26 readscript.c, 23
getuline()	utils.c, 50	interact()	interact.c, 29
inclass()	class.c, 43	match()	interact.c, 34
interact()	interact.c, 29	main()	eliza.c, 21
islistempty()	list.c, 46	crack()	interact.c, 30
keyfind()	interact.c, 39	crack() linkmemory() punt()	interact.c, 30 readscript.c, 27 interact.c, 34
keyrespond()	interact.c, 32	interact() punt()	interact.c, 29 interact.c, 34

Dynamic Graphics Project	Eliza: The Program	Chapter 12:	Section 12.3:	Printed 2 Jun 17:04
University of Toronto, with		Indices	Callee Index	
Aaron Marcus and Associates				
Berkeley				

linkmemory()	readscript.c, 27	main()	eliza.c, 21
listbottom()	list.c, 44	crack()	interact.c, 30
listclear()	list.c, 46	crack()	interact.c, 30
listdump()	list.c, 46	interact()	interact.c, 29
listinspect()	list.c, 45	interact()	interact.c, 29
listpop()	list.c, 45	interact()	interact.c, 29
listtop()	list.c, 44	crack() listbottom()	interact.c, 30 list.c, 44
match()	interact.c, 34	match() patrespond() stash()	interact.c, 34 interact.c, 32 interact.c, 31
memorize()	memory.c, 40	respond()	interact.c, 33
newkwd()	readscript.c, 25	readscript()	readscript.c, 23
patrespond()	interact.c, 32	interact() keyrespond()	interact.c, 29 interact.c, 32
punt()	interact.c, 34	patrespond() respond()	interact.c, 32 interact.c, 33
putline()	interact.c, 39	interact() respond()	interact.c, 29 interact.c, 33
readscript()	readscript.c, 23	main()	eliza.c, 21
remember()	memory.c, 41	interact()	interact.c, 29
respond()	interact.c, 33	patrespond() stash()	interact.c, 32 interact.c, 31
same()	utils.c, 51	keyfind() match()	interact.c, 39 interact.c, 34
setmemsize()	memory.c, 41	newkwd()	readscript.c, 25
stash()	interact.c, 31	interact()	interact.c, 29

Dynamic Graphics Project
University of Toronto, with
Aaron Marcus and Associates
Berkeley

Eliza: The Program

Dynamic Graphics Project
University of Toronto
Toronto, Ontario, Canada

Aaron Marcus and Associates
Berkeley, California, USA

Eliza: The Program

Highlights

- Eliza carries on a dialogue with a user in a limited subset of English.

- The nature of the dialogue is controlled by a script.

- A sample script, "Doctor,"allows Eliza to simulate to a limited extent a Rogerian therapist.

- Complete source code of Eliza and Doctor is included.

- Instructions on the use and maintenance of Eliza and Doctor, and on the art of writing scripts, are also included.

Eliza is a program that carries on a dialogue with a user and pretends to a very limited extent to understand English language input. Driven by the "Doctor" script, it tries to simulate a Rogerian therapist.

Eliza operates with a very simple keyword and pattern-matching scheme that sometimes enables it to appear to recognize significant phrases. It reuses these phrases in a dialogue, thus sometimes conveying the illusion of comprehension. Extensive or even modest use of Eliza should make apparent to even the most naive of users that one is not communicating with an intelligent entity but merely with a simple-minded automaton.

Nonetheless, Eliza can be used for very canned English-like dialogues, and also presents an interesting case study of simple natural language processing.

The original implementation of Eliza was done by **Joseph Weizenbaum,** later to become a Professor of Computer Science at M.I.T. The version published in this book is a re-implementation in C by **Henry Spencer** of the University of Toronto Department of Zoology. **Alan Rosenthal** of the University of Toronto Dynamic Graphics Project modified and further enhanced Spencer's code. This work was carried out under the supervision of **Ronald M. Baecker**, a Professor of Computer Science at the University of Toronto, and **Aaron Marcus,** Principal of Aaron Marcus and Associates, with the assistance of **D. Hugh Redelmeier** and **Ilona R. Posner** of the Dynamic Graphics Project.

Natural Language Dialogue Systems/Conversational Systems Dynamic Graphics Project Software Distributing ISSN 0-123-45678-9

Section 5.5

Examples and Variations of Program Views

Program Source Text

Methods to enhance the appearance and usability of program source text were introduced in Chapters 1, 3, and 4. These methods can be and have been automated.

Program Page Metadata

Also located on the program pages are two kinds of secondary text. Program page *headers* include metadata selected by the user, for example, the location of the file being listed, the date and time of last update, and the revision number. Program page *footnotes* could include cross-references to the definitions and uses of global identifiers. These concepts have already been illustrated and discussed in Chapters 1, 3, and 4. Program metadata can be added to program pages automatically.

User Documentation

Among the numerous possible user documents, there are four essential ones that appear frequently.

A *tutorial guide* is a step-by-step introduction to the purpose and usage of the major features of the system. A skeletal tutorial guide to Eliza, expressed in terms of the "Doctor" script, which enables Eliza to simulate a Rogerian psychiatrist, appears as Section 1.1 of the program book.

A *command summary* is a terse listing of the method of usage of all system features. In the case of a program operating under the UNIX operating system, this command summary is often included in the manual page, or "man page." [†] By convention, one such page is written to correspond to each UNIX utility or command installed on the system. Section 1.2 of the program book is a prototype manual page for Eliza.

A *user manual* is a practical, not necessarily logically organized summary of the major features of the system, often oriented to a set of practical tasks. We illustrate this concept in terms of Eliza in Section 1.3 of the program book, which includes a complete listing of the "Doctor" script.

A *reference manual* is a "contract with the user," a comprehensive information source on all system features, usually organized in terms of the program's functionality. UNIX manual pages often contain brief reference manuals, as is the case with Section 1.2 of the Eliza program book.

Programmer Documentation

There are two essential program documents among the many possible ones, an installation guide and a maintenance guide. In the UNIX world, a README file is by convention included in any software distribution. This file is the first read by the programmer upon receipt of the system, and thus should be a guidebook to what is in the distribution and to the locations of the installation guide and the maintenance guide. Section 11.1 of the Eliza program book is its README file.

An *installation guide* describes how to install a system; in the UNIX world, a "Makefile" file is used by the UNIX "make" program to facilitate system recompilation and regeneration. Thus we include the Eliza Makefile as Section 11.2 of the program book.

A *maintenance guide* contains instructions on how to maintain the system. Section 11.3 of the Eliza program book is a maintenance guide.

[†]   A UNIX man page may actually consist of many physical pages, although the tradition is one that emphasizes terseness often at the expense of clarity and usability.

Program Introductions

A program published in book form may need a *cover page* identifying it and depicting it with an attractive illustration. The Eliza cover page appears on page 147 of this book. At this point we have entered a book within a book, and begin numbering anew, adding the prefix "E" before each page number.[†]

A *title page* (see page Ei/149) presents the most important metadata, such as the program's title, author, company and address of the author, version, date, publishing source, level of confidentiality, and copyright notice.[††]

A *colophon* (see page Eii/150) presents production information, details about the typesetting, printing, and distribution of the document.

An *abstract* of the program summarizes what it does, how it accomplishes it, and why it does it. (See page Eiii/151.)

A *program history* presents the history of the system from conception to implementation through recent modification. (See page Eiii/151.)

An *authors and personalities page* (see page Eiv/152) lists the authors and other important personalities (e.g., augmenters and maintainers) associated with the program, gives their postal and network addresses, their phone numbers, and potentially also their photographs (Pike and Presotto, 1985).

User documentation, programmer documentation, and program introductions cannot be generated automatically; they all require human authors.

Program Overviews

A *Table of Contents* enumerates the major component parts of a program publication. In the case of a C program, the table of contents should list the components of program metatext: the introductions, user documentation sections, program overviews, programmer documentation sections, and indices, in order of their occurrence, and it should give their locations within the document. The list should also cover the program source text: the directories, files, and major user-defined program elements. These elements include functions, global variables and file static variables, preprocessor macros, defined types, and structure tags.

An example Eliza table of contents appears on pages Ev/153 through Evii/155 of the program book. As in the design of individual program pages, we had to apply graphic design principles and carry out systematic design variations in order to develop the most effective presentations of program structure and meaning. One step along the way toward our table of contents of program text is shown as Figure 5.2.

If the table of contents becomes too long and cumbersome, it may be advantageous to include a simplified and then a more elaborate version. A *Detailed Table of Contents* (DTOC), therefore, is a table of contents providing more detail about the contents of a program book than does the standard table of contents.[†††] Because of the multiplicity of choices in the contents of the DTOC, it is desirable to have them computed upon demand. Examples will be discussed later in this section (see also Section 2.1 of the Eliza program book and Figure 5.12).

[†]   Actually, both numbers are shown in the Eliza book page headers. Page number references in Eliza source text footnotes refer only to the "E" number.

[††]   Traditional book conventions usually place the copyright notice on the obverse side of the title page, but we believe it deserves more prominence.

[†††] The two parts of the Eliza table of contents already illustrate the concept. The first part details program metatext, whereas the second part expands the contents of program source text. See also Baecker and Buxton (1987), where the concept is applied to a book.

Eliza: The Program

		Files and Functions		Data Objects

✂ -

Figure 5.2: *Table of contents of Eliza program text, an early variation.*

Function-like elements are on the left. Object-like elements are on the right.
Because we have listed the elements in the most compact form possible, the
method of presentation has the disadvantage that the order of occurrence of
elements in the table is not always identical to their occurrence in the program. We repair this problem and thereby improve the depiction to achieve
the recommended form shown on pages Evi/154 and Evii/155 of the Eliza
program book. Although each line of the table now lists only one element, the
resulting form is clearer, because the order of occurrence in the table strictly
preserves the order of occurrence in the program.

A *signature* is a compact graphic symbol computed from the program that encapsulates and communicates certain aspects and properties of the program and its author.[†]

A *condensation* is a perceptual zoom-out, a signature computed by shrinking or compressing the displays of individual program pages into small images. This is done in order to include multiple pages on a single sheet of paper and to facilitate quick scanning of a large program. Figures 5.3 through 5.6 show a series of condensations in which the pages are compressed by factors of 2.5, 5, 12.5, and 50. What is remarkable, even when text is compressed by a factor of 12.5 in both dimensions, is the degree to which information and clues about the structure and contents of the program are still perceptible even though none of the text is legible or readable. The condensation by a factor of 50, however, does not seem to work, although it might serve as the basis for an effective execution profile display (see Figure 5.11 and the accompanying discussion).

A *map* is a condensation that has been annotated so that the names of the major constituent parts of the program are readable. An illustration of this concept appears as Section 2.1 of the Eliza program book. Clearly, the map can also serve as a graphically enhanced table of contents.

A *diagram* is an abstract representation of structure and process not immediately apparent and not necessarily easily computable.[††]

A *call hierarchy* (see Section 2.2 of the Eliza program book) is a diagram that shows the nesting of function calls, detailing which functions could potentially call which other functions. It is a description of the static structure of the program source text. Our example call hierarchy includes only Eliza functions, and no library functions. Thus we see that "main()" can call "STREQ()," "readscript()," "linkmemory()," and "interact()," "readscript()" can call "err()," "getsline(), " "blank()," etc.

A *regular expression control diagram* (devised by Hugh Redelmeier) illustrates the control structure of various functions and the appearance of calls on other functions in the context of that control structure. An example appears as Section 2.3 of the Eliza program book. Our example diagram includes both Eliza functions and library functions. Iterative execution is denoted by curly braces, conditional execution by the "or" bar, and a return from a function by a carat.

A *function call history*, or *trace*, of the program, shows the nesting of function calls during a particular execution of the program. This device is a description of the dynamic structure of the program source text. Section 2.4 of the Eliza program book is an example. The trace is based on the execution of Eliza as it carries out the dialogue of the first example in the Eliza tutorial guide which is Section 1.1 of the Eliza program book. Only functions that appear in "interact.c" are shown. Repetitive occurrences of function calls are described compactly and meaningfully. Understanding of the program's behavior is further aided by interspersing its input and output in the marginalia column.

Computer scientists have researched various *metrics* (Gilb, 1977; Perlis, Sayward and Shaw, 1981) that encapsulate significant properties or qualities of a program. These can be displayed as tables or charts that convey aspects of one or more large programs in a single figure or on a single page.

[†]   For examples, refer to the discussion on metrics that follows.

[††]   See also Martin and McClure, 1985.

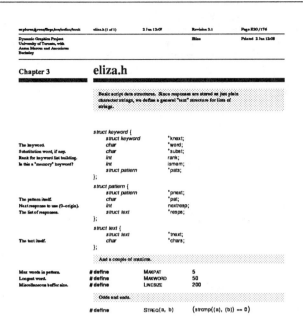

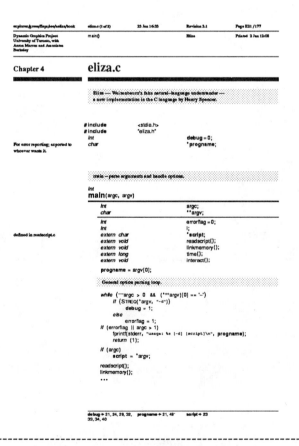

Figure 5.3: *Condensation by a factor of 2.5.*

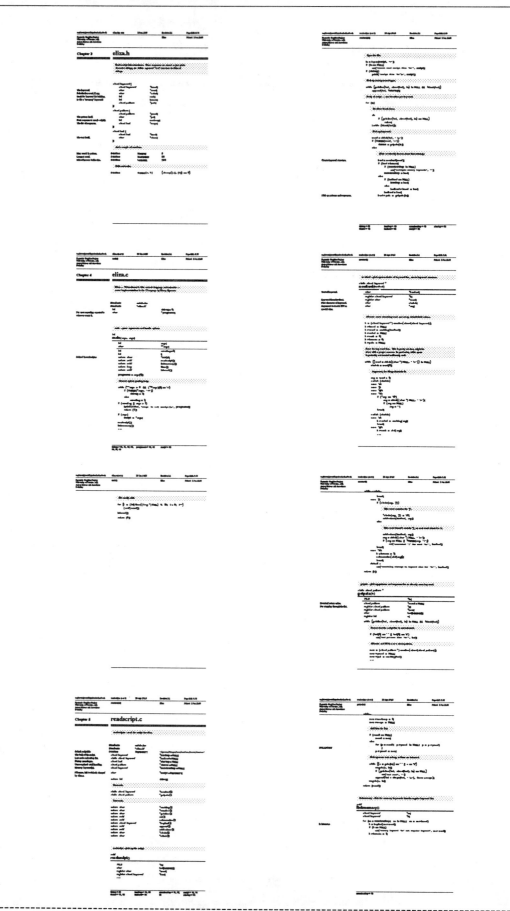

Figure 5.4: *Condensation by a factor of 5.*

Figure 5.5: *Condensation by a factor of 12.5.*

Figure 5.6: *Condensation by a factor of 50.*

Although software engineers and human factors specialists must do more work to determine the proper content and form of program metrics, we shall illustrate the concept using a set of seven prototypical metrics that capture and describe some of the variability in C programs:

- The *length* of the program in lines of source text.
- The *conditional compilation complexity*, defined as the number of conditional compilation commands.
- The *number of functions* defined within the source text.
- The *average function length*, defined as the number of *program commands* divided by the number of defined functions.[†]
- The *control flow density*, defined as the number of control flow reserved words divided by the number of commands.
- The *non-local reference density*, defined as the number of references to non-local variables divided by the total number of references to variables.
- The *comment density*, defined as the number of comment lines divided by the length of the program.

We make no claims about the excellence or ultimate utility of these metrics, other than they are useful to illustrate how metrics could be presented.[††]

We therefore include as Figures 5.7 and 5.8 tables in which these metrics are applied to three compilers, the UNIX Edition Eight Portable C Compiler (PCC) (Johnson, 1979), the Gnu C compiler (Free Software Foundation, 1988) and the Red C compiler (Redelmeier, 1989). In each case, the tables present metrics for the entire program as well as metrics for the individual files comprising the program, listed in order of decreasing length.[†††]

The data reveal a number of facts of particular interest:

- PCC is by the far the shortest compiler.[††††]
- Over 2% of the lines of code within PCC are conditional compilation commands.
- There are a number of files (some machine-generated), such as "c-parse.tab.c" and "insn-recog.c" within Gnu C, with significant numbers of very large functions and very few comments.
- Control flow in Red C is relatively simple compared to that in PCC and Gnu C.
- Use of non-local variables is relatively high in "pcc/cgram.c" and "mip/scan.c" within PCC, in "preproc.c," "strtab.c," and "diag.c" within Red C, and in "insn-extract.c" and "toplev.c" within Gnu C.
- There is great variability in the occurrence of comments in the three compilers, ranging from the quite sparsely commented PCC to the relatively densely commented Red C.

[†]   A program command is a statement. A line of C source code typically contains several statements. For example, "*if* (k>0) k=0;" counts as two commands.

[††]   It is easy to be cynical about program metrics. For example, Berry and Meekings (1985) propose a set of metrics for C programs and a method of combining them into a "goodness" score that is severely flawed. Not only do their techniques not always measure what they claim to be measuring, but it is easy to devise simple and terrible C programs that result in a high score. On the other hand, metrics that apply to cars and displays of them such as appear in *Consumer Reports* give us hope that a more mature computer science will possess meaningful program metrics and sensible ways of depicting and using them.

[†††] A more conventional order would be that in which the files would occur in their program book. On the other hand, the use of order of decreasing file length makes visible interesting properties of the programs.

[††††] One reason for this is that PCC handles only traditional C, whereas the other two compilers are designed for ANSI C. Also, the Gnu C compiler is much more machine-independent and does more optimization. The cost of this in lines of code is staggering!

Eighth Edition UNIX Portable C Compiler (PCC)

	length	conditional compilation complexity	number of functions	average function length	control flow density	non-local reference density	comment density
mip/pftn.c	1924	49	41	37.37	0.38	0.27	0.10
mip/trees.c	1527	23	26	44.46	0.47	0.06	0.09
pcc/cgram.c †	1383	14	10	121.10	0.37	0.54	0.03
mip/reader.c	1319	27	19	41.16	0.45	0.14	0.11
cpp/cpp.c	1190	54	24	55.50	0.35	0.42	0.18
pcc/local2.c	1155	10	38	20.29	0.36	0.07	0.13
mip/scan.c	1109	17	11	64.82	0.42	0.49	0.13
pcc/table.c	831	3	0	–	–	–	0.02
mip/match.c	637	19	6	47.33	0.62	0.13	0.20
pcc/local.c	596	16	26	13.23	0.40	0.18	0.12
mip/allo.c	558	18	15	28.67	0.35	0.23	0.10
pcc/order.c	527	0	17	23.94	0.37	0.09	0.17
pcc/code.c	494	6	24	12.33	0.23	0.20	0.16
cpp/cpy.c †	385	8	1	246.00	0.39	0.24	0.07
mip/optim.c	182	0	4	37.00	0.46	0.02	0.08
mip/xdefs.c	103	1	1	8.00	0.38	0.29	0.36
pcc/rodata.c	34	0	0	–	–	–	0.00
cpp/rodata.c	9	0	0	–	–	–	0.00
mip/comm1.c	5	0	0	–	–	0.00	0.00
total of all files	13968	265	263	36.73	0.39	0.25	0.11

† automatically generated

Red C Compiler

	length	conditional compilation complexity	number of functions	average function length	control flow density	non-local reference density	comment density
codegen.c	7018	53	109	41.31	0.18	0.20	0.28
expr.c	3357	49	26	97.46	0.31	0.14	0.20
decl.c	2412	19	26	65.19	0.27	0.19	0.22
preproc.c	1910	34	26	58.15	0.28	0.52	0.19
objfile.c	1468	19	32	23.88	0.20	0.35	0.27
stmt.c	998	15	7	100.00	0.26	0.33	0.23
type.c	906	13	9	45.11	0.33	0.15	0.30
lex.c	781	10	6	87.83	0.42	0.26	0.29
opinfo.c	669	0	0	–	–	–	0.17
literal.c	589	6	5	87.40	0.33	0.12	0.18
init.c	398	4	3	97.00	0.35	0.16	0.24
filein.c	374	12	5	35.40	0.26	0.46	0.28
size.c	372	7	7	15.14	0.32	0.21	0.43
driver.c	326	14	4	49.25	0.25	0.34	0.26
strtab.c	320	8	14	13.71	0.15	0.48	0.14
name.c	256	4	7	18.00	0.25	0.16	0.16
space.c	246	13	5	32.40	0.20	0.12	0.14
token.c	215	0	0	–	–	–	0.57
diag.c	98	2	7	3.43	0.04	0.50	0.15
univ.c	79	1	3	10.00	0.40	0.00	0.18
syn.c	63	0	2	17.00	0.44	0.38	0.22
total of all files	22855	283	303	47.58	0.25	0.23	0.24

Figure 5.7: *A table of metrics of the PCC compiler and the Red C compiler.*

Gnu C Compiler

	length	conditional compilation complexity	number of functions	average function length	control flow density	non-local reference density	comment density
insn-output.c †	5448	80	148	8.74	0.48	0.19	0.01
cccp.c	5234	34	62	52.65	0.33	0.14	0.23
expr.c	4804	93	49	44.59	0.33	0.10	0.19
loop.c	4538	9	30	71.50	0.37	0.13	0.23
c-parse.tab.c †	3676	37	13	198.15	0.36	0.30	0.09
insn-recog.c †	3643	0	8	603.25	0.48	0.21	0.00
cse.c	3492	4	36	49.25	0.40	0.15	0.24
c-typeck.c	3469	3	49	38.37	0.45	0.10	0.16
stmt.c	3449	28	61	22.79	0.26	0.18	0.24
c-decl.c	3346	8	41	36.00	0.28	0.25	0.24
reload.c	2827	13	18	72.39	0.40	0.17	0.24
insn-extract.c †	2777	1	267	3.31	0.00	0.67	0.00
combine.c	2447	10	21	59.33	0.39	0.21	0.21
reload1.c	2336	18	16	70.31	0.32	0.26	0.28
tree.c	2058	3	66	11.92	0.36	0.36	0.20
flow.c	1951	18	17	51.71	0.29	0.19	0.27
optabs.c	1930	170	22	35.68	0.28	0.30	0.08
integrate.c	1686	5	11	80.55	0.43	0.15	0.19
toplev.c	1663	22	28	33.00	0.25	0.50	0.15
insn-emit.c †	1656	0	146	4.50	0.24	0.11	0.00
varasm.c	1583	9	30	26.87	0.33	0.32	0.18
fold-const.c	1578	0	16	62.44	0.41	0.01	0.14
emit-rtl.c	1547	11	52	13.23	0.36	0.24	0.19
jump.c	1510	5	24	30.54	0.38	0.05	0.21
expmed.c	1443	22	13	48.00	0.30	0.08	0.22
final.c	1356	36	17	56.53	0.38	0.32	0.21
cexp.c †	1258	33	6	85.83	0.41	0.16	0.20
gcc.c	1254	11	23	23.35	0.29	0.42	0.21
symout.c	1217	5	22	27.82	0.24	0.20	0.13
local-alloc.c	1139	7	16	33.88	0.31	0.29	0.27
dbxout.c	1112	11	14	33.71	0.27	0.44	0.26
recog.c	1009	6	25	25.20	0.50	0.05	0.20
global-alloc.c	1000	6	14	34.36	0.26	0.28	0.26
sdbout.c	899	21	0	–	–	–	0.17
stor-layout.c	882	3	16	23.69	0.30	0.11	0.21
regclass.c	863	6	11	43.91	0.38	0.20	0.19
print-tree.c	580	4	12	33.67	0.26	0.31	0.06
explow.c	552	4	20	21.65	0.38	0.04	0.24
stupid.c	462	3	4	55.25	0.25	0.25	0.28
c-convert.c	363	1	4	42.75	0.53	0.05	0.26
insn-peep.c †	68	0	1	68.00	0.62	0.19	0.03
version.c	1	0	0	–	–	–	0.00
total of all files	84106	760	1449	29.71	0.36	0.21	0.17

† automatically generated

✂ --

Figure 5.8: *A table of metrics of the Gnu C compiler.*

Such dense numerical data can better be displayed as charts and graphs. For example, Figure 5.9 shows the metrics of the individual files of the three compilers depicted as bar charts. Figure 5.10 shows the summary data for each compiler portrayed in three ways: as bar charts, as "star charts" (Human Synergistics, 1980), and as gray tone bars. The star charts are a concise method of displaying and facilitating the comparison of sets of multi-dimensional data. The gray tone bars are a very compact form of depicting program metrics of gross value distinctions (close to 0%, low, medium, high, close to 100%). Such a display would permit as many as hundreds of programs to be registered on a single page.

A gray tone bar display of these same metrics applied to Eliza appears on the title page, page Ei/149, of the program book.

An example of an important metric is an *execution profile* of a program. This is a diagram showing the relative frequency of execution of different parts of the source code. It is a description of the dynamic behavior of the program that is somewhat more global than the trace. A traditional representation of an execution profile of Eliza function calls appears as Section 2.5 of the program book. A more dramatic display, superimposing a line-by-line execution profile on a condensation, is shown as Figure 5.11. Note the appearance of "hot spots" within the program.[†] Color depiction would dramatically enhance this kind of display.

Program overviews can be generated automatically.

Program Indices

A *cross-reference index* lists every identifier, indicates where it is defined and where it is declared, and points to every occurrence of that identifier in the program. A portion of the Eliza cross-reference index appears as Section 12.1 of the program book.

Two especially useful subsets of a cross-reference index show, for each function, all the functions that it calls (the *Caller Index*, illustrated in Section 12.2 of the Eliza program book), and for each function, every function that calls it (the *Callee Index*, illustrated in Section 12.3). Although this information can be laboriously extracted from a typical cross-reference index and from the program source code, we recommend the production of special-purpose crisp portrayals of caller and callee data such as those that appear in Sections 12.2 and 12.3.[††]

Key Word In Context (KWIC) listings show all program tokens alphabetically in the context of their surrounding text. Although one would probably not include such a listing in a paper program publication, computing, displaying, and printing sections upon demand might be very useful in certain program development, reading, and maintenance situations. Figure 5.12 is an example of a portion of a KWIC index applied to Eliza. Seeing at a glance the entire set of ways in which a particular token is used in the program and where these uses occur can be very illuminating.

Program indices can also be generated automatically.

[†]   Our use of line width in this illustration is reminiscent of that in the classic graphic by Minard depicting the fate of Napoleon's army in Russia, as reproduced and discussed in Tufte (1983).

[††]   Caller and callee data could also be combined in a single table.

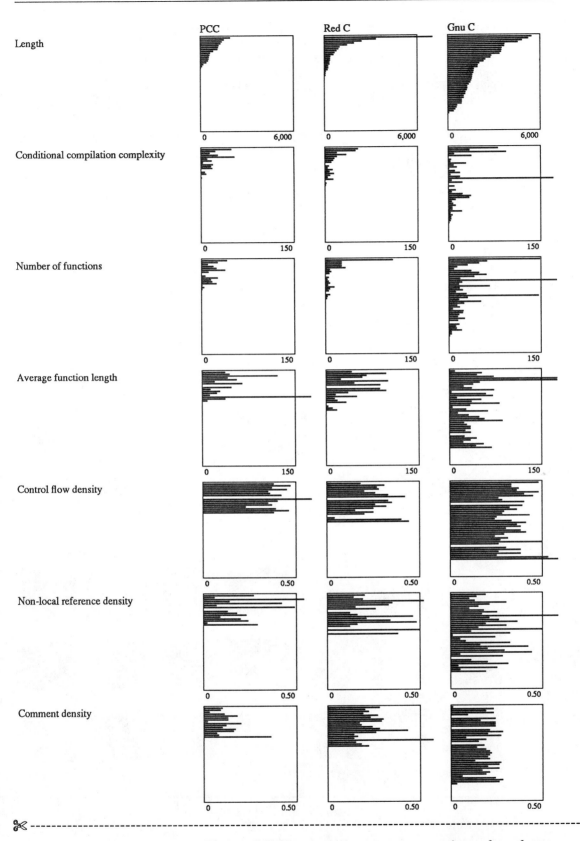

Length

PCC   Red C   Gnu C

Conditional compilation complexity

Number of functions

Average function length

Control flow density

Non-local reference density

Comment density

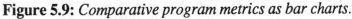

Figure 5.9: *Comparative program metrics as bar charts.*

The data of Figures 5.7 and 5.8 are presented as bar charts. Each bar corresponds to one metric of one file. Files are ordered according to decreasing length. Any data value that exceeds 7/6 times the "maximum" value within a chart is displayed as a line that extends only to 7/6 times that maximum value.

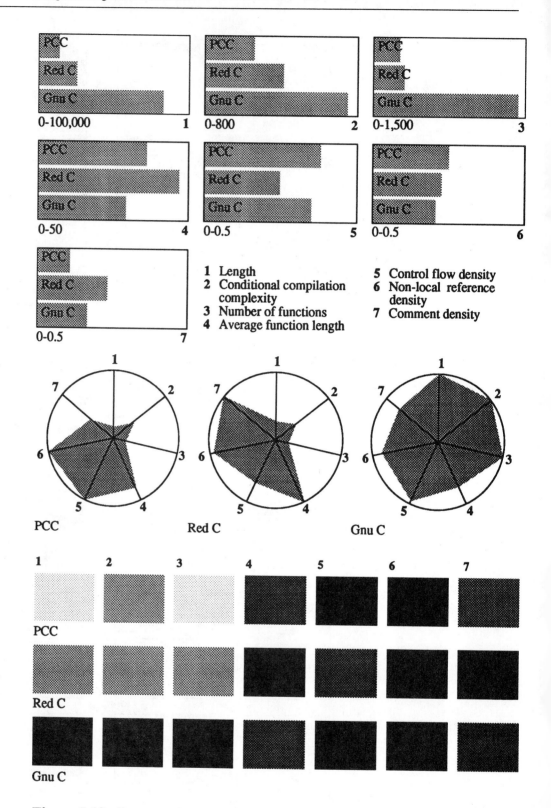

Figure 5.10: *Comparative program metrics as bar charts, star charts, and gray tone bars.*

The summary data for the three compilers taken from Figures 5.7 and 5.8 are displayed in three different ways. The star charts plot relative, normalized values (0.0–1.0) of the seven calculated metrics for each of the three programs. The gray tone bars take these values and map them into five gray tones based on the ranges 0.0–0.2, 0.2–0.4, 0.4–0.6, 0.6–0.8, and 0.8–1.0.

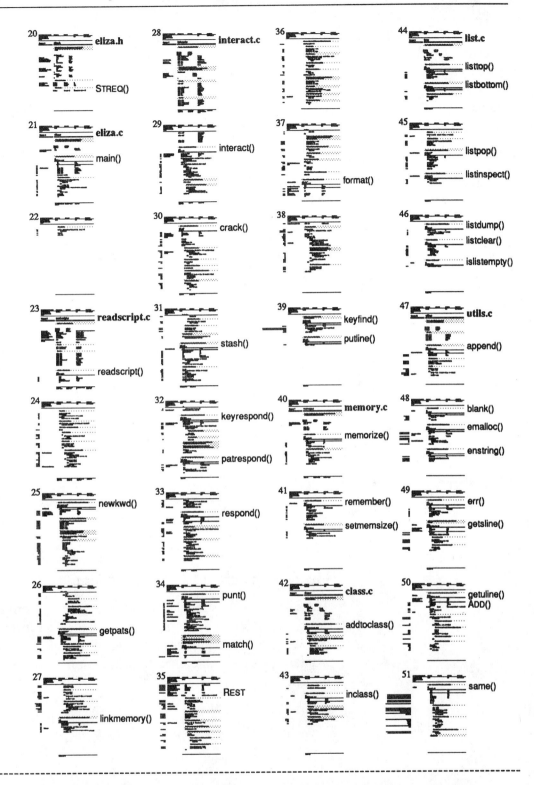

Figure 5.11: *Program execution profile superimposed on a program map.*

Beside each line of the Eliza source text is a straight line representing the number of times that source code line was executed in a particular run of Eliza. No straight line appears beside comments or declarations which are not executable. Each line of executable code that is not reached is represented by a straight line that is 3 pixels long. Each line of code that is executed *n* times is represented by a straight line that is $3 + \sqrt{n}$ pixels long. Data presented in this figure can be compared and related to that presented in the program execution profile of Eliza functions that appears on page E19/175.

readscript.c,23	*extern struct keyword* *keyfind();
readscript.c,27	k = keyfind(m → word);
interact.c,28	*extern struct keyword* *keyfind();
interact.c,30	k = keyfind(word);
interact.c,30	k = keyfind(word);
interact.c,34	newkey = keyfind(nword);
interact.c,39	**keyfind**(word)
eliza.h,20	*struct keyword* *knext;
readscript.c,24	lastkwd → knext = kwd;
readscript.c,25	k → knext = NULL;
readscript.c,27	...**memkwdtop**; m != NULL; m = m → knext)
interact.c,31	...(k = **memkwdtop**; k != NULL; k = k → knext)
interact.c,39	...**kwdtop**; scan != NULL; scan = scan → knext)
readscript.c,25	**newkwd**(kwdtext)
readscript.c,25	*char* *kwdtext;
readscript.c,25	k → word = enstring(kwdtext);
readscript.c,26	addtoclass(kwdtext, arg);
readscript.c,26	addtoclass(kwdtext, arg);
readscript.c,26	err(`"unmatched '[' for word '%s'"`, kwdtext);
readscript.c,26	`...hing strange on keyword line for '%s'`", kwdtext);
readscript.c,23	*struct keyword* ***kwdtop** = NULL;
readscript.c,24	**kwdtop** = kwd;
interact.c,28	*extern struct keyword* ***kwdtop**;
interact.c,39	*for* (scan = **kwdtop**; scan != NULL; scan = ...

✂ --

Figure 5.12: *Partial KWIC index of Eliza.*

The concept is illustrated using four identifiers from Eliza, the name of a defined function, a structure member names, a function parameter, and a global variable. Typographic attributes of the tokens have been preserved; horizontal positions of the lines have been shifted so that "key words" line up in the center of the page.

**Structured Program
Excerpts**

When one is reading a program, a central issue that affects one's understanding is the cognitive availability of the appropriate *context*. Context may include such information as the type of an identifier, the arguments and types of a function name, the purpose and/or code defining a procedure, the various invocations of a function, or the information provided in comments attached to some declaration or procedure definition. Unfortunately, when one is examining a particular section of program code, the appropriate context is often not physically adjacent, and thus it is not concurrently visible on the page or the display.[†]

Various solutions have been proposed to deal with the problem of the visibility of source code context, usually in the domain of interactive code display. These include the use of multiple windows (Shneiderman, et al., 1985, 1986), *holophrasting* (Smith, Barnard, and MacLeod, 1984), and *fisheye views* (Furnas, 1982, 1986). The central concept usually involves the use of *elision* (Mikelsons, 1981; Teitelman, 1984; Cordy, et al., 1987; Small, 1989), that is, the display of sections of code with sub-sections omitted and replaced by symbols such as "...".[††]

An example of this concept is yet another Detailed Table of Contents, one that lists every function header with its associated external comment. The Computer Graphics Laboratory of the University of Pennsylvania (Badler, 1988) actually uses such a document to help in the maintenance and use of their large body of graphics software. Applying this technique to Eliza results in Figure 5.13.[†††]

Another approach to the construction of meaningful structured program fragments through the use of ellipses is illustrated in Figure 5.14. It shows a *code overview*, a selection of key code and comments from within the file that provides a top-level description of the contents of the file. Embedded within Figure 5.14 is an example of a *data overview*, a structured excerpt from the initial declarations within a file that "captures the essence" of the key data used by that section of code.

Finally, Figure 5.15 shows a fisheye view of a portion of Eliza. A fisheye view simulates that provided by a fisheye lens, which shows "nearby" places in great detail while still showing "more remote" regions in successively less detail. Furnas (1982, 1986) applies this concept to the display of large information structures by defining a "degree-of-interest" function which determines, for a particular task and for each element within the structure, how interested the user is in seeing that element. The degree-of-interest function for a fisheye view is based on the *a priori* importance of a structure element and on its distance from the current point of focus.

Structured program excerpts can be generated automatically, but typically require some degree of user control to specify a point of focus or level of detail.

[†]   One way to deal with the need for context is to reduce the size of the type so that more is visible on the page or the display. The most extreme form of this with which we are familiar is Henry Spencer's listing program which uses 10 x 14 dot matrix characters (roughly 5-point type) in order to print roughly 300 lines of code on each 8.5" x 11" page (Spencer, 1989). On the other hand, this doesn't solve the problem, but only reduces the frequency of its occurrence.

[††]   In an interactive hypertext environment, we could link to and display appropriate program context in windows other than the main code window (see Section 6.8). Nonetheless, screen space will always be at a premium, and it will be important to invoke cleverer methods of source code display than the sequential listing of every line of code.

[†††]   The use of systematic commenting conventions facilitates the automatic construction of views such as these.

Chapter 5

readscript.c

readscript.c – read the script for eliza.

Forwards.

Externals.

readscript – pick up the script.

void
readscript()

newkwd – pick up remainder of keyword line, create keyword structure.

static struct keyword *
newkwd(kwdtext)

Text of keyword.

char	*kwdtext;

getpats – pick up patterns and responses for an already–seen keyword.

static struct pattern *
getpats(in)

FILE	*in;

linkmemory – link the memory keywords into the regular keyword list.

void
linkmemory()

✂ ---

Figure 5.13: *Table of contents with function headers and external comments.*

This structured program excerpt provides a brief overview of the Eliza file
"readscript.c". This view should be compared to pages E23–E27 of the Eliza
program book.

crack -- analyze and transform input string.

static void
crack()

Current scan point.
Keyword struct if found.
Was word a substitution
keyword?

int	rank;
register char	*word;
struct keyword	*k;
int	wassubst;

...
for (;;)

    Handle punctuation in input string.

    ...

    If no more words, we're finished.

    ...

    Else find this word's keyword struct.

    ...

    Do synonym substitutions (substitutions without patterns).

    ...

    If it's a keyword, add it to the list.

    ...

        And substitute if appropriate.

       ...

    Put it into the definitive version.

    ...

Trim trailing blank off.

if (sentence[0] && sentence[strlen(sentence) − 1] == ' ')
    ...

✄ --

Figure 5.14: *Code overview of a portion of Eliza.*

This structured program excerpt provides a brief overview of the Eliza function "crack()." It includes all internal comments, all declarations in the function header, and all code at the first level of nesting. This view should be compared to pages E30–E31 of the Eliza program book.

> Pick out next word of pattern.

```
plen = strcspn(pp, " \t");
strcpy(pword, "");
strncat(pword, pp, plen);
pp += plen;
```

> Deal with an annoying special case.

Only "*" can match null.

```
if (*sp == '\0' && !STREQ(pword, "*"))
    ...
```

> Break by pattern type, recursing (via REST) as necessary.

```
if (STREQ(pword, "*"))
    ...
else if (pword[0] == '(')
    ...
else if (pword[0] == '[')
    ...
else
```

> Simple case – just match a word. First split off this word into
> sword. Use strncat rather than strncpy because it makes
> zero–terminated strings.

```
slen = strcspn(sp, " \t");
strcpy(sword, "");
strncat(sword, sp, slen);
```

> If the word doesn't match the pattern word, we fail.

Point of Focus ☞

```
if (!same(pword, sword))
    return (0);
```

> Otherwise, try to match the rest.

```
if (!REST)
    ...
```

> Store into parts at current position.

```
if (slen == 0)
    ...
else
    ...
```

> If we've got to here, we've succeeded so return true.

```
return (1);
```

✂ - ✂ - - - - - - - - - -

Figure 5.15: *Fisheye view of a portion of Eliza.*

This first order tree fisheye view of the Eliza function "match()" has been
applied at the line of C source code labelled as the "point of focus." The result
is a view of C source in which one can see the adjacent lines of C source
within the current control construct, and all the control constructs within
which the current line is embedded. This view should be compared to pages
E35–E37 of the Eliza program book.

**Program Change
Descriptions**

Figures 5.16 through 5.20 deal with the process of program preparation, and the relationship of the current state of the program to its previous state. Several different methods for depicting which code has changed since the last version are presented.[†] In a UNIX environment, this information is gathered and managed by systems such as the Source Code Control System (SCCS) (Rochkind, 1975) and the Revision Control System (RCS) (Tichy, 1982).

We first consider, in Figures 5.16 and 5.17, how one might depict code which has been inserted since the previous version. Next, in Figure 5.18, we consider methods of depicting code deletion. If code that is added is substituted for some "similar" code that is removed, this is a replacement. Figure 5.19 illustrates methods of depicting code replacement.

Another aspect of the process of program preparation that requires methods of visualization (Sproull, 1988) is the creation of various parallel and supporting classes of code that are not necessarily required in the final version but whose existence is still reflected in the source text. These classes include debugging code, test code, and "clean" versions of algorithms that are later replaced by efficient versions. Figure 5.20 illustrates the movement of debugging code and conditionally compiled version-dependent code into footnotes where they are less disruptive of the process of reading and understanding the program.

Program change descriptions can be generated automatically.

Program Annotation

Normally, the reader of a program's source text has readily available only the code and comments included in that text. Other commentary and explanatory text appears separately as documentation. Yet there is no reason that program source text cannot be modified automatically or by a human editor for purposes of clarification.

Figure 3.47 shows one example. Suspicious control flow is marked by arrows located at the offending statements. The particular arrow representing each case indicates the nature of the problem.

Figure 5.21 contains two annotations. One points to a suspicious control construct. The other warning marginalia comment has been generated by the UNIX style-checking program LINT (Johnson, 1978), and then merged into the TROFF file by a programmer.[††]

These kinds of annotations can be added automatically. Others must be constructed by programmers. For example, in Figure 5.22, we show an annotation appearing as a footnote that represents a contribution from a reader or maintainer of the program. Thus program books can evolve, with layers upon layers of commentary, to embody the history of their construction, maintenance, and use, and to contain the collective wisdom of those who have written and carefully studied them.[†††]

[†]   We present only methods that employ black-and-white printing, although color would clearly be very helpful. See, for example, the inside front and back covers.

[††]   LINT detects unused variables and functions, variables used before they are set, unreachable parts of the program, and mismatches between function declarations and uses in terms of the the number and types of arguments.

[†††]   Note the similarity of this concept to the Talmud. See Figure 2.9.

readscript – pick up the script.

void
readscript()

FILE	*in;
char	buf[LINESIZE];
register char	*word;
register struct keyword	*kwd;

Open the file.

```
in = fopen(script, "r");
if (in == NULL)
    err("cannot read script file '%s'", script);
if (debug)
    printf("script file '%s'\n", script);
```

Pick up startup monologue.

```
while (getsline(buf, sizeof(buf), in) != NULL && !blank(buf))
    append(buf, &startup);
```

✂ --

readscript – pick up the script.

void
readscript()

FILE	*in;
char	buf[LINESIZE];
register char	*word;
register struct keyword	*kwd;

Open the file.

```
in = fopen(script, "r");
if (in == NULL)
    err("cannot read script file '%s'", script);
if (debug)
    printf("script file '%s'\n", script);
```

Pick up startup monologue.

```
while (getsline(buf, sizeof(buf), in) != NULL && !blank(buf))
    append(buf, &startup);
```

✂ --

Figure 5.16: *Added code denoted by a different typeface or by boldface.*

The use of the new typeface at the top of this figure clearly fails to distinguish the appropriate lines. Boldface or gray tone would work, but they clash with other uses we have made for these conventions, as can be seen at the bottom of the figure.

readscript – pick up the script.

void
readscript()

```
FILE                            *in;
char                            buf[LINESIZE];
register char                   *word;
register struct keyword         *kwd;
```

Open the file.

```
in = fopen(script, "r");
if (in == NULL)
    err("cannot read script file '%s'", script);
if (debug)
    printf("script file '%s'\n", script);
```

Pick up startup monologue.

```
while (getsline(buf, sizeof(buf), in) != NULL && !blank(buf))
    append(buf, &startup);
```

✂ -

readscript – pick up the script.

void
readscript()

```
FILE                            *in;
char                            buf[LINESIZE];
register char                   *word;
register struct keyword         *kwd;
```

Open the file.

```
in = fopen(script, "r");
if (in == NULL)
    err("cannot read script file '%s'", script);
```
```
{ if (debug)
    printf("script file '%s'\n", script);
```

Pick up startup monologue.

```
while (getsline(buf, sizeof(buf), in) != NULL && !blank(buf))
    append(buf, &startup);
```

✂ -

Figure 5.17: *Added code denoted by underlining or by Zapf Dingbats.*

This figure depicts two methods that are much more effective. Underlining is shown at the top of the figure. The bottom of the figure presents the most striking variation, employing two symbols out of the Zapf Dingbats typeface to highlight the new code.

readscript – pick up the script.

```
void
readscript()
```

```
FILE                    *in;
char                    buf[LINESIZE];
register char           *word;
register struct keyword *kwd;
```

Open the file.

```
in = fopen(script, "r");
if (in == NULL)
    err("cannot read script file '%s'", script);
if (debug)
    printf("script file '%s'\n", script);
```

Pick up startup monologue.

```
while (getsline(buf, sizeof(buf), in) != NULL && !blank(buf))
    append(buf, &startup);
```

✂ --

readscript – pick up the script.

```
void
readscript()
```

```
FILE                    *in;
char                    buf[LINESIZE];
register char           *word;
register struct keyword *kwd;
```

Open the file.

```
in = fopen(script, "r");
if (in == NULL)
    err("cannot read script file '%s'", script);
if (debug)
    printf("script file '%s'\n", script);
```

Pick up startup monologue.

```
while (getsline(buf, sizeof(buf), in) != NULL && !blank(buf))
    append(buf, &startup);
```

✂ --

Figure 5.18: *Deleted code denoted by strike-through or by reduced point size.*

Strike-through, a technique used in legal and engineering documentation, is illustrated at the top of this figure. The illustration at the bottom of the figure keeps the text that has been removed, but reduces it to 5-point type.

readscript – pick up the script.

void
readscript()

FILE	*in;
char	buf[LINESIZE];
register char	*word;
register struct keyword	*kwd;

Open the file.

```
in = fopen(script, "r");
if (in == NULL)
      err("cannot read script file '%s'", script);
if (debug)
                                      script
      printf("script file '%s'\n", scrtipt);
```

Pick up startup monologue.

```
while (getsline(buf, sizeof(buf), in) != NULL && !blank(buf))
      append(buf, &startup);
```

✂ -

readscript – pick up the script.

void
readscript()

FILE	*in;
char	buf[LINESIZE];
register char	*word;
register struct keyword	*kwd;

Open the file.

```
in = fopen(script, "r");
if (in == NULL)
      err("cannot read script file '%s'", script);
if (debug)
      printf("script file '%s'\n", scrtipt script);
```

Pick up startup monologue.

```
while (getsline(buf, sizeof(buf), in) != NULL && !blank(buf))
      append(buf, &startup);
```

✂ -

Figure 5.19: *Replaced code denoted by strike-through and insertion and by strike-through and underlining.*

The top of this figure illustrates one method of depicting replacement by combining strike-through with the appearance of the new code on a blank line right above the code that it is replacing. The combination of deleted code denoted by strike-through followed by inserted code that is underlined is illustrated at the bottom of the figure.

readscript -- pick up the script.

void
readscript()

```
FILE                              *in;
char                              buf[LINESIZE];
register char                     *word;
register struct keyword           *kwd;
```

Open the file.

①

```
in = fopen(script, "r");
if (in == NULL)
    err("cannot read script file '%s'", script);
```

②

Pick up startup monologue.

while (getsline(buf, *sizeof*(buf), in) != NULL && !blank(buf))
    append(buf, &startup);

Body of script — one iteration per keyword.

for (;;)

    Swallow blank lines.

    do
        if (getsline(buf, *sizeof*(buf), in) == NULL)
            return;

```
①  #ifdef      PIPESCRIPTS
       if (script[0] == '!')
           in = popen(script + 1, "r");
       else
    #endif

②      if (debug)
           printf("script file '%s'\n", script);
```

✂ -

Figure 5.20: *Conditionally compiled and debugging code shown in footnotes.*

Conditionally compiled version-dependent code and debugging code have
been moved into footnotes. Circled numbers mark the spots of the removals,
with the text removed shown as footnotes at the bottom of the page.

main – parse arguments and handle options.

```
int
main(argc, argv)
```

| int | argc; |
| char | **argv; |

int	errorflag = 0;
int	i;
extern char	*script;
extern void	readscript();
extern void	linkmemory();
extern long	time();
extern void	interact();

defined in readscript.c

```
progname = argv[0];
```

General option parsing loop.

```
while (--argc > 0  && (*++argv)[0] == '-')
    if (STREQ(*argv, "-d"))
            debug = 1;
    else
            errorflag = 1;
if (errorflag || argc > 1)
        fprintf(stderr, "usage: %s [-d] [script]\n", progname);
        return (1);

if (argc)
        script = *argv;

readscript();
linkmemory();
```

Warning: Early return
(Suspicious Control Guru)

Stir rand() a bit.

```
for (i = (int) time((long *) NULL) % 19;  i > 0;  i--)
        (void) rand();

interact();

return (0);
```

**Warning: Long assignment
may lose accuracy**
(Lint)

✂ --

Figure 5.21: *Warning annotations that could be automatically generated.*

This figure shows two annotations that could be automatically generated by a hypothetical program that checks for suspicious control flow and by the UNIX style-checking program LINT (Johnson, 1978).

If no more words, we're finished.

```
if (word == NULL)
    break;
```

Else find this word's keyword struct.

```
k = keyfind(word);
```

Do synonym substitutions (substitutions without patterns).

```
wassubst = 0;
if (k != NULL && k→pats == NULL && k→subst != NULL)
    word = k→subst;
    k = keyfind(word);
    wassubst = 1;
```

If it's a keyword, add it to the list.

```
if (k != NULL)
    if (k→rank > rank)
        listtop(k);
        rank = k→rank;
    else
①        listbottom(k);
```

And substitute if appropriate.

```
if (k→subst != NULL && !wassubst)
    word = k→subst;
```

Put it into the definitive version.

```
strcat(sentence, word);
strcat(sentence, " ");

word = strtok((char *) NULL, " \t");
```

Trim trailing blank off.

```
if (sentence[0] && sentence[strlen(sentence) − 1] == ' ')
    sentence[strlen(sentence) − 1] = '\0';
```

① I think this deviates from the Weizenbaum article. The keyword should be inserted into the list in the correct order by rank, because the patterns are tested in that order later on. Instead, it is only ever added to the top or bottom of the list. However, this will only rarely make a difference in practice, I think.
        — flaps@dgp (12 February 1989)

✂ --

Figure 5.22: *A footnote that is the annotation from a reader.*

The maintainer of the Eliza program has discovered what he believes is a flaw in the implementation. His annotation, recorded as a footnote, discusses the problem.

Program Illustration

Often illustrations would be more meaningful than text for elucidating program function, structure, or process. These too can be automatically generated and inserted into a program publication. When standard system-defined diagrams are not adequate, a programmer or documentation specialist will need to design and produce illustrations specifically tailored to the situation.

Figure 5.24 is an example in which an illustration is used to explain the state of data stored in the Eliza data structure listed in Figure 5.23. Another illustration, a figure depicting program execution history rather than the state of program data, appears as Figure 5.25.[†]

Program Animation

If program illustrations are dynamic, mirroring the execution history of the program in response to particular inputs or operating upon particular data, the result is what we call *program animation* (see also Baecker, 1973, 1975, 1981; Brown and Sedgewick, 1984, 1985; Brown, 1988a,b; London and Duisberg, 1985; Duisberg, 1986; Bentley and Kernighan, 1987; Eisenstadt and Brayshaw, 1987; Buchanan, 1988; Baecker and Buchanan, under review).

If we redesigned Figure 5.25 to include more intermediate states and displayed these rapidly and appropriately on a display screen, the result would be program animation.[††]

As with program illustration, program animation will usually require special design to achieve the optimum utility and effect.

[†]   These two figures were produced using the Movie/Stills system of Bentley and Kernighan (1987).

[††]   We have created and displayed such animation on a Sun workstation.

Data Structures

```
                        struct keyword {
                            struct keyword        *knext;
The keyword.                char                  *word;
Substitution word, if any.  char                  *subst;
Rank for keyword list building.  int              rank;
Is this a "memory" keyword?  int                  ismem;
                            struct pattern        *pats;
                        };

                        struct pattern {
                            struct pattern        *pnext;
The pattern itself.         char                  *pat;
Next response to use (0–origin).  int             nextresp;
The list of responses.      struct text           *resps;
                        };

                        struct text {
                            struct text           *tnext;
The text itself.            char                  *chars;
                        };
```

Input Data

```
    ...

    remember @5
    * you remember *
                        Do you often think of #4?
                        Does thinking of #4 bring anything else to mind?
                        What else do you remember?
                        Why do you remember #4 just now?
                        What in the present situation reminds you of #4?
                        What is the connection between me and #4?
    * do I remember *
                        Did you think I would forget #5?
                        Why do you think I should recall #5 now?
                        What about #5?
                        > what
                        You mentioned #5.

    ...
```

✂ ---

Figure 5.23: *Data structures and data essential to the operation of Eliza.*

The code fragment that defines the data structures for storing the Eliza text patterns and responses appears at the top of this figure. One section of the "Doctor" script appears at the bottom of the figure.

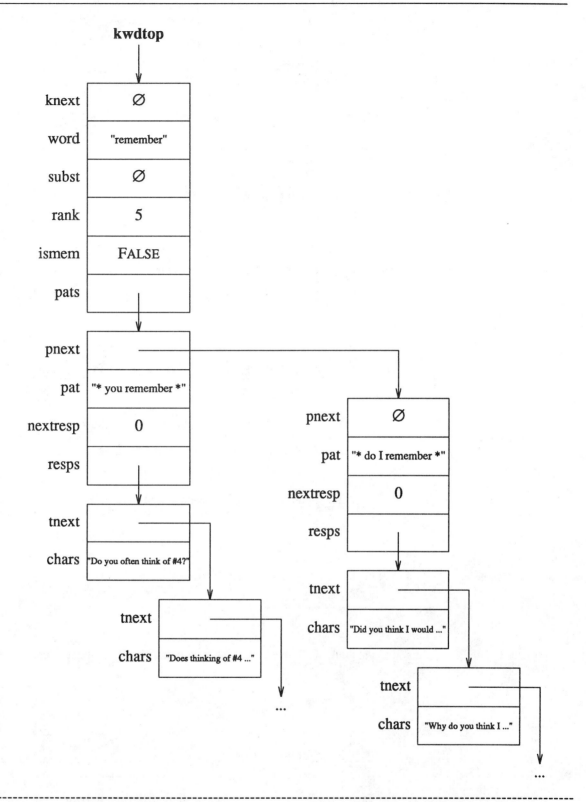

Figure 5.24: *An illustration of program state corresponding to Figure 5.23.*

We can more easily understand how the script shown in Figure 5.23 is processed into a usable internal representation defined by the data structures shown in Figure 5.23 by seeing a picture of what this representation looks like. Such a picture appears as the above figure.

```
I think I think I am  a computer        I think I think I am  a computer
*   I  * think I  am  *                  *   I  * think I  am  *


I think I think I am  a computer        I think I think I am  a computer
*   I  * think I  am  *                  *   I  * think I  am  *


I think I think I am  a computer        I think I think I am  a computer
*   I  * think I  am  *                  *   I  * think I  am  *


I think I think I am  a computer        I think I think I am  a computer
*   I  * think I  am  *                  *   I  * think I  am  *


I think I think I am  a computer        I think I think I am  a computer
*   I  * think I  am  *                  *   I  * think I  am  *


I think I think I am  a computer        I think I think I am  a computer
*   I  * think I  am  *                  *   I  * think I  am  *


I think I think I am  a computer        I think I think I am  a computer
*   I  * think I  am  *                  *   I  * think I  am  *


I think I think I am  a computer        I think I think I am  a computer
*   I  * think I  am  *                  *   I  * think I  am  *


I think I think I am  a computer        I think I think I am  a computer
*   I  * think I  am  *                  *   I  * think I  am  *


I think I think I am  a computer        I think I think I am  a computer
*   I  * think I  am  *                  *   I  * think I  am  *
```

Figure 5.25: *An illustration of program processing.*

This illustration shows how the "match()" procedure works as it attempts to match the sentence "I think I think I am a computer" against the pattern "* I * think I am *". The illustration sheds light on the peculiar recursive operation of "match()." Matches are indicated by arrows; progress in matching is reinforced by underlining that portion of the pattern that has been matched. In the case shown above, the procedure erroneously matches the second star to a null string (in the 4th frame) and gets two words further ahead before correcting the mistake by backtracking.

Section 5.6

Guidelines and Specifications for C Program Books

We have introduced and illustrated kinds of program metatext that enrich the comprehensibility and usability of complex computer programs. Just as they do in complex English texts and in the program pages discussed in Chapter 1, 3, and 4, these components must be designed and presented in a systematic, organized format. This presentation will eventually require developing guidelines and specifications similar to those presented in Chapter 4 and Appendix D, although such work would currently be premature and is beyond the scope of this book.

Section 5.7

Summary and Synthesis

We have presented a comprehensive set of abstractions and views of a program designed to facilitate its understanding and use. Looked at individually, only some of these techniques are new. Yet the breadth and scope of the integrated vision is new: as such, we believe that our framework represents a significant advance.

Integration is a key concept of program literature. Our proposals are not isolated and unrelated tricks, but a coherent body of technique. Relationships among the various methods and views can be seen in the following tables, in which we illustrate the framework by classifying a sample set of views along a number of dimensions.

Each entry in the table details the name of the view, what is represented by the view, how it is represented, and what questions the view answers.[†]

Most views are *static*, that is, they represent information about the program source text independent of program execution. We explicitly indicate those that are *dynamic*, that portray behavior of a particular program execution.[††]

The method of representation can be varied greatly; where we feel that a particular description does not do full justice to the possibilities, we tag it with a "+", as, for example, "prose+", which indicates prose that could occasionally include diagrams or images.

In the table entries listing questions, we cite only examples; our experience in using many of these views has shown us that such use often suggests new questions that the views are able to answer.

Documentation

Our system encompasses traditional documentation: that for the user, that providing detailed introductions to the program's source text for the maintenance or support programmer, and that providing auxiliary information for the programmer.

---

†   Goldberg (1987) presents a complementary formulation expressed in terms of twelve reading-comprehension questions that a system should be able to answer.

††   Ultimately, program views will be *multi-media*, incorporating text, graphics, animation, video, and sound.

User Documentation

View	*What is represented?*	*How is it represented?*	*What are some of the questions that the view answers?*
Command summary	Functionality	Prose+	To what commands does each program respond? How does the user issue each command?
Tutorial guide	Functionality	Prose+	How can one get started using the system?
User manual	Functionality	Prose+	How are various important tasks accomplished using the program?
Reference manual	Functionality	Prose+	What, in detail, does each aspect of the program accomplish? How is each feature activated and used?

Programmer Documentation

View	*What is represented?*	*How is it represented?*	*What are some of the questions that the view answers?*
Installation guide	Setting up the system	Prose+	How does one install the program to make it operational?
Maintenance guide	Fixing the system	Prose+	How does one understand the internals of the system so as to be able to fix bugs and add new features?

Program Introductions

View	*What is represented?*	*How is it represented?*	*What are some of the questions that the view answers?*
Title page	Identifying metadata	Text	What is the name of the program? Who are its author and publisher? When was it published?
Colophon	Identifying metadata	Text	What are the most significant facts about the copyright, typesetting, and printing of the program?
Abstract	Purpose functionality	Prose+	What, briefly stated, is the purpose of the program? What are its most salient features?
Design history	History of design and evolution	Prose+	What have been the major steps in the program's design, construction, maintenance, and modification?
Authors and personalities	Identifying metadata	Text and images (photos or cartoons)	Who have been the major players involved in the design, construction, maintenance, and support of the system?

Overviews and Indices

Program overviews and indices provide additional views of the program's functionality, structure, and processing. Program overviews are generally organized with respect to the order in which program elements appear in the program source or are used during a particular execution of the program; program indices are generally organized alphabetically.

Program Overviews

View	What is represented?	How is it represented?	What are some of the questions that the view answers?
Table of contents	Major program elements	Table	What is the overall structure of the source text and metatext comprising the program? Where may each element be found in the source listing?
Detailed table of contents	Other constituent program elements	Table	What other important constituent elements are in the program? Where may they be found in the source listing?
Signature	Program properties (static/dynamic)	Graphic symbol	What symbol identifies and conveys the spirit of the program? In whose style is the program written? What's out of the ordinary about this program?
Condensation	Program shape and structure	Graphic symbol	What does the entire source code of the program look like?
Map	Program shape and labeled structure	Graphic symbol plus text	What does the entire source code of the program look like; what are its major constituent elements, and where may they be found in the source listing?
Diagram	Program structure or behavior (static/dynamic)	Diagram	How is the program organized? How does it work?
Call hierarchy	Function call structure (static)	Text	Which functions are potentially called by other functions; in what order do such calls appear within the program source?
Regular expression control diagram	Control and function call structure	Text: Regular expression	How do such function calls appear within major control structures within the program source?
Function call history (Trace)	Function call structure (dynamic) + associated I/O or data structures	Text+	Which functions are called in a particular execution of the program and in what context do these appear?

| Metrics | Program properties | Tables, charts | What key measurements characterize and describe the program along a number of dimensions? |
| Execution profile | Execution times | Table or chart | What are some of the performance characteristics of the executing program? What are and are not the bottlenecks? |

Program Indices

View	*What is represented?*	*How is it represented?*	*What are some of the questions that the view answers?*
Cross-reference index	Identifier relationships	Table	For each identifier, where are all its definitions and uses to be found?
Caller index	Caller–callee relationships	Table	Which functions does a particular function call?
Callee index	Caller–callee relationships	Table	Which functions call a particular function?
Key word in context index	Source text context	Table	How and where is each token used in the program?

Structured Program Excerpts

Structured program excerpts present portions of the code (elided code) in a useful context, uncluttered by the usual surrounding code.

View	*What is represented?*	*How is it represented?*	*What are some of the questions that the view answers?*
Commented table of contents	Function headers and external comments	Table	What functions comprise the source text? How are they to be used? (What are their headers?) What do they do? (What external comments describe them?)
Fisheye view	Structurally (rather than lexically) nearby code	Text	What code is "near to" a particular section of code in terms of its distance along the syntax tree of the code?
Code overview	The structure of the code	Text	What is the top-level structure of the code, as expressed by key code fragments and associated comments?
Data overview	The structure of the data	Text	What is the top-level structure of the data, as expressed by key declarations and associated comments?

Program Change Descriptions

Program change descriptions present the recent history of source code revisions and changes.

View	What is represented?	How is it represented?	What are some of the questions that the view answers?
Code additions	Source text	Text	What code has been added since the last version, and where? Who broke it, and when?
Code deletions	Source text	Text	What code has been deleted since the last version, and where? Who broke it, and when?
Code replacements	Source text	Text	What code has replaced what other code since the last version, and where? Who broke it, and when?

Other Views

Our remaining classes of program views cannot be as easily systematized; they represent idiosyncratic attempts to clarify and elucidate code through annotation, illustration, and animation. Future work should strive to develop a more detailed understanding and a taxonomy of applicable methods and their benefits.

Conclusions

In concluding this discussion of a proposed system of program literature, we reiterate that we have presented a framework, not a polished structure. We have tried to raise as many new questions as we have provided answers. Future work will need to consider these ideas in the context of interactive programming environments (see Section 6.7). Researchers will also need to consider how techniques are influenced by concepts such as hypertext and hypermedia (see Section 6.8). The result of further investigations should be significant progress in our ability to help programmers visualize and manage the continuously increasing complexity of modern computer programs. The bright future of program visualization is discussed in the next, concluding chapter of the book.

Chapter 6

Future Issues in Program Presentation

"Programmer as reader is a statement of a problem, not a description of a solution. The problem is the programs are not readable. This does not mean that programs are prone to run-time error. They may in fact have been proven to be error-free. Error-free programs have no write-and-run bugs. They may still have read bugs...

"Why care about the readability of programs? Readability is an issue because we read to learn to write, and we read in order to rewrite. By reading the programs that implement a system, a programmer learns technique and style, as well as information about available functionality. Effective use of a program development system means that the programmer should be able to read the system in order to find existing parts that can be reused or modified. And a programmer needs to be able to read the system in order to maintain the existing parts and relationships..."

Adele Goldberg, Programmer as Reader, *IEEE Software* 4(5), p. 62. Copyright © 1987, IEEE. Reprinted with permission.

Section 6.1

Summary of Results

In this book, we have presented and explored a wide variety of issues affecting the legibility and readability of C program source text. We have seen that there are complex interactions of visible language attributes both among themselves and in relation to the C programming language. Despite this, the task of developing a recommended form has proven to be tractable, and we have been able to do many experimental variations (see Section 3.5) before recommending conventions for an improved appearance.

Our approach to developing a visible language schema for the appearance of C source text was as follows: We began by developing taxonomies of visible language (Section 3.2 and Appendix B) and of the C programming language (Section 3.3). We then presented some graphic design principles (Section 3.4) and some design variations (Section 3.5). We used the variations to explore methods of applying the design principles to achieve an effective visual presentation of C. This presentation is described by a graphic design manual for C, which consists of a set of graphic design guidelines (Section 4.2) and a set of detailed typographic specifications (Sections 4.3–4.4 and Appendix D).

We can therefore assert that a comprehensive, consistent, and effective visible language schema for the appearance of C is desirable to improve program legibility and readability, that we have demonstrated the feasibility of developing such a schema,[†] and that a graphic design manual for the visible language characteristics is an appropriate vehicle in which to present the resulting recommended conventions. As more programmers use the conventions, as they are refined and improved through use, and as more human factors knowledge about program literature becomes available from research, the conventions may mature into effective standards.

In carrying out our work, we have also encountered many unforeseen conceptual and technical difficulties. When we began the project, we originally desired a solution for the general problem of typographic and diagrammatic representation of programming languages for formats that were both static and dynamic. We soon realized that even the more restricted problem of determining static, typographic representations was a challenge. At the time, a wide variety of laser printer fonts of high quality was not readily available, and it was difficult to create even manually composed pages. We have also had to tackle many serious algorithmic problems (see Section 6.4), and to combat recalcitrant technology (see Section 6.6).

We believe that the approach and many of the concrete recommendations for C can be transferred to other programming languages (see Section 6.5). We must advise those attempting such designs, however, that the task will require extremely careful attention to each language's unique characteristics. By studying these characteristics, it will be possible to design effective visualizations that take advantage of visible language and of the computer language's full potential.

One of the primary difficulties encountered in making graphic design evaluations is that we have only very limited theories and understanding of programmers' tasks, motivations, strategies, and capabilities in reading, comprehending, and using code (see Section 6.2). As a result, it is not yet

---

†   As stated in the Preface, we do not assert that the proposed conventions are the best possible, only that they represent an improvement over current practice, and a first step towards further improvement.

possible to base decisions among functionally equivalent appearances on any scientific criteria. We present and review in Section 6.3 what we have been able to find or produce in the way of experimental evidence on the advantages and disadvantages of our conventions.

Were we to have merely designed unique prototypes for improvement, this would have had some value. However, we have gone beyond this to build a flexible tool for generating automatically improved appearance for most C programs, and for editing and refining the appearance of these automatically produced program visualizations. Our SEE compiler is one of the most elaborately tunable visible language processing engines ever developed, employing both the technology of the Portable C Compiler (Johnson, 1979) and the text manipulation capabilities of TROFF (Kernighan, 1982). We have pushed these tools as far as they can go in directions for which they were never intended. Future developers will therefore need to provide SEE's functionality in a far more appropriate and robust implementation than our prototype (see Section 6.6).[†]

Thus our approach and our major accomplishment have been to design the best possible appearance for the C programming language within technical and time constraints as well as to prototype an effective tool for automating, editing, and refining this appearance. Although this tool produces visualizations in a "batch" manner on paper, our research points the way towards a comparable interactive implementation on a workstation with a bit-mapped display (see Section 6.7).

The more we have looked at the potential of enhanced visualization of program source text, "visualization in the small," the more we have been drawn towards the development of higher level abstractions of program function, structure, and process, "visualization in the large." Chapter 5 presented a number of prototype examples of this kind and explored through concepts and a large sample document the potential of the *program publication*, an integrated body of program text and surrounding metatext which clarifies, explains, and enriches the experience of program reading, understanding, and use. Further research in this direction is proposed in Section 6.8.

Section 6.2 — Understanding Program Reading and Program Understanding

To what extent is our work rooted in or supported by scientific evidence about how programmers read, comprehend, and use programs? A predictive information processing model of program reading and understanding would greatly assist the design of better methods of program presentation.

To develop such a model, we must begin by recognizing that program "reading and understanding" consists of a variety of tasks, including, for example, reading, skimming, searching, returning, page turning, memorizing, remembering, simulating, guessing, answering, and "problem solving." These tasks may in fact be carried out in different ways depending upon the context in which they occur, in other words, within programming activities such as sketching, writing, revising, documenting, familiarization, reading, reviewing, and debugging.

---

†   Because our prototype is so fragile, we regretfully cannot make it available to other investigators.

The development of an appropriate predictive model is probably beyond what is possible given our current understanding. Nonetheless, we shall review for the readers' benefit a number of scientific fields that should be relevant: reading research; document design; the psychology of perception, cognition, and memory; information processing psychology; and the psychology of programming.

The field of reading research illustrates the problem. Most reading research (Huey, 1968; Kieras, 1978; Frase and Schwartz, 1979; Hartley, 1980, 1985) deals only with the readability and comprehensibility of prose. When investigators in the field study the role of format, they typically consider only simple variations such as the role of typeface, case, line length, and leading (Tinker, 1963, 1965).[†]

Document design (Wright, 1977, 1978; Felker, et al., 1980, 1981; Jonassen, 1982; Hartley, 1985; Duffy and Waller, 1985) is a synthetic discipline very much in the spirit of graphic design. Although document design principles and guidelines add very little that goes beyond those presented in this book, reading their formulations is a helpful learning exercise.

The science of psychology (Lindsay and Norman, 1977; Hagen, 1988), especially the fields of perception, cognition, and memory, deals with issues at far too low a level to tell us how programmers read and understand.[††] Even when developed from an engineering-oriented, systems and information processing perspective, as in Card, Moran, and Newell (1983), psychological theories are still too primitive for the task of modelling program reading and understanding.

Nonetheless, there has developed in recent years a field known as *software psychology*, or the *psychology of programming* (Shneiderman, 1980; Curtis, 1985; Curtis, et al., 1986). One central concern has been the effect of program format on program comprehensibility, yet results have been widely scattered and inconsistent.[†††] For example, Miara, et al. (1983; see also Norcio, 1982; Kesler, et al., 1984) report the result of an experiment which showed that a moderate level of indentation, namely four to eight spaces in a conventional fixed-width font, increases program comprehension and user satisfaction. They also review a number of human factors experiments concerning the effect of program indentation on program comprehensibility. Although results are mixed, there is some experimental evidence supporting our hypothesis, which is that a program's appearance affects its comprehensibility and usability.

Another central concern of software psychology has been the development of theories of program understanding; however, theories developed to date have been of little predictive and scientific value (Shneiderman, 1977; Shneiderman and Mayer, 1979; Brooks, 1977, 1982, 1983).

---

†   There are a few notable exceptions, such as the work of Sloboda (1976, 1981) on the perception of music notation.

††   Crosby and Stelovsky (1989) suggest the use of eye-tracking to help us gain insight into viewing and reading habits and strategies.

†††   Most of the work has attempted to measure the value of flowcharts and other two-dimensional notations and methods of visual organization for the specification of algorithms and programs (Wright and Reid, 1973; Blaiwes, 1974; Kammann, 1975; Mayer, 1976; Shneiderman, et al., 1977; Brooke and Duncan, 1980a, 1980b; Sheppard, et al, 1981, 1982; Arbblaster, 1982; Klerer, 1984; Gilmore and Smith, 1984; Schmidt, 1986; Foss, et al., 1987; Boehm-Davis, et al., 1987; Cuniff and Taylor, 1987; Patrick and Fitzgibbon, 1988). Typically, these papers present only the results of experiments, and not attempts to validate predictive theories. Larkin and Simon (1987) is an interesting attempt to formulate a theory of the value of diagrams.

The field has taught us a number of important lessons. One is the extent to which programmer skills are characterized by huge individual differences, often amounting to one to two orders of magnitude (Curtis, 1984). Another is the danger of extrapolating from the behavior of student programmers working on tiny problems to the behavior of real programmers working on real problems (Curtis, 1986). A third lesson is the extent to which programmer behavior and programmer performance is affected by the *task* that he is asked to carry out (Brooke and Duncan, 1980b; Gilmore and Green, 1984; Gilmore and Smith, 1984).

Research psychologists have not directed much attention to the problem of the design of appropriate and maximally communicative notation. One notable exception has been the work of T.R.G. Green and his colleagues (Sime, et al., 1973; Green, 1977; Sime, et al., 1977; Green, 1980a,b; Green, et al., 1980; Green, et al., 1981; Fitter and Green, 1981; Green, 1982; Green and Payne, 1982; Gilmore and Green, 1984; Payne, et al., 1984). These papers provide evidence that we are on the right track:

> "*Notation matters.* [Italics added for emphasis.] There are no two ways about that. A few experiments in doing arithmetic using Roman numerals should be enough to persuade anybody. Yet the Roman system had a very long life, and indeed it was a considerable advance over the system used by the Greeks in which each letter of the alphabet denoted a different number. How come all those Romans and early Europeans, right up to the Middle Ages, failed to think of the Arabic system? More urgently, how can we be sure that our programming notations are not just as backward?" (Green, 1980, p. 274)

> "*The details of the notation profoundly influence its usability*, much more so than one would at first suspect... [Italics added for emphasis.] How well the eye is guided from one place to another on the page, how clearly the different areas are bounded and separated, how easy it is to travel backwards as well as forwards — all affect performance...

> "We should therefore be looking much harder at detail. Can typographical cues be introduced?... How easy is it to use each notation as a thinking tool to clarify a design or to convey a point in conversation using the traditional back of an envelope? How easy is it to produce a properly laid-out version? Are the layout conventions too lax for the typographer's comfort, so that two typographers will probably produce quite different looking versions, making it hard to recognize old friends on new pages; or are the conventions too rigid, making it hard or impossible to meet the constraints of page formats without chopping the diagram up mercilessly?...

> "The problem of recognizing old friends takes us into a deeper set of questions. What should such notations consist of?... *Obviously the nature of the intended readership is highly relevant...* [Italics added for emphasis.]

> It would be nice to imagine that orthodox psychological research might offer us some guidance, but at present that seems unlikely..." (Green, 1982, p. 34)

Section 6.3

Experimental Verification

Since it has thus far been impossible to establish a hard scientific foundation for our work, we sought to provide an empirical one. Can we confirm experimentally that the application of these techniques makes a difference? Do our display conventions make programs more readable, intelligible, appealing, memorable, and maintainable? If so, by how much are these measures improved? We have begun a series of experiments to test the following:

* *Reading Speed*: Does enhanced presentation increase the speed with which programmers are able to read code?
* *Reading Comprehension*: Does enhanced presentation increase the comprehension or understanding achieved in the reading of code?
* *Appeal*: Do programmers prefer the enhanced presentation?
* *Memorability*: Do programmers remember more of what they read some time after they have read it when they use the enhanced presentation?
* *Maintainability*: Are programmers better able to maintain programs with the enhanced presentation in the senses of being better able to diagnose errors, fix bugs, and/or make simple additions and modifications?
* *Learnability*: Can novice programmers learn more easily or more quickly if they are using the enhanced presentation?

It is not easy to design and carry out valid experiments to answer these questions. There are literally thousands of ways in which our new format differs from the conventional one. We cannot test the effect of each of our changes and decide which of them is positive, which neutral, and which negative, but we can test the effect of all of them combined. We must be very careful in the choice of the difficulty and content of the test programs and of the background and experience of the subjects. We must also be very careful to exclude any possible confounding artifacts. Despite these cautions, the results of our first experiment are very encouraging.

Experiment One

For an initial experiment, forty-four subjects were drawn from a third year programming course at the University of Toronto. By the time of the experiment, all had acquired reasonable familiarity with writing and debugging short C programs formatted in the conventional manner.

Two short C programs, each consisting of about 200 lines of code and comments that span the functionality and features of C, were selected. The programs were taken from standard textbooks on C (Wortman and Sidebottom, 1984; Schildt, 1986) and, with one small exception, were not modified for the purposes of the experiment.[†] Hardcopy listings of the code in both conventional and SEE-produced format were used as the test materials.[††] Each program occupied about the same physical area over four to five pages of 8.5″ x 11″ paper in each of the two formats.

The independent variable in the experiment was the output format of the C source code presented to the subjects. The dependent variables being measured were the number of questions the subjects answered correctly and the time required to answer them. The times proved not to be meaningful, since all subjects took all of the available forty minutes to skim a program,

---

[†]   The exception is that one program was simplified slightly so that the two programs would be more comparable in length and difficulty.

[††] The SEE version differed from the standard presented and recommended in this book in one respect only: Prologue, external, and internal comments were formatted using boxes and brackets (see Figure 3.7) rather than using gray tone.

read eighteen questions, and then attempt to answer the questions.

The experimental design was composed of two 2 x 2 replicated Latin Squares. Subjects were randomly assigned to one of four groups, and the groups were randomly assigned to the rows of the Latin Squares. Individuals in the first group were given the first program in the SEE format followed by the second program in the familiar format. Individuals in the second group were given the first program in the familiar format followed by the second program in the SEE format. Individuals in the third group were given the second program in the SEE format followed by the first program in the familiar format. Individuals in the fourth group were given the second program in the familiar format followed by the first program in the SEE format.

The mean number of correct answers for the SEE-produced format at 7.83 was significantly higher than the mean number for the conventional format at 6.46 [$F(1, 40) = 15.29$, $p < 0.001$, MSe = 2.82]. There was no effect of program or presentation order. In short, we found that the enhanced source text presentation increased the programs' readability by 21% as measured by the subjects' performance on a comprehension test.

There was also a significant interaction between format and program [$F(1, 40) = 21.09$, $p < 0.0001$, MSe = 2.82]. For the second program, the mean number of correct answers with the conventional format was 5.80, and with the new format was 8.78. However, the mean number of correct answers for the first program with the conventional format was 7.11, and with the new format was 6.87. In short, the effect of the presentation format can depend dramatically upon the task that the programmer carries out and upon the program being used.[†]

Experiment Two

We are carrying out a second experiment, although results are not yet available. Twenty subjects have been selected from the population of moderately experienced C programmers who have several person-years of C programming experience and have written thousands of lines of C code.

Two C programs (one of them, a slightly simplified version of Eliza) of about 1500 lines, or twenty-five pages each, have been selected. The standard form of the programs has been improved to make its level and style of commenting and formatting far better than the average C program.[††] A SEE version of the program has then been produced. It has been modified to incorporate those aspects of the recommended presentation standard that are not yet handled automatically (inclusion of the nesting information, ellipses, and the cross-reference data in the footnotes). Both versions of the program occupy roughly the same number of pages.

As before, the independent variable in the experiment is the output format of the C source code presented to the subjects. This time there are several dependent variables, to be detailed below. The experimental design is again composed of two 2 x 2 replicated Latin Squares. Subjects are randomly assigned to one of four groups, and the groups are randomly assigned to the rows of the Latin Squares. The four groups differ in terms of the order of presentation of the programs and the assignment of a format to a program.

[†]   Why was the readability of only the second program increased by the new format? It is impossible to say with certainty. There were many differences between the two programs. The second one consisted of much "denser" code. It also contained greater numbers of embedded comments. The first program seemed relatively "clean" even in the conventional format.

[††]   The form of this version of the program is consistent with the Indian Hill standard for C program listings (Cannon, et al., 1987).

Subjects work in two sessions separated roughly by one day. Each session consists of roughly 3 1/2 hours and is comprised of a series of tasks, chosen to reflect the kinds of activities that real programmers carry out while working on real programs:

- Reading the experiment instructions, reading an explanation of the program format as illustrated by applying it to a short sample program, and carrying out a series of familiarization tasks on that program.
- Reading a description of the purpose, I/O behavior, and organization of the experiment program, and skimming the first few pages of the code.
- Answering, as quickly and accurately as possible, a series of questions about the experiment program.
- Answering, as quickly and accurately as possible, a series of deeper questions about the program.
- Attempting to find and correct, as quickly as possible, a series of bugs that were seeded into the program. Input-output pairs that elicit the bugs are provided.
- Attempting to define, as quickly and accurately as possible, changes that must be made to the program in order to maintain and enhance it in a set of prescribed ways.
- Filling out a questionnaire designed to elicit the subject's feelings about the experiment, the program, and the presentation format of the program.
- After a few minutes, attempting to recall as accurately as possible certain facts about the program without looking at the program.
- Given a fresh copy of the program, finding certain described entities within the program as quickly as possible.

Results from this experiment will be reported in Baecker, et al. (in preparation).

Some Other Relevant Experiments

Our experiments have dealt only with the effect of the enhanced presentation of source code, the work described in Chapters 3 and 4, and not with the utility of the program publication and program view concepts, the work described in Chapter 5. Oman and Cook (1989) have recently completed a series of experiments that also shed some light on these latter issues.

As in our work, Oman and Cook define a book format for source code. They describe this format in terms of "macro-" and "micro-typographic" style factors:

> "Macro-typographic factors used in the book format paradigm include creation of a preface, table of contents, chapter divisions, pagination, and indices... Micro-typographic factors used in the book format paradigm include identification and/or creation of code segments, code paragraphs, sentence structures, and intramodule comments. To do this, micro-typographic factors such as blank lines, embedded spaces, type styles, and in-line comments, are used to achieve our desired principles of good micro-typographic formatting."

Oman and Cook then present the results of four experiments:

- A macro-typographic rearrangement of a 1000-line Pascal program resulted in improved programmer performance on a maintenance task consisting of writing a new procedure and identifying where it is called.
- A micro-typographic rearrangement of a 100-line Pascal program resulted in statistically significant improvements in comprehension test score, test performance (score/time), and subjective readability rating.

- A micro-typographic rearrangement of a 100-line C program resulted in statistically significant improvements in comprehension test score and test performance (score/time).
- A macro- and micro-typographic rearrangement of a 1000-line C program resulted in improved programmer performance both on an oral comprehension test and on a written exercise to complete a call graph for the program.

Section 6.4   Research on Program Visualization Algorithms

Our work on the enhanced presentation of program source text led us into certain issues in automatic formatting that proved particularly difficult. These are the automatic introduction of white space, appropriate automatic line breaking, appropriate automatic page breaking, incorporation of programmer formatting intentions, display of programming language expressions, display of warnings and annotations, display of program history, and display of diagrammatic representations of program structures. Our work also raised the issue of the inadequacy of current typefaces for program visualization. We discuss each of these issues below.

Introduction of White Space

Good programmers add blank lines (white space) to enhance the readability of their code. A program visualizer should do automatically and correctly as much of this as is possible to automate. An effective algorithm will note the transitions between different kinds of program source text, classifying each line as, for example, a comment, a preprocessor command, a component of a function header, a statement within a function body, a component of a structure or union definition, and a component of any other kind of declaration. The visualizer may then introduce white space at transitions between a line of one kind and a line of another kind.

Presently, SEE adds two blank lines only when it encounters a transition from top-level declarations to function definitions, and from one function definition to another. SEE also interprets $n + 1$ successive programmer newlines as an explicit request for n half lines of white space. Whether SEE should add space on its own initiative more aggressively is a subject for future research.

Line Breaking

No matter how much space exists for a line on a page, some programmers will write some statements that will need to be "broken" and wrapped to the next line. The result is not ideal, but an appropriate line-breaking algorithm can minimize the visual chaos and damage that results. An effective algorithm will scan backwards from the point representing the most text that will fit on the line, will examine the precedence of various operators that precede that point, and will try to find an operator of "relatively low" precedence that is not "too far" from that point as the place at which to make the break. The algorithm will be complicated by the occurrence of lines that are very deeply indented and long string constants that should not be broken.

Presently, SEE scans backwards only until it finds the last operator of "low enough" precedence on the line (see Section 3.5 and Figures 3.44 and 3.45) and makes the break at that point. SEE is also willing to break lines at places where programmers break their lines, which allows programmers to control the appearance of long lines where this is desirable.

Pagination and Page Breaking

Automatic page breaking and pagination is an even more difficult problem. An implementation problem with the current generation of text formatters (see Section 6.6) is the need for a great deal of look-ahead in order to do the page breaking properly. There are also severe conceptual problems. The basic idea is that there should ideally never be less than two or three lines in a related "group" of statements at the top or the bottom of the page. The notion of a group here is related to the concept of the "kind" of source text line defined two paragraphs above. The algorithm becomes difficult for several reasons: because it is not always possible to fulfill this condition, because we want to break the page at a point that is as shallowly nested as possible, because we want to avoid separating an external or internal comment from the code following it to which it typically refers, and because we want at almost any cost to avoid breaking in places such as in the middle of a comment, a function header, a structure definition, or an expression.[†]

Presently, SEE forces a page break only to avoid breaking a function header or to keep an external comment together with a function header. The programmer can explicitly request a page break by including a formfeed character.

Programmer Formatting Intentions

The above discussion has emphasized a point made vividly through some of the examples of Section 3.5: We cannot automate the entire formatting process and achieve a satisfactory result. We must allow and heed programmer *formatting intentions*. In other words, the visualizer should heed the directions of programmers when they insert carriage returns in the middle of statements, formfeeds or extra carriage returns between statements, and tabs or carriage returns in the middle of initializers. What is interesting is how much control the programmer can exercise with very little work! A subject for future research is how to reconcile these programmer specifications with the default automated decisions of the visualizer, when the two are in conflict.

Expressions

One area that should be suitable for total automation, but where more work is still required, is in the display of expressions. Our series of variations (see Section 3.5, and Figures 3.48–3.53) has illustrated the importance of variable wordspacing around binary operators, the use of superscripts for unary operators, letterspacing adjustments in multi-character operators, and, in general, great attention to typographic detail. Although these specific experiments were instructive, our solution is not the final word on the subject.[††]

Annotation

The introduction of symbols pointing at "abnormal" control flow or at conditions currently detected by the LINT program (see Section 5.5) illustrates the need to develop mechanisms for the automatic addition of warnings and annotations. Researchers in *automatic programming* should be able to propose far more substantive ways in which a *programmer's assistant* can detect features of a program and write its suggestions on the listing for consideration by the programmer.

[†] This is like the widow and orphan problem for typesetting paragraphs, except the equivalent of paragraph structure is recursively nested.

[††] For example, our algorithm which adds space around binary operators based on the structure of the syntax tree of an expression currently adds extra space if unary operators appear in the expression. This was only noticed in the final stages of preparing this book. We believe this is a visual bug, but further research is needed to be sure.

Display of Program History

Another important topic is the display of program history. A good example is the need to know what code has changed since the last version. An effective algorithm may employ conventions (see Section 5.5, Figures 5.16–20) such as the use of a new font or underlining to highlight code that has been added, and a diagrammatic convention such as a strike-through line to show where code has been deleted and what has been removed. Similar conventions are used in technical documentation and legal texts, but program creation suggests new demands. For example, how do we depict an entire series of changes, or sets of changes made by several authors and maintainers?[†]

Diagrammatic Representations

Finally, despite the inclusion of our hand-generated program illustrations in Section 5.5, we have in this work not tackled the problem of the automatic generation of effective diagrammatic representations of program structure, code, and data. There is a rich variety of techniques to be considered (see, for example, Martin and McClure, 1985). Future research is required to select the most valuable representations and to devise algorithms for automatic conversion between source code and diagram.

Typefaces for Program Visualization

Finally, as stated in Section 3.5 (see Figures 3.59–63), program visualization requires typefaces chosen with great care and attention to the fine detail that occurs in computer program source text. The design of fonts that are optimal for the display of computer programs rather than English prose is therefore another task for future research. Lucida® (Bigelow and Holmes, 1986) is an attractive candidate with which to begin our search, because it has been designed in compatible forms for both serif and sans-serif fonts, and for printers and bit-mapped displays.

Section 6.5

Visualization of Other Programming Languages

Our work needs to be extended to programming languages other than C. The extension to other ALGOL-like languages such as Pascal will be straightforward. Conceptual work is required on the effective representation of operator overloading, exceptions, generic packages, and multi-tasking in Ada.

Languages such as LISP, Prolog, and Smalltalk present a greater challenge. For example, designers will have to combat the sea of parentheses presented by LISP, and will need to consider the rich program structures of Smalltalk and the rule-driven control mechanisms of Prolog.

To illustrate the feasibility of applying the concepts developed in this book to other programming languages, we include as Figures 6.1 and 6.2 (see also Figures 6.5 and 6.6) attempts to apply them to COBOL (Small, 1986) and LOGO (Buchanan, 1988). In each case, the designs are relatively preliminary ones carried out by computer science students who were familiar with the concepts of the work presented in this book but had no formal graphic design training. Yet their designs seem to embody such Principles as Economy, Consistency, Relationships, Distinctiveness, and Emphasis (see Section 3.4).

---

†   Consider the example of the Talmud. (See Figure 2.9.)

Section 6.6

Implementation of Program Visualization Processors

The Current Implementation

The SEE processor has been implemented as a modified version of PCC, the Portable C Compiler (Johnson, 1979).

The first pass has been modified in a number of ways. Unlike the original PCC, which sometimes directly generates assembly language, our first pass produces syntax trees for all C constructs. Comments are recognized and passed through instead of being stripped out. SEE's Pass 1 is also modified and supported by a special preprocessing pass in order to be able to handle C preprocessor statements.

The second pass has also been significantly modified in order to output instructions for the Device Independent TROFF document formatter (Kernighan, 1982) instead of assembler instructions. This output consists of C source code and comments interspersed with calls on TROFF macros that determine how code and comments are to be formatted.

SEE is heavily parameter-driven and thereby able to produce a wide variety of program appearances under control of the user. Typographic variations are determined by table entries that may be set and modified through the use of a special interactive editor. The table entries currently allow control of the following (see Sections 3.5, Sections 4.2–4.4, and Appendix D):
- presentation style for comments;
- indentation styles for statements;
- spacing, weight, and size variations for expressions;
- mappings of token classes onto typefaces and typographic attributes;
- spacing control for token classes and pairs of adjacent tokens; and
- symbol, size, and weight choices for punctuation.

Implementation Critique

Implementing SEE by making modifications and extensions to the Portable C Compiler resulted in a flawed and fragile implementation. Visual compiling is a very different problem from standard compilation, even though it shares common elements such as the need to do lexical analysis and the need to do parsing.

One constant problem was that PCC throws away too much information before the second pass, and thus the TROFF macros could not make use of this information. This includes comments (which are of no interest to the compiler), newlines, and parentheses (which are redundant in the tree structure of PCC intermediate code). Furthermore, preprocessing has already been done: preprocessor commands are gone, and macro invocations have been substituted.

A more serious problem was that the formatting task was split between the second pass of PCC and TROFF. The PCC part could not query TROFF about typographic issues such as the typeset size of a chunk of tokens, so it could not decide on line breaking or page breaking reasonably, with due regard for what would fit. On the other hand, TROFF is not sufficiently programmable to decide line breaking or page breaking reasonably, with due regard for program syntax.[†] It also cannot print the annotations, such as ellipses, that are needed at the break. In fact, the nature of TROFF's

---

†   For example, a line break should subsume any adjacent white space; since it fails to do so for the "horizontal motion" that SEE uses, the resulting lines include extraneous white space in the form of spurious indentation. We have had to remove this manually where it mattered.

processing of text makes formatting that requires look-ahead, such as line breaking and page breaking, very difficult. It is impossible to do conversational, interactive document formatting with TROFF; since all text must be processed from the very beginning of the document, it is hard to get TROFF to typeset chunks of code on a provisional basis so that layout decisions can be made.

As an experimental system, the degree of user control was fine; for a production system, it would be excessive. Whenever users wanted to deviate from the default presentation style, they found themselves presented with a bewildering array of options.

A New Implementation Strategy

As we have seen above, there are a great many problems remaining to be solved before a system such as SEE can be implemented with ease. Nonetheless, we now propose an implementation strategy that we feel would lead to a far more malleable, robust, and usable system than our prototype.

The proposed implementation strategy asserts that the C formatter should be broken into two phases: analysis and synthesis. The analysis phase should parse the C program, much as a compiler would. The result of this phase would be a stream of tokens, embedded in a parse tree. Unlike a normal C compiler, the analysis phase must output preprocessor tokens (commands and macro invocations), not their result. Comments and white space must be preserved. Even apparently invalid input should be accepted gracefully, something the current implementation fails to do.

The synthesis phase would map the parse tree onto typeset pages. Much of this mapping is straightforward and is spelled out in Chapter 4 and Appendix D, which detail the desired appearance. The hard issues are what to do about page and line breaking. To make these decisions well requires simultaneous knowledge of the dimensions of typeset code (to decide when breaking is needed) and of the parse of the code (to determine reasonable places to break the code). This structural information might be represented as a "cost to break" at each possible breaking point.[†]

Section 6.7

Interactive Enhancements of Source Text

Even more interesting is the extension of this work to the interactive display and manipulation of program source text (Shneiderman, et al., 1985, 1986; Goldberg, 1987; Small, 1989).

Display Quality

One immediate problem that must be faced is the lower resolution (typically, no more than 80–100 dots-per-inch) of interactive display devices. This will probably require modification of the techniques that employ type at very small point sizes or very fine rules or symbols.

However, the problem is not as serious as it may seem. We illustrate this in Figure 6.3, which shows a program visualization (similar to that at the bottom of Figure 3.58) rendered on a workstation using 1 bit per pixel, and in Figure 6.4, which shows a similar visualization rendered on a workstation using anti-aliased fonts and 8 bits per pixel. Figure 6.4 illustrates how the

---

[†]   This is reminiscent of T_EX's "glue" and "penalty" concepts, but not the same (Knuth and Plass, 1981). Although glue would appear to give T_EX advantages over TROFF as an implementation vehicle, we suspect that one is just as monolithic and intractable as the other. A better tool for implementing parts of the synthesis phase might be a lower-level programmable text processor such as Postscript™ (Adobe, 1985).

use of anti-aliased gray-valued fonts can increase the apparent spatial resolution of a display (see, for example, Naiman and Fournier, 1987). We can therefore produce, using the current generation of display technology, screen softcopy comparable in utility to the paper hardcopy presented in this book.[†]

Interactive Control

Interactive program visualization offers a host of new opportunities to incorporate dynamics, animation, color, and sound. We are no longer faced with the difficult problem of establishing "the best" mapping between token types and typographic styles, for the program can be easily re-displayed with different settings. Figures 6.5 and 6.6 show multiple views of a Turing (Holt and Cordy, 1985, 1989) program displayed in response to user requests by the VIPER system (Small, 1989).

The design of interactive visualizers also raises new implementation issues that go beyond those encountered in this work (Small, 1989).[††]

Dynamic Visualization

We can also depict, through image dynamics and through animation, features of the program *in execution*. This is, quite literally, an entire new dimension of program visualization (see Section 2.3, Figure 2.14, and Figure 5.25).

The Use of Color

Most program presentation devices are monochrome. As color hardcopy devices and screen displays with acceptable spatial resolution and appropriate colors become more available, conventions for "polychrome" programs will need to be developed (Marcus, 1984, 1986, 1987c; Reynolds, 1987).[†††]

When used correctly, color can call attention to specific items within code or comments, make and enhance distinctions, reduce errors of interpretation, and increase appeal. However, color selections must be made carefully. Figures B.34 and B.37 in Appendix B explain the basic terminology of color relationships. The following principles of effective color design for program visualization derive from Marcus (1986):

- *Use a maximum of five, plus or minus two, colors.* This small number of colors will assure that readers can maintain color distinctions in short term memory. Where appropriate, use the spectral order of colors (red, orange, yellow, green, blue, indigo, violet).
- *Use foveal (center) and peripheral colors appropriately.* The central focusing area of the eye (the fovea) has few blue receptors. Do not use medium to light blue on white backgrounds or medium to dark blue on black backgrounds for thin lines or text type. Medium blue is suitable for large background area of color. Do not use adjacent colors that differ only in the amount of blue.
- *Use colors that exhibit a minimum shift in color if the amount of color changes.* As color areas change size, they appear to change their value (lightness to darkness range) and chroma (purity). Text type should have a high contrast with the background color for legibility and readability.
- *Do not use high-chroma, spectrally extreme colors close together.* Strong contrasts of red/green, blue/yellow, green/blue, and red/blue can create

---

[†]   Display devices of higher resolution are also now available. For example, Megascan Corporation (1989) makes a black-and-white display with 300-dots-per-inch resolution and a gray scale display capable of representing 8 bits per pixel at 200-dots-per-inch.

[††]   Relevant technologies for work on interactive program visualizers include incremental compilers, syntax-directed editors (Reps and Teitelbaum, 1987), and incremental document formatters that maintain multiple representations (Chen and Harrison, 1988).

[†††]   Marcus (1984) includes a prototype for a polychrome display which was developed in 1981.

vibrations and afterimages that are disturbing to the viewer.

- *Use familiar, consistent color codings.* Typical associations are these: red for stop or danger, yellow for caution or warning, green for go or OK, gray for neutrality. Use color connotations with great care because interpretation can vary greatly among different kinds of viewers.

- *Use the same color for grouping related elements.* Having established a pattern for a group of tokens, do not use a particular color for any elements not related to the group. Be complete and consistent.

- *Use the same color code for all aspects of program visualization.* Screen display and hardcopy, code development and commercial use, documentation and training should all use consistent colors. Once the color coding is established, the same colors should be used throughout the life cycle of program creation and dissemination. This will necessitate careful selection of colors that can be displayed consistently across different display media.

- *Use high value, high saturation colors to draw attention.* Bright colors should be used for danger signals, or for getting the viewer's attention. When too many bright colors compete for the viewer's attention, however, confusion arises.

- *Use redundant coding of shape or size as well as color.* Do not rely solely on color distinctions because approximately 8% of Caucasian males are color-deficient and because there may be distortions in the display media.

- *Use color to enhance black-and-white information.* Color can assist in conveying the information in a monochrome visualization, improving the viewer's processing time and the appeal of the display, although purely monochrome versions may still also be required.

The color plates on the inside front and back cover show a number of color depictions of the fragment of C code that was used in Figures 3.54–3.58. The color selections in these plates are explained and discussed in Appendix F, on the very last page of the book, opposite the inside back cover.

Section 6.8

Fully Electronic Program Publishing

The concepts developed in this book, although illustrated by "linear" examples appearing on paper, may be applied in far richer, non-linear, computer-based program development and maintenance environments.

Hypertext environments (Conklin, 1987) such as Apple's Hypercard™ (Goodman, 1987), Brown's Intermedia (Yankelovich et al, 1988), Shneiderman's Hyperties (Marchionini and Shneiderman, 1988), and Tektronix's Hypertext Abstract Machine and Dynamic Design Development Environment (Bigelow and Riley, 1987; Bigelow, 1988) provide a glimpse of program documents as complex entity and relationship structures. As documentation and publication management systems (Walker, 1988; Schlichter and Miller, 1988) evolve, the creation and distribution of electronic program documents will become a part of routine programming practice.

Fully electronic program publishing raises new opportunities and poses new issues:

- Representations of programs may be computed upon demand.
- Representations of programs can be automatically updated as the programs are changed.
- Multiple formats for possibly arbitrary window shapes and sizes are

required.

- We are therefore better able to exploit the use of concurrent multiple representations.
- Links between representations are required.
- It is important to be able to navigate among the multitude of representations with ease.

It is our hope that electronic program documents do not need to endure four decades of inadequate appearance as have paper program documents, with the consequent inefficiency of communication.

Section 6.9   Towards Literate Programming

Knuth (1984) has proposed the concept of "literate programming" and stressed the need for "a main concern with exposition and excellence of style." In a sense, our approach has been less ambitious than his. WEB users, with access to the full descriptive power of T_EX, can produce more sophisticated documents than can users of SEE.[†] To achieve this sophistication, the programmer must do far more work. On the other hand, our approach is more ambitious in the sense that we have developed mechanisms for the automatic production of enhanced program appearance that is generally far superior to that which most programmers likely would create by hand.

The two approaches are complementary and could be made synergistic. We can imagine a "SEEWEB" system which allows WEB's top-down structured exposition and documentation of a program, presented using SEE's designs and formats with escapes to WEB-like appearance control when desired, all augmented with sets of SEE-like program views such as those presented in Chapter 5.

Although one cannot deny the virtue of programmer production of literate programs, lovingly crafted with every attention to details of content, style, and appearance, it is important to remember that creators of fine literature have typically not also been their own typesetters, illustrators, and printers. Programs of the future will increasingly be created partially by human programmers and partially by automated procedures (Balzer, et al., 1983). Program typesetting, illustration, and printing will likewise be the result of a mixture of automated technique and manual control, incorporating libraries of appearance templates and *clip art* (Marcus, 1987d) designed by professional designers who specialize in program visualization. We must therefore develop a new discipline of program typesetting, illustration, and printing, a discipline that is sensitive to the characteristics of the human readers of programs. We hope that the work presented in this book will be a significant step towards the creation of such a discipline.

[†]   The same statement can be made about Cweb (Thimbleby, 1986), a WEB-like system that deals with C rather than Pascal and uses TROFF rather than T_EX.

```
01  MVVBUSIN.
    02  MVVBUS-KEY.
        04  MVVBUS-RECORD-KEY PIC S9(3) COMP-3.
            88  MVVBUS-START-FIS-MONTH VALUE -99.
            88  MVVBUS-END-FIS-MONTH VALUE +99.
            88  MVVBUS-PREV-BUSI-DAY VALUE -1.
            88  MVVBUS-CURRENT-BUSI-DAY VALUE +0.
            88  MVVBUS-CURRENT-PLUS-1 VALUE +1.
            88  MVVBUS-CURRENT-PLUS-2 VALUE +2.
            88  MVVBUS-CURRENT-PLUS-3 VALUE +3.
            88  MVVBUS-CURRENT-PLUS-4 VALUE +4.
            88  MVVBUS-CURRENT-PLUS-5 VALUE +5.
            88  MVVBUS-CURRENT-PLUS-6 VALUE +6.
            88  MVVBUS-CURRENT-PLUS-7 VALUE +7.
            88  MVVBUS-CURRENT-PLUS-8 VALUE +8.
            88  MVVBUS-CURRENT-PLUS-9 VALUE +9.
            88  MVVBUS-CURRENT-PLUS-10 VALUE +10.
        04  MVVBUS-DATE-YYMMDD PIC S9(7) COMP-3.
    02  MVVBUS-FISCAL-YYMM PIC S9(5) COMP-3.
    02  MVVBUS-FISCAL-WEEK-DAY PIC S9(3) COMP-3.
    02  MVVBUS-FISCAL-WORK-DAY PIC S9(3) COMP-3.
    02  MVVBUS-FISCAL-START-YYMMDD PIC S9(7) COMP-3.
    02  MVVBUS-FISCAL-END-YYMMDD PIC S9(7) COMP-3.
    02  MVVBUS-PREV-BUSI-YYMMDD PIC S9(7) COMP-3.
    02  MVVBUS-NEXT-BUSI-YYMMDD OCCURS 10 TIMES PIC S9(7) COMP-3.
    02  MVVBUS-TOT-WORK-DAY-THIS-MO PIC S9(3) COMP-3.
    02  FILLER PIC X(13).
```

7	01 **MVVBUSIN.**			
8	02 **MVVBUS-KEY.**			
9	04 **MVVBUS-RECORD-KEY**		S9(3) COMP-3.	
10	88 *MVVBUS-START-FIS-MONTH*			−99.
11	*MVVBUS-END-FIS-MONTH*			+99.
12	*MVVBUS-PREV-BUSI-DAY*			−1.
13	*MVVBUS-CURRENT-BUSI-DAY*			+0.
14	*MVVBUS-*	*-PLUS-1*		+1.
15	*MVVBUS-*	*-2*		+2.
16	*MVVBUS-*	*-3*		+3.
17	*MVVBUS-*	*-4*		+4.
18	*MVVBUS-*	*-5*		+5.
19	*MVVBUS-*	*-6*		+6.
20	*MVVBUS-*	*-7*		+7.
21	*MVVBUS-*	*-8*		+8.
22	*MVVBUS-*	*-9*		+9.
23	*MVVBUS-*	*-10*		+10.
24	04 MVVBUS-DATE-YYMMDD		S9(7) COMP-3.	
25	02 MVVBUS-FISCAL-YYMM		S9(5) COMP-3.	
26	MVVBUS-	-WEEK-DAY	S9(3) COMP-3.	
27	MVVBUS-	-WORK-DAY	S9(3) COMP-3.	
28	MVVBUS-	-START-YYMMDD	S9(7) COMP-3.	
29	MVVBUS-	-END-YYMMDD	S9(7) COMP-3.	
30	MVVBUS-PREV-BUSI-YYMMDD		S9(7) COMP-3.	
31	MVVBUS-NEXT-BUSI-YYMMDD		S9(7) COMP-3	
32	OCCURS 10 TIMES.			
33	MVVBUS-TOT-WORK-DAY-THIS-MO		S9(3) COMP-3.	
34	FILLER		X(13).	

Figure 6.1: *An enhanced display of a COBOL variable declaration.*

Small (1986) includes a reasonably complex set of design variations in the display of a COBOL variable declaration. The version at the top of the figure represents the conventional form. The version at the bottom of the figure illustrates the improvements possible through the use of typographic encoding, tabular formatting, elision of repetitive elements, and inclusion of rules.

```
% Code to solve the Towers of Hanoi problem.  The solution is the
% traditional recursive one.
To Hanoi :Number :From :To :Using
%
% A standard solution to the Towers of hanoi problem
%
If Equalp :Number 0 [ Stop ]                  % If there are no disks to move then stop
Hanoi Difference :Number "1 :From :Using :To  % Move top disks to other post
MoveDisk :Number :From :To                    % Print disk movement.
Hanoi Difference :Number "1 :Using :To :From  % Move the top disks to target post.
END
TO MoveDisk :Number :From :To
%
% Move the disk from the From post to the To post
%
Type  "Move\ disk\ number\
Type :Number
Type "\ from\
Type :From
Type "\ to\
Print :To
End
```

% Code to solve the Towers of Hanoi problem. The solution is the
% traditional recursive one.

Hanoi

To **Hanoi** :Number :From :To :Using
%
% A standard solution to the Towers of hanoi problem
%
If Equalp :Number 0 [Stop]   % If there are no disks to move then stop
Hanoi *Difference* :Number "1 :From :Using :To % Move top disks to other post
MoveDisk :Number :From :To   % Print disk movement.
Hanoi *Difference* :Number "1 :Using :To :From % Move the top disks to target post.
END

MoveDisk

To **MoveDisk** :Number :From :To
%
% Move the disk from the FROM post to the TO post
%
Type "Move\ disk\ number\
Type :Number
Type "\ from\
Type :From
Type "\ to\
Print :To
End

Figure 6.2: *An enhanced display of a LOGO function.*

Buchanan (1988) implements a method for the enhanced presentation of LOGO source text. The conventional version is shown at the top of the figure. At the bottom of the figure is an enhanced presentation which uses typographic encoding and rules.

```
static STATUS
keyrespond(key)
    struct keyword                          *key.
    register struct pattern                 *pat,
    register STATUS                         ret.

    for (pat = key→pats; pat != NULL; pat = pat→pnext)
        ret = patrespond(pat).
        if (ret == S_DONE || ret == S_NEXT)
            return (ret).
    if (debug)
        printf("---no match\n").
    return (S_FAIL).
```

For stepping through pattern list.
Eventual return value.

Figure 6.3: *A program visualization rendered with 1 bit per pixel on a raster display.*

We can achieve a reasonable facsimile of our enhanced appearance even on today's 80–100 dots-per-inch displays with their 1 bit per pixel representation of text. The above program visualization, which should be compared to that at the bottom of Figure 3.58, was rendered on a Silicon Graphics interactive workstation displaying Postscript fonts and using 1 bit per pixel. Character quality is uneven and often very poor due to the low spatial resolution of the display.

```
static STATUS
keyrespond(key)
    struct keyword                          *key;
    register struct pattern                 *pat;
    register STATUS                         ret;

    for (pat = key→pats; pat != NULL; pat = pat→pnext)
        ret = patrespond(pat);
        if (ret == S_DONE || ret == S_NEXT)
            return (ret);
        if (debug)
            printf("---no match n");
    return (S_FAIL);
```

For stepping through pattern list.
Eventual return value.

Figure 6.4: *A program visualization rendered with 8 bits per pixel on a raster display using anti-aliased fonts.*

This figure shows a visualization similar to that at the bottom of Figure 3.58 and similar to that in Figure 6.3. It was rendered on a Sun interactive workstation displaying anti-aliased fonts and using 8 bits per pixel. It illustrates how the use of anti-aliased gray-valued fonts can increase the apparent resolution and improve the appearance of individual characters on a display (Naiman and Fournier, 1987). The uneven character spacing apparent in this image could be removed if we had slightly smarter typesetting software.

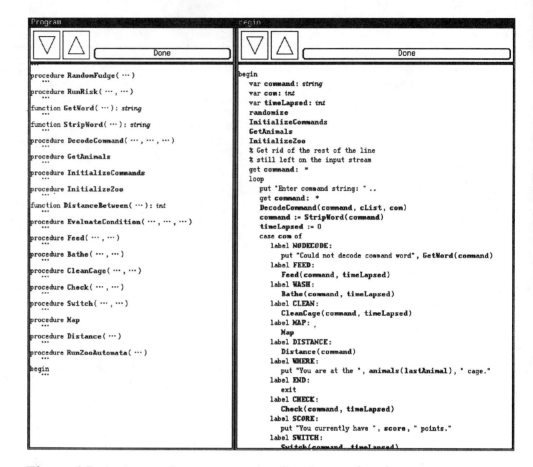

Figure 6.5: *An interactive program visualization rendered on a raster display.*

Small (1989) is an investigation of the application and extension of the concepts and methods presented in this book to an interactive display environment. This figure, a laser printer snapshot of what is seen on an interactive display by a user of the VIPER system, illustrates two of the many advantages achievable in such an environment: multiple representations of the same program may co-exist simultaneously within different windows on a workstation; the contents and appearance of code in these windows may be controlled by the user through the specification of visualization attributes and source code filters. Thus the elided view on the left is a kind of table of contents of an entire program written in the Turing language; the view on the right simultaneously shows the program's main routine.

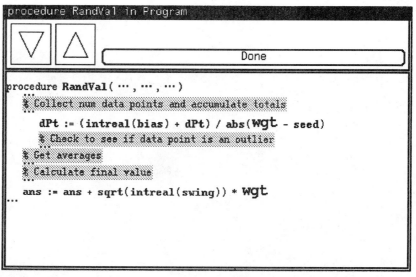

Figure 6.6: *Another interactive program visualization rendered on a raster display.*

The default visualization of the "RandVal" procedure shown by the VIPER system (Small, 1989) appears at the top of the figure. The representation at the bottom of the figure is achieved by highlighting the "Wgt" identifier with a larger point size, and by applying a syntactic filter that selects only lines that contain this identifier and a semantic filter that looks for identifiers of type integer.

Appendix A

References and Bibliography

Adobe Systems, Inc. (1985). *PostScript Language Reference Manual*. Reading, Mass.: Addison-Wesley.

Amit, N. (1984). A Different Solution for Improving the Readability of Deeply Nested IF-THEN-ELSE Control Structure. *SIGPLAN Notices* 19(1), 24–29.

Aron, J.D. (1983). *The Program Development Process. Part II: The Programming Team*. Reading, Mass.: Addison-Wesley.

Arblaster, A. (1982). Human Factors in the Design and Use of Computing Languages. *International Journal of Man-Machine Studies* 17, 211–224.

AT&T Bell Laboratories (1985). *The C Programmer's Handbook.*, Prentice-Hall.

Badler, N. (1988). Personal communication.

Baecker, R.M. (1973). Towards Animating Computer Programs: A First Progress Report. *Proceedings of the Third NRC Man-Computer Communications Conference*, 4.1–4.10.

Baecker, R.M. (1975). Two Systems Which Produce Animated Representations of the Execution of Computer Programs. *SIGCSE Bulletin*, 7(1), February 1975, 158–167.

Baecker, R.M. (1981). *Sorting Out Sorting*. 30 minute color sound film, Dynamic Graphics Project, Computer Systems Research Institute, University of Toronto, 1981. Distributed by Morgan Kaufmann, Publishers. (Excerpted in *SIGGRAPH Video Review 7*, 1983.)

Baecker, R.M. (1988). Enhancing Program Readability and Comprehensibility with Tools for Program Visualization. *Proceedings of the 10th International Conference on Software Engineering*, IEEE Press.

Baecker, R.M. (under review). Program Visualization Through Multiple Views.

Baecker, R.M., et al. (in preparation). The Effect of the Enhanced Presentation of Source Text on a Program's Readability and Usability: Results of Two Experiments.

Baecker, R.M. and Buchanan, J. (under review). A Visually Enhanced and Animated Programming Environment.

Baecker, R.M. and Buxton, W.A.S. (1987). *Readings in Human-Computer Interaction: A Multidisciplinary Approach*. Los Altos, Calif.: Morgan Kaufmann.

Baecker, R.M. and Marcus, A. (1983). On Enhancing the Interface to the Source Code of Computer Programs. *Proceedings of the Conference on Human Factors in Computing Systems* (CHI '83), ACM, 251–255.

Baecker, R.M. and Marcus, A. (1986). Design Principles for the Enhanced Presentation of Computer Program Source Text. *Proceedings of the Conference on Human Factors in Computing Systems* (CHI'86), ACM, 51–58.

Baecker, R.M., Marcus, A., Arent, M., Longarini, J., Macintosh, A., and Tims, T. (1985). Enhancing the Presentation of Computer Program Source Text. Final Report of the Program Visualization Project to the Defense Advanced Research Projects Agency, submitted by HCR Corporation and Aaron Marcus and Associates, 6 volumes, 1985.

Baker, F.T. (1972). Chief Programmer Team Management of Production Programming, *IBM Systems Journal* 11:1 (1972), 56–73.

Balzer, R., Cheatham, T.E., and Green, C. (1983). Software Technology in the 1990's: Using a New Paradigm. *IEEE Computer* 16(11), 39–45.

Barstow, D. (1987). Artificial Intelligence and Software Engineering. *Proceedings of the 9th International Conference on Software Engineering*, IEEE Computer Society Press, 200–211.

Basili, V.R. and Rombach, H.D. (1987). Tailoring the Software Process to Project Goals and Environments. *Proceedings for 9th International Conference on Software Engineering*, IEEE Computer Society Press, 345–357.

Bates, R.M. (1981). A Pascal Prettyprinter With a Different Purpose. *SIGPLAN Notices* 16(3), 10–17.

Beach, R. (1986). Personal communication.

Belady, L.A. and Lehman, M.M. (1976). A Model of Large Program Development.

IBM Systems Journal 15(3).

Berry, R.E. and Meekings, B.A.E. (1985). A Style Analysis of C Programs. *Communications of the ACM*, 28(1), 80–89.

Bentley, J.L. (1986a). Programming Pearls: Literate Programming. *Communications of the ACM* 29(5), 364–369.

Bentley, J.L. (1986b). Programming Pearls: A Literate Program. *Communications of the ACM* 29(6), 471–483.

Bentley, J.L. and Kernighan, B.W. (1987). A System for Algorithm Animation. Computing Science Technical Report No. 132, AT&T Bell Laboratories, Murray Hill, N.J., January 1987.

Bigelow, C. and Holmes, K. (1986). The Design of Lucida®: an Integrated Family of Types for Electronic Literacy. Appears in van Vliet, J.C. (Ed.) (1986). *Text Processing and Document Manipulation*. Cambridge, England: Cambridge University Press, pp. 1–17.

Bigelow, J. (1988). Hypertext and CASE. *IEEE Software* 5(2), 23–27.

Bigelow, J. and Riley, V. (1987). Manipulating Source Code in Dynamic Design. *Proceedings of Hypertext '87*, 397–406.

Blaiwes, A.S. (1974). Formats for Presenting Procedural Instructions. *Journal of Applied Psychology* 59(6), 683–686.

Böcker, H.D., Fischer, G., and Nieper, H. (1986). The Enhancement of Understanding through Visual Representations. *CHI'86 Proceedings*, 44–50.

Boehm, B.W. (1981). *Software Engineering Economics*. Englewood Cliffs, N.J.: Prentice-Hall.

Boehm-Davis, D.A., Sheppard, S.B. and Bailey, J.W. (1987). Program Design Languages: How Much Detail Should They Include? *International Journal Man-Machine Studies* 27, 337–347.

Brooke, J.B. and Duncan, K.D. (1980a). An Experimental Study of Flowcharts as an Aid to Identification of Procedural Faults. *Ergonomics* 23(4), 387–399.

Brooke, J.B. and Duncan, K.D. (1980b). Experimental Studies of Flowchart Use at Different Stages of Program Debugging. *Ergonomics* 23(11), 1057–1091.

Brooks, R. (1977). Towards a Theory of the Cognitive Processes in Computer Programming. *International Journal of Man-Machine Studies* 9, 737–751.

Brooks, R. (1982). A Theoretical Analysis of the Role of Documentation in the Comprehension of Computer Programs. *Proceedings of Human Factors in Computer Systems* (CHI'82), ACM, 125–129.

Brooks, R. (1983). Towards a Theory of the Comprehension of Computer Programs. *International Journal of Man-Machine Studies* 18(6), 543–554.

Brown, G., Carling, R., Herot, C.F., Kramlich, D.A., and Souza, P. (1985). Program Visualization: Graphical Support for Software Development. *IEEE Computer* 18(8), 27–35.

Brown, M. (1988). An Interactive Tool for Literate Programming. CHI'88 Poster Session.

Brown, M.H. (1988a). Algorithm Animation. Cambridge, Mass.: MIT Press.

Brown, M.H. (1988b). Exploring Algorithms Using Balsa-II. *IEEE Computer* 18(8), 27–35.

Brown, M.H. and Sedgewick, R. (1984). A System for Algorithm Animation. *Computer Graphics* 18(3), 177–186.

Brown, M.H. and Sedgewick, R. (1985). Techniques for Algorithm Animation. *IEEE Software* 2(1), January 1985, 28–39.

Buchanan, J. (1988). LogoMotion: A Visually Enhanced Programming Environment. M.Sc. Thesis, Department of Computer Science, University of Toronto.

Cannon, L.W., et al., and Spencer, H. (1987). Indian Hill C Style and Coding Standards (as Amended for U of T Zoology UNIX). AT&T Bell Laboratories and University of Toronto Department of Zoology Memo, last updated November 1987.

Card, S.K., Moran, T.P., and Newell, A. (1983). *The Psychology of Human-Computer Interaction*. Hillsdale, N.J.: Lawrence Erlbaum Associates.

Carter, R., Day, B., and Meggs, P. (1985). *Typographic Design: Form and Communication*. New York: Van Nostrand Reinhold.

Chang, S.-K. (1987). Visual Languages: A Tutorial and Survey. *IEEE Software* 4(1), January 1985, 29–39.

Chaparos, A. (1981). *Notes for a Federal Design Manual*, Washington, D.C.:

Chaparos Productions.

Chen, P. and Harrison, M.A. (1988). Multiple Representation Document Development. *IEEE Computer* 21(1), 15–31.

Chikofsky, E.J. (1988). Software Technology People. *IEEE Software* 5(2), 8–10.

Chikofsky, E.J. and Rubenstein, B.L. (1988). CASE: Reliability Engineering for Information Systems. *IEEE Software* 5(2), 11–16.

Clifton, M.H. (1978). A Technique for Making Structured Programs More Readable. *SIGPLAN Notices* 13(4), 58–63.

Conklin, J. (1987). Hypertext: An Introduction and Survey. *IEEE Computer* 20(9), 17–41.

Cordy, J.R., Eliot, N., and Robertson, M.G. (1987). TuringTool: A Knowledge-based User Interface to Aid in the Maintenance Task. Queen's University Department of Computer Science Technical Report 87–193, Kingston, Ontario.

Crosby, M. and Stelovsky, J. (1989). The Influence of User Experience and Presentation Medium on Strategies of Viewing Algorithms. *Proceedings of the 22nd Annual Hawaii International Conference on System Sciences*, Vol. II, IEEE Computer Society Press, 438–446.

Cunniff, N. and Taylor, R.P. (1987). Graphical vs. Textual Representation: An Empirical Study of Novices' Program Comprehension. Appears in Olson, G.M., Sheppard, S. and Soloway, E. (Eds.) (1987), *Empirical Studies of Programmers: Second Workshop*, Norwood, N.J.: Ablex Publishing Co., 114–131.

Curtis, B. (1984). Fifteen Years of Psychology in Software Engineering: Individual Differences and Cognitive Science. *Proceedings of the 7th International Conference on Software Engineering*, IEEE Computer Society Press, 97–106.

Curtis, B. (Ed.) (1985). *Tutorial: Human Factors in Software Development*. Second Edition. IEEE Computer Society Press.

Curtis, B. (1986). By the Way, Did Anyone Study Any Real Programmers? Appears in Soloway, E. and Sitharama, I (Eds.) (1986), *Empirical Studies of Programmers*, Norwood, N.J.: Ablex Publishing Co., 256–268.

Curtis, B., et al. (1986). Software Psychology: The Need for an Interdisciplinary Program. *Proceedings of the IEEE* 74(8), 1092–1106.

Dahl, O.-J., Dijkstra, E.W., and Hoare, C.A.R. (1972). *Structured Programming*. London: Academic Press.

Dart, S.A., Ellison, R.J., Feiler, P.H., and Habermann, A.N. (1987). Software Development Environments. *IEEE Computer* 20(11), 18–28.

Dondis, D.A. (1973). *A Primer of Visual Literacy*, Cambridge: MIT Press.

Duffy, T.M. and Waller, R. (Eds.) (1985). *Designing Usable Texts*. Orlando, Florida: Academic Press.

Duisberg, R.A. (1986). Animating Graphical Interfaces Using Temporal Constraints. *Proceedings of the Conference on Human Factors in Computing Systems* (CHI '86), ACM, 131–136.

Eco, U. (1976). *Theory of Semiotics*, Bloomington: Indiana University Press.

Eisenstadt, M. and Brayshaw, M. (1987). The Transparent Prolog Machine, Technical Report No. 21a, Human Cognition Research Laboratory, Open University.

Elshoff, J.L., Marcotty, M. (1982). Improving Computer Program Readibility to Aid Modification. *Communications of the ACM* 25(8), 512–521.

Felker, D.B. (Ed.) (1980). *Document Design: A Review of the Relevant Research*. Washington, D.C.: American Institutes for Research.

Felker, D.B. (Ed.) (1981). *Guidelines for Document Design*. Washington, D.C.: American Institutes for Research.

Fitter, M.J. and Green, T.R.G. (1981). When do Diagrams Make Good Computer Languages? Appears in Coombs, M.J. and Alty, J.L. (Eds.) (1981), *Computing Skills and the User Interface*, Academic Press, 253–287.

Foss, D.J., Smith-Kerker, P.L., and Rosson, M.B. (1987). On Comprehending a Computer Manual: Analysis of Variables Affecting Performance. *International Journal of Man-Machine Studies* 26, 277–300.

Frase, L.T. and Schwartz, B.J. (1979). Typographical Cues That Facilitate Comprehension. *Journal of Educational Psychology* 71(2), 197–206.

Free Software Foundation (1988). Gnu C

Reference Manual.

Furnas, G.W. (1982). The Fisheye View: A New Look at Structured Files. Bell Laboratories, October, 1982.

Furnas, G.W. (1986). Generalized Fisheye Views. *Proceedings of the Conference on Human Factors in Computing Systems* (CHI '86), ACM, 16–23.

Gerstner, K. (1965). *Designing Programs.* Switzerland: Niggli, Teufen.

Gerstner, K. (1978). *Compendium for Literates*, Cambridge: MIT Press.

Gilb, T. (1977). *Software Metrics.* Cambridge: Winthrop Publishers.

Gilmore, D.J. and Smith, H.T. (1984a). An Investigation of the Utility of Flowcharts During Computer Program Debugging. *International Journal of Man-Machine Studies* 20, 357–372.

Gilmore, D.J. and Smith, H.T. (1986b). Comprehension and Recall of Miniature Programs. *International Journal of Man-Machine Studies* 21, 31–48.

Goldberg, A. (1987). Programmer as Reader. *IEEE Software* 4(5), 62–70.

Goodman, Danny (1987). *The Complete Hypercard Handbook.* New York: Bantam Books.

Graham, T.C.N. and Cordy, J.R. (1989). Conceptual Views of Data Structures as a Model of Output in Programming Languages. *Proceedings of the Hawaii International Conference on System Sciences*, January 1989, 1–11.

Green, T.R.G. (1977) Conditional Program Statements and Their Comprehensibility to Professional Programmers. *Journal of Occupational Psychology* 50(2), 93–109.

Green, T.R.G. (1980a). Programming as a Cognitive Activity. Appears in Smith, H.T. and Green, T.R.G. (Eds.)(1980), *Human Interaction with Computers*, New York: Academic Press, 271–320.

Green, T.R.G. (1980b). Ifs and Thens: Is Nesting just for the Birds? *Software — Practice and Experience* 10(5), 373–381.

Green, T.R.G. (1982). Pictures of Programs and Other Processes, or How to Do Things With Lines. *Behaviour and Information Technology*, 1(1), 3–36.

Green, T.R.G. and Payne, S.J. (1982). The Woolly Jumper: Typographic Problems of Concurrency in Information Display. *Visible Language* 16(4), 391–403.

Green, T.R.G., Sime, M.E., and Fitter, M.J. (1980). The Problems the Programmer Faces. *Ergonomics* 23(9), 893–907.

Green, T.R.G., Sime, M.E., and Fitter, M.J. (1981). The Art of Notation. Appears in Coombs, M.J., and Alty, J.L. (Eds.)(1981), *Computing Skills and the User Interface*, New York: Academic Press, 221–251.

Grogono, P. (1979). On Layout, Identifiers and Semicolons in Pascal Programs. *SIGPLAN Notices* 14(4), 35–40.

Gustafson, G.G. (1979). Some Practical Experiences Formatting Pascal Programs. *SIGPLAN Notices* 14(9), 42–49.

Gutz, S., Wasserman, A.I., and Spier, M.J. (1981). Personal Development Systems for the Professional Programmer. *IEEE Computer* 14(8), April 1981, 45–53.

Hagen, M.A. (1988). Experimental Psychology and Human-Computer Interaction. Conference on Human Factors in Computing Systems (CHI'88) Tutorial Notes.

Harbison, S.P. and Steele, Jr., G.L. (1984). *C: A Reference Manual*, Englewood Cliffs, N.J.: Prentice-Hall.

Hartley, J. (1978). *Designing Instructional Text*, Second Edition. London: Kogan Page Ltd.

Hartley, J. (1980a). Spatial Cues in Text. *Visible Language* 14(1), 62–79.

Hartley, J. (Ed.) (1980b). *The Psychology of Written Communication*. London: Kogan Page Ltd.

Herot, C.F., Brown, G.P., Carling, R.T., Friedell, M., Kramlich, D., and Baecker, R.M. (1982). An Integrated Environment for Program Visualization. In *Automated Tools for Information Systems Design*, H.-J. Schneider and A.I. Wasserman (Eds.), North-Holland, 237–259.

Higgins, David A. (1979). *Program Design and Construction*, Englewood Cliffs, N.J.: Prentice-Hall.

Holt, R.C. and Cordy, J.R. (1985). The Turing Language Report. Technical Report CSRI-153, Computer Systems Research Institute, University of Toronto, Revised July 1985.

Holt, R.C. and Cordy, J.R. (1989). The Turing Programming Language. *Communications of the ACM* 31(12), 1410–1423.

Horowitz, E. and Williamson, R.C. (1986a). SODOS: A Software Documentation Support Environment — Its Definition. *IEEE Transactions on Software Engineering* SE-12(8), 849–859.

Horowitz, E. and Williamson, R.C. (1986b). SODOS: A Software Documentation Support Environment — Its Use. *IEEE Transactions on Software Engineering* SE-12(11), 1076–1087.

Hudlicka, E. (to appear). Visual System Browser. *SIGPLAN Notices*

Hueras, J. and Ledgard, H. (1977). An Automatic Formatting Program for Pascal. *SIGPLAN Notices* 12(7), 82–84.

Huey, E.B. (1968). *The Psychology and Pedagogy of Reading*. Cambridge: MIT Press.

Human Synergistics (1980). *Life Styles Interpretations Manual*, Plymouth, Mass.

International Paper Co. (1987). *Pocket Pal*, N9.

Jackel, M. (1983). Context Sensitive Formatting. *SIGPLAN Notices* 18(2), 65–68.

Johnson, S.C. (1978). LINT, A C Program Checker. *UNIX Programmer's Manual*, Volume 2.

Johnson, S.C. (1979). A Tour Through the Portable C Compiler. *UNIX Programmer's Manual*, Volume 2.

Jonassen, D.H. (1982). *The Technology of Text: Principles for Structuring, Designing, and Displaying Text*. Englewood Cliffs, N.J.: Educational Technology Publications.

Kammann, R. (1975). The Comprehensibility of Printed Instructions and the Flowchart Alternative. *Human Factors* 17(2), 183–191.

Kernighan, B.W. (1982). A Typesetter-independent TROFF. *Bell Laboratories Computing Science Series Technical Report No. 97*, March 1982.

Kernighan, B.W. and Plauger, P.J. (1976). *Software Tools*, Reading, Mass.: Addison-Wesley.

Kernighan, B.W. and Ritchie, D.M. (1978). *The C Programming Language*, Englewood Cliffs, N.J.: Prentice-Hall.

Kesler, T.E, et al. (1984). The Effect of Indentation on Program Comprehension. *International Journal of Man-Machine Studies* 21, 415–428.

Kieras, D.E. (1978). Good and Bad Structure in Simple Paragraphs: Effects on Apparent Theme, Reading Time, and Recall. *Journal of Verbal Learning and Verbal Behavior* 17(1), 13–28.

Klerer, M. (1984). Experimental Study of a Two-Dimensional Language vs. Fortran for First-Course Programmers. *International Journal of Man-Machine Studies* 20, 445–467.

Knuth, D.E. (1984a). Literate Programming. *The Computer Journal* 27(2), 97–111.

Knuth, D.E. (1984b). *The $T_EX$book*. Reading, Mass.: Addison-Wesley.

Knuth, D.E. (1986a). *METAFONT: The Program*. Reading, Mass.: Addison-Wesley.

Knuth, D.E. (1986b). *T_EX: The Program*. Reading, Mass.: Addison-Wesley.

Knuth, D.E. and Plass, M.F. (1981). Breaking Paragraphs into Lines. *Software–Practice and Experience* 11, 1119–1184.

Kurtenbach, G.P. (1988). Hierachical Encapsulation and Connection in a Graphical User Interface: a Music Case Study. M.Sc. Thesis, Department of Computer Science, University of Toronto.

Landin, P.J. (1966). The Next 700 Programming Languages. *Communications of the ACM* 9(3), 157–166.

Larkin, J.H. and Simon, H.A. (1987). Why a Diagram is (Sometimes) Worth Ten Thousand Words. *Cognitive Science* 11(1), 65–99.

Leavens, G.T. (1984). Prettyprinting Styles for Various Languages. *SIGPLAN Notices* 19(2), 75–79.

Leinbaugh, D. (1980). Indenting for the Compiler. *SIGPLAN Notices* 15(5), 41–48.

Liebermann, H. (1984). Seeing What Your Programs Are Doing. *International Journal of Man-Machine Studies* 21, 311–331.

Lindsay, P.H. and Norman, D.A. (1977). *Human Information Processing: An Introduction to Psychology*, Second Edition. New York: Academic Press.

Lions, J. (1977). A Commentary on the UNIX Operating System, University of New South Wales, Australia.

London, R.L. and Duisberg, R.A. (1985). Animating Programs Using Smalltalk. *IEEE Computer* 18(8), 61–71.

Maier, M. (1977). *Basic Principles of Design.* New York: Van Nostrand Reinhold.

Marchionini, G. and Shneiderman, B. (1988). Finding Facts vs. Browsing Knowledge in Hypertext Systems. *IEEE Computer* 21(1), 70–80.

Marcus, A. (1984). Aaron Marcus: An Information Artist for the Light Age. *Atari Connection* 3(1), 26ff.

Marcus, A. (1986). The Ten Commandments of Color. *Computer Graphics Today,* 3(10), 7ff.

Marcus, A. (1987a). Studying the Classics: Required Reading for Desk Top Publishing. *Computer Graphics Today,* 4(5).

Marcus, A. (1987b). Classics Illustrated: More Required Reading. *Computer Graphics Today,* 4(6).

Marcus, A. (1987c). Recommended Reading: Workstation Design. *Computer Graphics Today,* 4(7).

Marcus, A. (1987d). Clip Art and Format Libraries: Keys to Successful Electronic Publishing. *Proceedings of NCGA 1987,* Fairfax, Virginia: NCGA.

Marcus, A. and Baecker, R.M. (1982). On the Graphic Design of Program Text. *Proceedings of Graphics Interface '82,* 302–311.

Martin, J. and McClure, C. (1985). *Diagramming Techniques for Analysts and Programmers,* Englewood Cliffs, N.J.: Prentice-Hall.

Mateti, P. (1983). A Specification Schema for Indenting Programs. *Software — Practice and Experience* 13, 163–179.

Mayer, R.E. (1976). Comprehension as Affected by Structure of Problem Representation. *Memory & Cognition* 4(3), 249–255.

Megascan Technology, Inc. (1989). Product Literature. Gibsonia, Pennsylvania.

Miara, R.J., Musselman, J.A., Navarro, J.A., and Shneiderman, B. (1983). Program Indentation and Comprehensibility. *Communications of the ACM* 26(11), 861–867.

Mikelsons, M. (1981). Prettyprinting in an Interactive Programming Environment. *SIGOA Newsletter* 2, 108–116.

Miles, J. (1987). *Design for Desktop Publishing: A Guide to Layout and Typography on the Personal Computer.* San Francisco: Chronicle Books.

Moriconi, M. and Hare, D.F. (1985a). Visualizing Program Designs Through PegaSys. *IEEE Computer* 18(8), 72–85.

Moriconi, M. and Hare, D.F. (1985b). PegaSys: A System for Graphical Explanation of Program Designs. *Proceedings of the ACM SIGPLAN 85 Symposium on Language Issues in Programming Environments,* ACM, 148–160.

Moriconi, M. and Hare, D.F. (1986). The PegaSys System: Pictures as Formal Documentation of Large Programs. *ACM Transactions on Programming Languages and Systems* 8(4), 524–546.

Müller-Brockman, J. (1981). *Grid Systems in Graphic Design.* Switzerland: Verlag Arthur Niggli.

Myers, B. (1986). Visual Programming, Programming by Example, and Program Visualization: A Taxonomy. *Proceedings of the Conference on Human Factors in Computing Systems* (CHI '86), ACM, 59–66.

Naiman, A. and Fournier, A. (1987). Rectangular Convolution for Fast Filtering of Characters. *Computer Graphics* 21(4), 233–242.

Nassi, I. and Shneiderman, B. (1973). Flowcharting Techniques for Structured Programming. *SIGPLAN Notices* 8(8), 12–26.

Naur, P. (Ed.) (1963). Revised Report on the Algorithmic Language ALGOL 60. *Communications of the ACM* 6(1), 1–17.

Norcio, A.F. (1981). Indentation, Documentation, and Programmer Comprehension. *Proceedings of the Conference on Human Factors in Computer Systems* (CHI'82), ACM, 118–120.

Oman, P.W. and Cook, C.R. (1989). Typographic Style is More than Cosmetic. Computer Science Department Technical Note #89-60-5. Oregon State University (under review).

Oppen, D.D. (1980). Prettyprinting. *ACM Transactions on Programming Languages and Systems* 2(4), 465–483.

Organick, E. and Thomas, J.W. (1974). Computer-generated Semantics Displays. *Proceedings of the IFIP Congress*, Applications Volume, 1974, 898–902.

Parnas, D. L. (1972). On the Criteria to be Used in Decomposing Systems into Modules. *Communications of the ACM* 15, 1053–1058.

Parnas, D.L. and Weiss, D.M. (1985). Active Design Reviews: Principles and Practices. *Proceedings of the 8th International Conference on Software Engineering*, August 1985, 132–136.

Patrick, J. and Fitzgibbon, L. (1988). Structural Displays as Learning Aids. *International Journal of Man-Machine Studies* 28, 625–635.

Payne, S.J., Sime, M.E., and Green, T.R.G. (1984). Perceptual Structure Cueing in a Simple Command Language. *International Journal of Man-Machine Studies* 21, 19–29.

Perlis, A., Sayward, F., and Shaw, M. (Eds.) (1981). *Software Metrics: An Analysis and Evaluation*, Cambridge: MIT Press.

Perlman, G. and Erickson, T.D. (1983). Graphical Abstractions of Technical Documents. *Visible Language*, XVII (4), 380–389.

Pike, R. and Presotto, D.L. (1985). Face the Nation. *Proceedings of the Summer 1985 Usenix Conference*, Portland, Oregon, June 1985, 81–86.

Plum, T. (1984). *C Programming Guidelines*. Cardiff, N.J.: Plum Hall Inc.

Raeder, G. (1985). A Survey of Current Graphical Programming Techniques. *IEEE Computer* 18(8), August 1985, 11–25.

Redelmeier, H. (1989). Personal Communication.

Reenskaug, T. and Skaar, A.L. (1989). An Environment for Literate Smalltalk Programming. Center for Industrial Research, Oslo, Norway.

Reiss, S.P. (1984). Graphical Program Development with PECAN Program Development Systems. *Proceedings of the ACM SigSoft/SigPlan Software Engineering Symposium on Practical Software Development Environments*, Pittsburgh, April 23–25, 1984.

Reiss, S.P. (1985). PECAN: Program Development Systems That Support Multiple Views. *IEEE Transactions on Software Engineering* SE-11(3), March 1985, 276–285.

Reiss, S.P. (1987). Working in the Garden Environment for Conceptual Programming. *IEEE Software* 4(6), 16–27.

Reiss, S.P. and Pato, J.N. (1987). Displaying Program and Data Structures. *Proceedings of the 20th Annual Hawaii International Conference on System Sciences*, 391–401.

Reps, T. and Teitelbaum, T. (1987). Language Processing in Program Editors. *IEEE Computer* 20(11), 29–40.

Reynolds, C.F. (1987). The Use of Color in Language Syntax Analysis. *Software — Practice and Experience* 17(8), 513–519.

Ritchie, D.M. (1989). Personal communication.

Rose, G.A. and Welsh, J. (1981). Formatted Programming Languages. *Software — Practice and Experience* 11, 651–669.

Rosen, B. (1976). *Type and Typography*. New York: Van Nostrand Reinhold.

Ross, D.T. (1977). Structured Analysis (SA): A Language for Communicating Ideas, *IEEE Transactions on Software Engineering* SE-3(1), 16–34.

Ross, D.T. (1985). Applications and Extensions of SADT. *IEEE Computer* 18(4), 25–34.

Rothkind, M.J. (1975). The Source Code Control System. *IEEE Transactions on Software Engineering* SE-1 (December 1975), 364–370.

Rubin, L. (1983). Syntax-Directed Pretty Printing — A First Step Towards a Syntax-Directed Editor. *IEEE Transactions on Software Engineering*, 9(2), 119–127.

Rubinstein, R. (1988). *Digital Typography: An Introduction to Type and Composition for Computer System Design*. Reading, Mass.: Addison-Wesley.

Ruder, E. (1977). *Typographie*. Third Edition. Switzerland: Verlag Arthur Niggli Teufen AR.

Sammet, J.E. (1981). An Overview of High-Level Languages. *Advances in Computers* 20, 199–259.

Sanger, D.E. (1987). The Computer Contribution to the Rise and Fall of Stocks, *New*

York Times, December 15, 1.

Schildt, H. (1986). *Advanced C*. Osborne McGraw-Hill, 112–117.

Schmidt, A.L. (1986). Effects of Experience and Comprehension on Reading Time and Memory of Computer Programs. *International Journal of Man-Machine Studies* 25(4), 399–409.

Schlichter, J.H. and Miller, L.J. (1988). FolioPub: A Publication Management System. *IEEE Computer* 21(1), 61–69.

Shapiro, S.C. and Kwasny, S.C. (1974). Interactive Consulting Via Natural Language. Computer Science Technical Report No. 12, Indiana University, Bloomington, June 1974.

Shapiro, S.C. and Kwasny, S.C. (1975). Interactive Consulting Via Natural Language. *Communications of the ACM*, 18(8), 459–462.

Sheppard, S.B., Kruesi, E., and Curtis, B. (1981). The Effects of Symbology and Spatial Arrangement on the Comprehension of Software Specifications. *Proceedings of the 5th International Conference on Software Engineering*, IEEE Computer Society Press, 207–214.

Sheppard, S.B., Kruesi, E., and Bailey, J.W. (1982). An Empirical Evaluation of Software Documentation Formats. *Proceedings of Human Factors in Computer Systems* (CHI'82), ACM, 121–124.

Shneiderman, B. (1977). Measuring Computer Program Quality and Comprehension. *International Journal of Man-Machine Studies* 9(4), 465–478.

Shneiderman, B. and Mayer, R. (1979). Syntactic/Semantic Interactions in Programmer Behavior: A Model and Experimental Results. *International Journal of Computer and Information Sciences* 8(3), 219–238.

Shneiderman, B., Mayer, R., McKay, D., and Heller, P. (1977). Experimental Investigations of the Utility of Detailed Flowcharts in Programming. *Communications of the ACM* 20(6), 373–381.

Shneiderman, B., Shafer, P., Simon, R., and Weldon, L. (1985). Display Strategies for Program Browsing. *Proceedings of the IEEE Conference on Software Maintenance*, Silver Spring, Md., November 11–13, 1985, 136–143.

Shneiderman, B., Shafer, P., Simon, R., and

Weldon, L. (1986). Display Strategies for Program Browsing: Concepts and Experiment. *IEEE Software* 3(3), 7–15.

Shu, N.C. (1988). *Visual Programming*. New York: Van Nostrand Reinhold.

Sime, M.E., Green, T.R.G., and Guest, D.J. (1973). Psychological Evaluation of Two Conditional Constructions Used in Computer Languages. *International Journal of Man-Machine Studies* 5, 105–113.

Sime, M.E. Green, T.R.G., and Guest, D.J. (1977). Scope Marking in Computer Conditionals — A Psychological Evaluation. *International Journal of Man-Machine Studies* 9, 107–118.

Sloboda, J. (1976). Visual Perception of Musical Notation: Registering Pitch Symbols in Memory. *Quarterly Journal of Experimental Psychology* 28, 1–16.

Sloboda, J. (1981). The Uses of Space in Music Notation. *Visible Language* 15(1), 87–110.

Small, I.S. (1986). Program Visualization: Enhancing the Readability of COBOL Source Code. B.A.Sc. Thesis, Division of Engineering Science, Faculty of Applied Science and Engineering, University of Toronto.

Small, I.S. (1989). Program Visualization: Static Typographic Visualization in an Interactive Environment. M.Sc. Thesis, Department of Computer Science, University of Toronto.

Smith, S.R., Barnard, D.T., and Macleod, I.A. (1984). Holophrasted Displays in an Interactive Environment. *International Journal of Man-Machine Studies* 20, 343–355.

Smullyan, R. (1983). *5000 B.C. and Other Philosophical Fantasies*, New York: St. Martin's Press.

Spencer, H. (1989). Personal communication.

Sproull, R.F. (1988). Personal communication.

Sproull, R.F. (1989). Personal communication.

Swartout, W. and Balzer, R. (1982). On the Inevitable Intertwining of Specification and Implementation. *Communications of the ACM* 25(7), 438–440.

Teitelman, W. (1979). A Display Oriented

Programmer's Assistant. *International Journal of Man-Machine Studies* ,11, 157–187.

Teitelman, W. (1984). The Cedar Programming Environment: A Midterm Report and Examination. Xerox Palo Alto Research Center Technical Report CSL-83-11.

Teitelman, W. (1985). A Tour Through Cedar. *IEEE Transactions on Software Engineering* SE-11(3), March 1985, 285–302.

Thimbleby, H. (1986). Experiences of 'Literate Programming' Using Cweb (a variant of Knuth's WEB). *The Computer Journal* 29(3), 201–211.

Tichy, W.F. (1982). Design, Implementation, and Evaluation of a Revision Control System. *Proceedings of the Sixth International Conference on Software Engineering*, IEEE Computer Society, Tokyo.

Tufte, E.R. (1983). *The Visual Display of Quantitative Information*. Cheshire, Conn.: Graphics Press.

Walker, J. (1988). Supporting Document Development with Concordia. *IEEE Computer* 21(1), 48–59.

Wasserman, A.I. (1981). *Tutorial: Software Development Environments*, IEEE Computer Society Press.

Webster (1981). *Webster's Third New International Dictionary of the English Language*. Encyclopedia Britannica, Inc.

Weinberg, G.M. (1971). *The Psychology of Computer Programming*, New York: Van Nostrand Reinhold.

Weizenbaum, J. (1969). Eliza — A Computer Program for the Study of Natural Language Communication between Man and Machine, *Communications of the ACM* 9(1), 36–45.

Weizenbaum, J. (1986). *Computer Power and Human Reason*, San Francisco: W.H. Freeman.

Weiser, Mark (1987). Source Code. *IEEE Computer*, 20(11), 73.

White, J.V. (1988). *Graphic Design for the Electronic Age*. New York: Watson-Guptill Publications.

Wirth, N. (1971). Program Development by Stepwise Refinement, *Communications of the ACM* 14(4), April 1971, 221–227.

Wirth, N. (1977). Modula: A Language for Modular Multiprogramming. *Software — Practice and Experience* 7(1), January 1977, 3–35.

Wortman, L.A. and Sidebottom, T.O. (1984). *The C Programming Tutor*, Robert J. Brady Co., 139–141.

Wright, P. (1977). Presenting Technical Information: A Survey of Research Findings. *Instructional Science* 6(2), 93–134.

Wright, P. (1978). Feeding the Information Eaters: Suggestions for Integrating Pure and Applied Research on Language Comprehension. *Instructional Science* 7(3), 249–312.

Wright, P. and Reid, F. (1973). Written Information: Some Alternatives to Prose for Expressing the Outcomes of Complex Contingencies. *Journal of Applied Psychology* 57(2), 160–166.

Yankelovich, N., Haan, B.J., Meyrowitz, N.K., and Drucker, S.M. (1988). Intermedia: The Concept and the Construction of a Seamless Information Environment. *IEEE Computer* 21(1), 81–96.

Yourdon, E. (1979). *Structured Walkthroughs*, Englewood Cliffs, N.J.: Prentice-Hall.

Appendix B

Taxonomy of Visible Language

The following Appendix presents selected visual examples of typical distinctions in the appearance of typographic and illustrated printed documents. The selection is not intended to be comprehensive, nor is it rigorously organized. It is intended as a practical compendium of relevant possibilities for the display of code, comments, and program publications. For further visual examples see Dondis (1973), Maier (1977), Gerstner (1978), Rosen (1976), Ruder (1977), Müller-Brockman (1981), Miles (1987), International Paper Company (1987), White (1988), Rubinstein (1988), and current Letraset™ or similar commercial catalogues. The general categories are:

Page characteristics
Page composition and layout
Typographic vocabulary
Typesetting
Symbolism
Color and texture

The specific categories are the following. Numbers in square brackets indicate figure numbers.

Page characteristics
  Page size and proportion
    American [B.1]
      Letterhead: 8.5″ x 11″
      Legal: 8.5″ x 14″
      Hardcover book: 6″ x 9″
      Softcover book: 4.25″ x 6.875″
      Half-letterhead horizontal: 5.5″ x 8.5″
      Half-letterhead vertical: 4.25″ x 11″
    European [B.1]
      A0 to A7 sizes
        Example: A4 = 8.25″ x 11.75″
    Alternative proportions [B.2]
      Square: 1:1
      CRT or video screen: 1:1.33
      Square root of 2: 1:1.414
      Photographic slide: 1:1.5
      Golden rectangle: 1:1.618
      Double square: 1:2

Page orientation
  Horizontal
  Vertical
Paper properties
  Weight (affects storage)
  Caliper (thickness)
  Bulk (affects thickness and folding)
  Grain direction (affects folding)
  Color (affects legibility of type)
  Opacity (affects page translucency
    and type show-through)
  Surface texture (affects clarity
    of reproduction)
  Coating (affects printed color)
  Strength (affects durability)
Binding [B.3]
  Sewn, perfect, side-stitched or
    saddle-stitched
  Three-ring notebook
  Plastic or metal spiral ring
  Plastic strip

Page composition and layout
  Grid [B.4]
    Symmetric
    Asymmetric
    Reflected about binding
    Translated about binding
  Layout [B.5]
    Primary text
      One primary column
      One primary column
        with secondary column
      Two primary columns
      Two primary columns
        with secondary column
      Three primary columns
    Secondary features
      Graphics
      Tables and lists
      Pagination, folio
      Field corners and outlines
      Edge of field indicators
      Headers
      Footers
    Example: Newsletter page [B.5]

American paper sizes

Standard trimmed page size in inches	Number of pages in a signature	Number of signatures from paper sheet	Standard paper sheet size in inches
5 1/2 x 8 1/2	4	16	35 x 45
	8	8	35 x 45
	16	4	35 x 45
	32	2	35 x 45
6 x 9	4	8	25 x 38
	8	4	25 x 38
	16	2	25 x 38
	32	2	38 x 50
8 1/2 x 11	4	4	23 x 35
	8	2	23 x 35
	16	2	35 x 45
9 x 12	4	4	25 x 38
	8	2	25 x 38
	16	2	38 x 50

European paper sizes

Standard trimmed page Size in millimeters	Name of size (A sizes)	Standard paper size in inches
841 x 1189	A0	33 1/8 x 46 3/4
594 x 841	A1	23 3/8 x 33 1/8
420 x 596	A2	16 1/2 x 23 3/8
297 x 420	A3	11 3/4 x 16 1/2
210 x 297	A4	8 1/4 x 11 3/4
148 x 210	A5	5 7/8 x 8 1/4

Figure B.1: *Selected typical American and European page sizes derived from single printed paper sheets.*

The table shows typical sizes for the final page size of books, or booklets, together with supplementary information, such as the number of printed pages in a signature (a folded, trimmed set of pages printed from a single large sheet of paper), the number of signatures cut from a single large sheet of paper, and the original size of the standard large sheets of paper.

The size of the original large sheet of paper, and the number of pages in a signature resulting from multiple folds of the sheet, determines economical page sizes in the printing process.

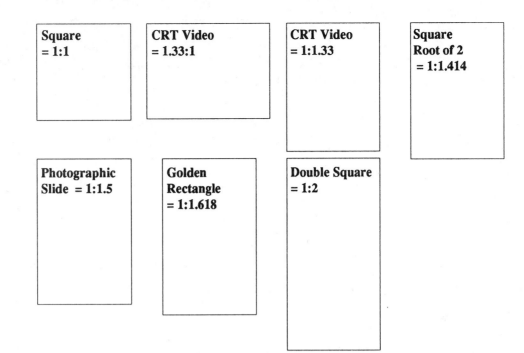

Figure B.2: *Alternative proportions of pages and screens.*

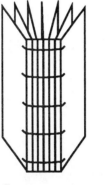 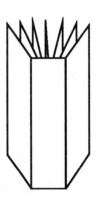 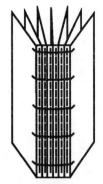

Sewn   **Side stitched**   **Perfect**   **Saddle stitched**

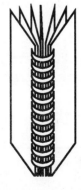

Spiral   **Three ring**

Figure B.3: *Book bindings.*

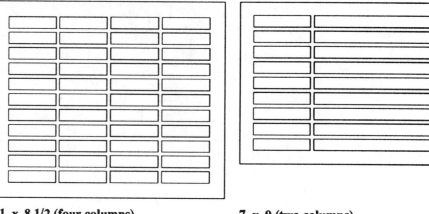

11 x 8 1/2 (four columns)   **7 x 9 (two columns)**

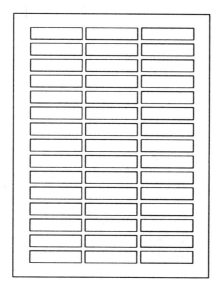

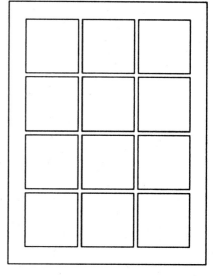

8 1/2 x 11 (three columns)   **8 1/2 x 11 (three columns)**

Figure B.4: *Layout grids within various page sizes.*

Horizontal and vertical lines of a layout grid within the page area organize columns of text, illustrations, and other annotation, such as page numbers, running heads, footnotes, marginalia, etc. The grid elements provide a basis for overall consistency of layout but also enable the varying amounts and types of contents to appear in flexible, attractive pages. The enclosed rectangular areas suggest modules for location, size, and proportion of figures.

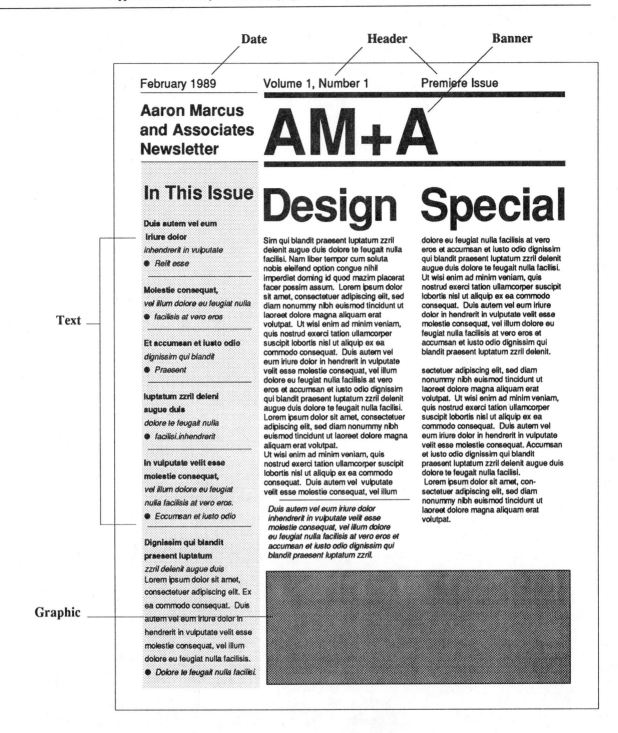

Figure B.5: *Typical page layout with primary and secondary features.*

Typographic vocabulary
  Character set of font
    Alphanumeric (ASCII) set
      Roman
      Greek
      Cyrillic
      Chinese
      Japanese
      Hebrew
      Arabic
    Case
      Upper
      Lower
      Mixed
      Initial capitals
      Small caps
    Supplementary characters
      Punctuation
      Foreign accents
      Mathematics [B.6]
      Special symbols [B.6]
  Spatial resolution [B.7]
    Low resolution dot matrix
      Example: 5 x 7, 7 x 9, 10 x 14
    Medium resolution: 80–300 dots-per-inch
    High resolution: above 600 dots-per-inch
  Typeface or style of lettering [B.8]
    Old Style
      Example: Garamond
    Modern
      Example: Bodoni
    Transitional
      Example: Baskerville
    Egyptian (square serif)
      Example: Clarendon
    Contemporary (serif)
      Example: Times Roman
    Contemporary (sans-serif)
      Example: Helvetica
    Script
      Example: Commercial
      Example: Chancery cursive
    Fixed-width
      Example: Courier
    Special
      Example: OCR-B
        (Optical character recognition)

  Size [B.9]
    Primary (display) sizes: 16–72 point
    Secondary (main text) sizes: 8–14 point
    Tertiary sizes: 4–8 points
      Examples:
        Marginalia
        Footnotes
        Annotation
        Sub/superscripts
  Weight [B.10]
    Light
    Normal
    Medium (semi-bold)
    Bold
    Extra bold
  Proportion [B.11]
    Condensed
    Normal
    Extended
  Slant [B.12]
    Roman
    Italic
    Reverse italic
  Orientation [B.13]
    Horizontal
    Vertical
    Angled: 30, 45, 60 degrees
  Special conditions [B.14]
    Reversed figure-field
    Textured
    Outlined
    Shadow
    Decorated
    Distorted
    Disjointed
    Mutilated
    Foreshortened

Typesetting
  Words
    Orientation [B.15]
      Horizontal
      Vertical (top to bottom,
        bottom to top)
      Angular: 30, 45, 60 degrees
      Curvilinear

Math Symbols

≐ = ! @ # $ % ˘ & * ( ) _ + ≠ ÷ ∑ ∈ ≅ ∴

⊆ ∪ ≡ → ‖ [ ] ⇔ ⊡ ⊄ ⇄ △ ↓ ↑ ∞ ⊢ ⊥ { } ≐ ∵ ≕ ⌐

⠒ ∩ ≠ ⊻ ± ; ' ∀ ‰ ∂ ∫ ∨ ∧ ¬ ⅄ ▱ ∶ " ◢ ⁀ ◎ ⊸

↝ ↜ ↦ ♪ ∅ △ ‶ ' ◇ ∠ ° ∿ ∫ ℵ ∇ , . / ⟨ ⟩ ?

⚑ ⚐ ⌢ ⌢ ⚑ ⊙ ≤ ≥ ÷ ´ \ ~ |

Special Symbols

¡ ™ £ ¢ ∞ § ¶ • ª º – ≠ ≠ Œ „ ‰ Â Ê Á Ë È Ø

∏ " ' Å Í Î Ï Ì Ó Ô Ò … Æ ' « ≤ ≥ ÷ Û Ù Ç

◊ ı ˆ ˜ ≤ ≥ ÷ ! @ # $ % ^ & * ( ) _ + { } : "

< > ? ~ |

Figure B.6: *Mathematical and special symbols.*

Figure B.7: *Low, medium, and high resolution characters.*

Avante Garde

This illustration shows different typographic styles. Type style is an important design consideration and helps give an overall look to the document.

Garamond

This illustration shows different typographic styles. Type style is an important design consideration and helps give an overall look to the document.

Bookman

This illustration shows different typographic styles. Type style is an important design consideration and helps give an overall look to the document.

Helvetica

This illustration shows different typographic styles. Type style is an important design consideration and helps give an overall look to the document.

Courier (fixed width serif typeface)

```
This illustration shows
different typographic styles.
Type style is an important
design consideration and
helps give an overall look to
the document.
```

Palatino

This illustration shows different typographic styles. Type style is an important design consideration and helps give an overall look to the document.

Futura

This illustration shows different typographic styles. Type style is an important design consideration and helps give an overall look to the document.

Times

This illustration shows different typographic styles. Type style is an important design consideration and helps give an overall look to the document.

Figure B.8: *Variable-width serif and sans-serif typefaces and a fixed-width serif typeface.*

Typical text sizes

5-point type
6-point type
7-point type
8-point type
9-point type
10-point type
11-point type
12-point type
14-point type
16-point type

Typical display sizes

18-point type
20-point type
24-point type
30-point type
36-point type
42-point type
48-point type
60-point type
72-point type

Figure B.9: *Commonly used type sizes.*

Light
Regular
Bold
Extrabold

Figure B.10: *Common variations in type weight.*

Condensed
Regular
Extended

Figure B.11: *Common variations in type proportion.*

Roman
Italic

Figure B.12: *The two most common typographic slants.*

Figure B.13: *Common orientations of individual typographic characters.*

Figure B.14: *Special conditions of individual typographic characters.*

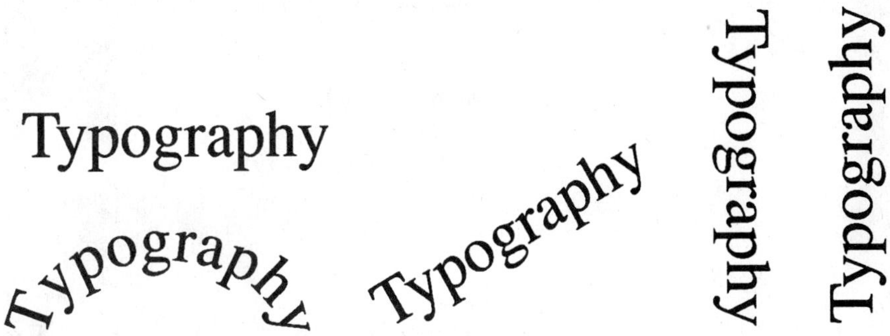

Figure B.15: *Common orientations of a word.*

Typesetting (continued)
  Words (continued)
    Letterspacing [B.16]
      Loose
      Normal
      Tight
      Kerned [B.17]
      Overlapping
    Special kinds of words
      Titles
      Labels, tables [B.18]
      Captions
      Notes
      Superscripts [B.19]
      Subscripts [B.19]
      Footnote content
      Marginalia
      Initial capitals [B.20]
  Lines
    Orientation [B.21]
      Horizontal
      Vertical
      Angled: 30, 45, 60 degrees
      Curvilinear
    Wordspacing [B.22]
      Tight
      Normal
      Loose
    Justification
      Justified right and left [B.23]
      Flush left, ragged right [B.24]
      Flush right, ragged left [B.25]
      Centered [B.26]
    Emphasis
      Indentation
      Exdentation
      Bullets
      Boxes
      Ruled lines
    Line length and line breaks
      Hyphenation
    Linespacing (leading) [B.27]
      Solid
      1 point
      2 points
      3 points
    Special kinds of lines [B.28]
      Text lines
      Titles

      Subtitles
       List, table headings
      Running heads
      Running footers
      Footnotes
      Labels
      Captions
      Notes
      Sentences
      Phrases
      Highlighted text
  Paragraphs
    Orientation [B.29]
      Horizontal
      Vertical
      Angled: 30, 45, 60 degrees
    Justification (see Line) [B.23-B.26]
    Emphasis [B.30]
      Indentation
      Exdentation
      Linespace
      Bullet
      Boxes
      Ruled lines
      Emboldened type
      Enlarged type
      Reduced type
      Italicized type
      Combinations
    Depth
      Column length
      Column breaking
      Page breaking
    Special kinds of paragraphs
      Main text body
      Marginalia
      Captions
      Footnotes
      Page edge notes
      Bibliographic references
      Comments
    Lists and tables
      Single column
      Multi-column
      Row labels
      Column labels
    Forms
      Simple
      Complex

-4 Units	Letterspacing is variable and can be adjusted.
-3 Units	Letterspacing is variable and can be adjusted.
-2 Units	Letterspacing is variable and can be adjusted.
-1 Unit	Letterspacing is variable and can be adjusted.
-.5 Unit	Letterspacing is variable and can be adjusted.
Normal	Letterspacing is variable and can be adjusted.
+.5 Unit	Letterspacing is variable and can be adjusted.
+1 Unit	Letterspacing is variable and can be adjusted.
+2 Units	Letterspacing is variable and can be adjusted.
+3 Units	Letterspacing is variable and can be adjusted.
+4 Units	Letterspacing is variable and can be adjusted.

Figure B.16: *Common letterspacing in 100ths-of-em-units.*

Normal kerning	AV	Te	Yo	Y.
Kerned 3 units	AV	Te	Yo	Y.
Kerned 6 units	AV	Te	Yo	Y.
Kerned 9 units	AV	Te	Yo	Y.
Kerned 12 units	AV	Te	Yo	Y.
Kerned 15 units	AV	Te	Yo	Y.

Figure B.17: *Kerning in 100ths-of-em-units.*

C Construct	Typeface	Size/Leading
Marginalia comments	TR	8/12
All other comments	TR	10/12
Punctuation marks	HR	10/12
Preprocessor command names	HB	10/12
Macro names	HR	8-10/12
Reserved words	HI	10/12
Structure tags	HI	10/12
Defined types	HI	10/12
Global variables	HB	10/12
Other variables	HR	10/12
Function names in their definitions	HB	14/16
Other instances of functions names	HR	10/12
Other identifiers	HR	10/12
String constants	HR	8/12
Other constants	HR	10/12
File names	HB	18/21
Headers to program pages	TR	8/9
Footnotes to program pages	HR/HB	8/9

Figure B.18: *A table*.

The number at the end of this phrase is in superscript[123]
The number at the end of this phrase is in subscript[123]

Figure B.19: *Superscripts and subscripts.*

Drop intitials are set into the text, requiring that a number of lines be indented. Some phototypesetting machines have the capacity to set drop initials in position., others do not, in which case the text is set with the proper indent and the initials are set separately and stripped in later.

Raised initials represent the simplest and least-expensive method of setting display initials, especially if the typeface and typesize can be mixed on-machine.

Figure B.20: *Initial capitals.*

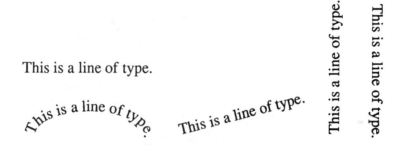

Figure B.21: *Common orientations of a line of text.*

-40 units	Wordspacingisvariableandcanbeadjusted.
-20 units	Wordspacingisvariableandcanbeadjusted.
0 units	Wordspacing is variable and can be adjusted.
+20 units	Wordspacing is variable and can be adjusted.
+40 units	Wordspacing is variable and can be adjusted.

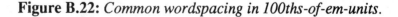

Figure B.22: *Common wordspacing in 100ths-of-em-units.*

Type set with all lines the same length and aligning on both the left and the right is referred to as justified type. In order to make the lines equal, the wordspacing is adjusted so that each line fills the entire measure. Because the number of words in each line varies, the wordspacing also varies from line to line. This uneven wordspacing, necessary to justify lines of type, is not noticeable if the type is properly set.

Figure B.23: *Justified type.*

Type set with lines of varying length and even wordspacing is referred to as unjustified type. If the lines of type align on the left, they will be ragged on the right. This arrangement is referred to as flush left, ragged right. Type can also be set flush right, ragged left. There are three major advantages to unjustified type. First, the even wordspacing creates a uniform overall texture. Second, it is ideal for setting type in narrow columns, and third, it reduces hyphenation to a minimum.

Figure B.24: *Flush left, ragged right type.*

Type set with lines of varying length and even wordspacing is referred to as unjustified type. If the lines of type align on the left, they will be ragged on the right. This arrangement is referred to as flush left, ragged right. Type can also be set flush right, ragged left. There are three major advantages to unjustified type. First, the even wordspacing creates a uniform overall texture. Second, it is ideal for setting type in narrow columns, and third, it reduces hyphenation to a minimum

Figure B.25: *Flush right, ragged left type.*

Another way to arrange lines of type is to center the lines on the page. Centered type, like unjustified type, has the advantage of even wordspacing. When using centered type, make sure the length of the lines varies enough to create an interesting silhouette. To control the shape of the setting, give the typesetter a minimum and maximum line length. Reading centered lines can be demanding, therefore centered type is better suited to small amounts of copy.

Figure B.26: *Centered type.*

Solid	Appearance. Linespacing affects the appearance of the printed piece. The more white space between the lines, the grayer the block of type. Conversely, the less white space, the blacker the printed piece will appear.
1 point linespacing	Appearance. Linespacing affects the appearance of the printed piece. The more white space between the lines, the grayer the block of type. Conversely, the less white space, the blacker the printed piece will appear.
3 point linespacing	Appearance. Linespacing affects the appearance of the printed piece. The more white space between the lines, the grayer the block of type. Conversely, the less white space, the blacker the printed piece will appear.

Figure B.27: *Common variations in linespacing.*

Figure B.28: *Typical page with varying typographic and line treatments.*

This shows common orientations of a paragraph. The orientations are horizontal, vertical moving up or down, and diagonal. The horizontal orientation is, of course, the most common and legible.

This shows common orientations of a paragraph. The orientations are horizontal, vertical moving up or down, and diagonal. The horizontal orientation is, of course, the most common and legible.

This shows common orientations of a paragraph. The orientations are horizontal, vertical moving up or down, and diagonal. The horizontal orientation is, of course, the most common and legible.

This shows common orientations of a paragraph. The orientations are horizontal, vertical moving up or down, and diagonal. The horizontal orientation is, of course, the most common and legible.

Figure B.29: *Common variations of paragraph orientation.*

This illustration shows the most common methods to emphasize a portion of a paragraph. *There are a variety of possible methods*. The choice is a matter of stylistic consideration for the designer.

This illustration shows the most common methods to emphasize a portion of a paragraph. **There are a variety of possible methods**. The choice is a matter of stylistic consideration for the designer.

This illustration shows the most common methods to emphasize a portion of a paragraph.

There are a variety of possible methods.

The choice is a matter of stylistic consideration for the designer.

This illustration shows the most common methods to emphasize a portion of a paragraph.

  There are a variety of possible methods.

The choice is a matter of stylistic consideration for the designer.

This illustration shows the most common methods to emphasize a portion of a paragraph.

- There are a variety of possible methods.

The choice is a matter of stylistic consideration for the designer.

This illustration shows the most common methods to emphasize a portion of a paragraph.

There are a variety of possible methods.

The choice is a matter of stylistic consideration for the designer.

Figure B.30: *Common means of emphasis in paragraphs.*

Symbolism
    Rules and leader lines [B.31]
    Pictograms and ideograms
        Bullets [B.32]
        Pi fonts [B.33]
        Boxes
    Figures
        Charts
        Maps
        Diagrams
        Illustrations
        Photographs
    Special kinds of symbols
        Display initials
        Delineation of zone or segment
        Folios (page, section,
            or chapter enumeration)
        Scientific or mathematical annotation

Color and texture [B.34]
    Hue
        Color on white/black
        White/black on color

        Color on color
        Polychrome on white/black
        White/black on polychrome
    Value [B.35]
        White on black
        Black on white
        Gray on white
        Black on gray
        Gray on gray
    Chroma
        Pure
        Dull
    Texture [B.36]
        Screen-tinted shapes and areas
        Textured shapes and areas
    Interaction [B.37]
        Brightness
        Contrast
        Harmony
            Monochrome
            Complementary
            Split complements
        Transparent overlap
        Translucent overlap

Dotted line	··
Scarser dots	· · · · · · · · · · · · · ·
Dash line	– – – – – – – – – – – – – – – – –
Larger dashes	— — — — — — — — — — — — —
Mixed dots and dashes	—·—·—·—·—·—·—·—·—
Hairline rule (.25 point)	———————————————
Fine rule (.5 point)	———————————————
1-point rule	———————————————
2-point rule	———————————————
3-point rule	———————————————
4-point rule	———————————————
5-point rule	———————————————
6-point rule	———————————————

Figure B.31: *Rules and leader lines.*

- 10-point Times Roman with small bullet.
- 10-point Times Roman with medium bullet.
- 10-point Times Roman with large bullet.
- ○ 10-point Times Roman with round outline bullet.
- □ 10-point Times Roman with square outline bullet.
- ■ 10-point Times Roman with square bullet.

Figure B.32: *Typographic bullets.*

Figure B.33: *Pi fonts and miscellaneous characters.*

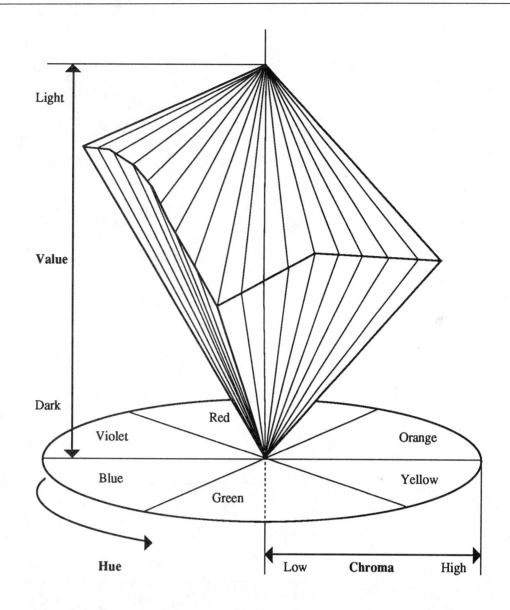

Figure B.34: *Color relationships.*

The three-dimensional model of colors depicted here is based on the Munsell system, which organizes colors along the axes of hue (the range of red, blue, green, etc.), value (the range of white to black), and chroma (the range of gray or dull to pure or highly saturated). Because of the characteristics of light-emitting and light-reflecting materials, and because of the physiological and perceptual characteristics of the light-sensitive rods and cones in the retina of the eye, the form of the bounding contour of visible colors in this scheme is not a regular solid.

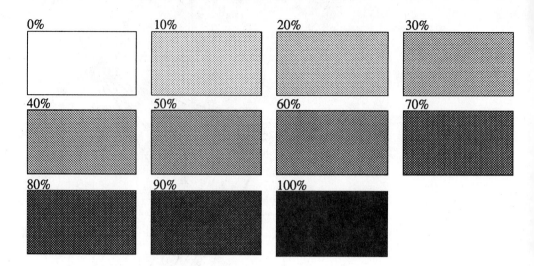

Figure B.35: *Variations of gray value.*

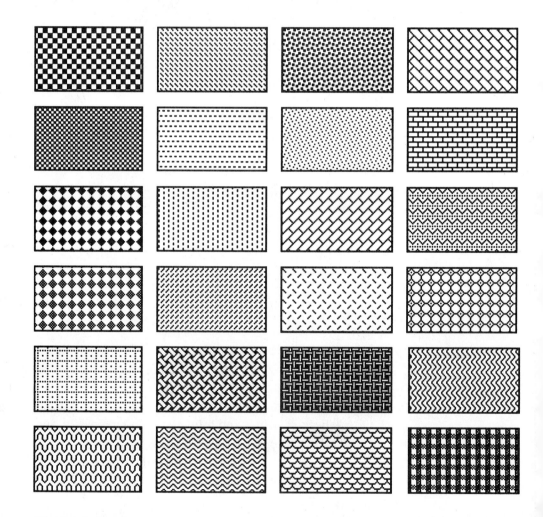

Figure B.36: *Textures.*

Adjacent hues

Varying values of a given hue

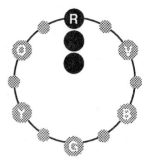

Varying chromas of a given hue

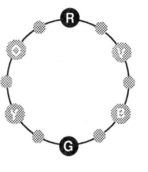

Opposing hues

Nearly opposing hues

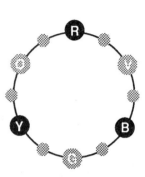

Equidistant hues

Figure B.37: *Color mixtures.*

These diagrams depict typical means of achieving clearly related sets of colors (left to right, top to bottom):

Adjacent hues: sections of the hue circle such as so-called warm colors (e.g., red-orange, red, red-violet) or cool colors (e.g., blue-violet, blue, blue-green).

Varying values of a given hue: so-called monochromatic colors (e.g., dark red, medium-value red, light red).

Varying chromas of a given hue: e.g., dull red, medium-chroma red, pure red.

Opposing hues: so-called complementary colors opposite each other on the hue circle (e.g., red, green).

Nearly opposing hues: so-called split-complementary colors comprising a hue and the two hues adjacent to its complement, e.g., red, blue-green, yellow-green.

Equidistant hues: so-called triadic colors equally spaced around the hue circle, e.g., red, blue, yellow.

An Essay on Comments

Appendix C

As discussed in Chapter 5, computer programs contain primary text, i.e., source code and comments, together with various secondary and tertiary text. This Appendix presents a discussion of the kinds of comments and commentaries that might accompany source code and of the visual appearance of such text.

Both comments and commentary have distinct characteristics. In current programming practice, comments sprinkled throughout the source code are text materials immediately and formally associated with the source code. In a sense the source code denotes the comments. Commentaries, on the other hand, have more far-ranging content with possible graphic materials that might explain, describe, and in other indirect and informal ways elaborate upon the significance of the code. In a sense, the source code connotes the commentaries. In this Appendix, the term *commentation* will refer to both kinds of text.

Mature program documents are likely to require diverse and extensive commentation. As program readership expands, levels of commentation may become oriented to different reader groups, e.g., lay or professional readers; or to frequency of reading, e.g., novice, occasional, or expert readers; or to reading objective, e.g., scanning, comparison, slow study, or leisure-time activity. The amount of commentation will probably increase, with more area of the page consequently required for its presentation.

In order to study further useful presentations of comments and commentary, it is helpful to construct a taxonomy of commentation. We conducted a preliminary study of such a taxonomy as an aid to our own investigation of program visualization. The study yielded an interesting set of possibilities for variations of content and form that secondary text may possess. In the sections that follow, we discuss these variations in terms of the semantic and syntactic relations between commentation and code. We begin by discussing the semantic dimension, because it is the content that visual appearance attributes must distinguish.

Semantics

As noted earlier in Section 3.1, semantics concerns the conceptual relationship between commentation and the source code to which it refers. Of particular importance in identifying semantic distinctions of commentation are these two questions: What is the referent, and what is the communication objective?

What is the Referent?

Attributes of semantics include the kind of source code entity, the level of importance, or the role of the referent. The referent may be any of the following scales of code contents:

An entire program: For example, a title page, major headline, or abstract refers to an entire program.

Parts or subparts of a program: For example, a subtitle may refer to an entire module or section of a program.

Function definition: The definition of a new function may require automatic generation of commentation identifying this component of the program.

Statement: Commentation may refer to one or more statements.

Expression: Commentation may refer to one or more expressions.

Token: Commentation may refer to one or more tokens.

Character or symbol: commentation may refer to one or more characters or symbols, e.g., a footnote may describe or explain an individual symbol.

What is the Communication Objective?

Another primary dimension that distinguishes commentation is the pedagogic (i.e., informative) or rhetorical (i.e., persuasive) motive of the authors in presenting the particular text or imagery. In general, the following kinds of commentation are found:

Identification: The reader's attention is called to the existence of a section of code.

Emphasis: Beyond prompting the reader to notice the existence of an item of code, the commentation calls attention to additional significance, e.g., age, status, or other characteristics.

Description: The commentation makes explicit more immediately intuitable attributes of a code item or fragment.

Explanation: The commentation clarifies the justification, function, or other less apparent attributes of a code item or fragment.

Amusement: For very long or difficult documents, it may be necessary to employ typical training or rhetorical strategies to relax, intrigue, jar, and/or even mystify the reader. Possible secondary text material includes: word and number games; crossword puzzles based on code words; dialogues (cf., those used by Plato or more recently by the philosopher Smullyan, 1983); jokes; cartoons; anecdotes (cf., in Donald Knuth's WEB programs, 1986a,b, he includes digressions of an historical or philosophical nature); epigrams (cf., in the characteristic page fillers of *Reader's Digest*); photographs or illustrations; and farcical statistics about the program in the style of Trivial Pursuit™ (e.g., how many function definitions are there?).

Summary and Review: The purpose of this material may be to reflect upon the preceding quantity of code or to review systematically the reader's progress. Such commentation may occur after small actions, function definitions, achievement of goals, module completion, or at the close of an entire program.

Announcements or Warnings: Such commentation would serve to inform the readers of recent changes, warnings, or cautionary remarks. For example, a portion of code that is not necessary for basic understanding of the program and/or that could confuse the mind of the reader could be indicated by a special symbol, color, or typographic treatment (e.g., reduced size of type) so that readers could be aware that they might safely skip over that portion of code.

Testing, Gaming, or Simulation: For long code documents, quizzes may be useful for readers to test their understanding of the program or diagnose potential areas of programming error during creation or interpretation stages of code development.

Measurement or Indexing: There are many possibilities for new metrics of program structure or process (see Section 5.5). Among items that might be indicated to the reader are: the program's or program section's fog index; its "hairiness"; its age/maturity; its degree of bugginess, or fragility; its suitability for novice or occasional or expert readers; or other items of interest such as those discussed in Section 5.5. Some indicators might be shown by means of a special illustration of the entire program that appears within a small section of a single page, as illustrated on page Ei/149, the Eliza title page. Some measurements or indices might appear as charts, maps, or diagrams at the beginning of or throughout the program (see Figures 5.7 through 5.10). They could become part of a standardized set of visual key indicators (see Figure C.1) that program builders, maintainers, and readers would examine before, during, and after program perusal. By means of these program signatures (see Section 5.5), readers would be able to grasp levels of significance that are currently hard to visualize, to verbalize, and consequently to comprehend and remember.

Analogies, Metaphors, Parables: For long and complex code, it may be advisable to present verbal or visual material that helps the reader to understand otherwise impenetrable code. Following the example of Talmudic Judaism, Zen Buddhism, and other religious disciplines, it is possible that certain tales could be interspersed with or otherwise accompany the code that could help the reader to grasp the fundamental ideas of the primary text. Such commentation might appear as pages that introduce sections of code or that interrupt the code in order to provide graphic and mental relief.

Informal Remarks: Commentation might appear as spontaneous graffiti generated by past readers. Such secondary text should be visually distinguishable from the official, or more formal secondary text of comments and commentaries. For example, such remarks could appear in freehand writing and sketches rather than typeset characters and technical illustrations.

Major branch

Warning/Sensitive

Added code

Deleted code

Dangerous

Most recent version

Halt in code

Fragile code

Buggy code

Bug free code

Well structured

Foggy code

Major loop

Unreachable Code

Incomprehensible

Obsolete code

Changed code

Sturdy code

Well-commented

Hairy code

Figure C.1: *Possible indicator signs for use in indexing code.*

Syntax

Syntax refers to how textual and graphic elements appear and are arranged within the page. The following brief categorization lists identify various modes by which secondary text material may be distinguished:

Typography aspects
   Typefont
      Typeset characters
      Typewritten characters
      Handwritten characters
   Size and column width
      Small, medium, large sizes
      Narrow, medium, wide columns
Extent
   Character or sign
   Word
   Single line
   Several lines
   Paragraph
   Multiple paragraphs
   Pages
Location
   Above
   Below
   Interspersed
   Left
   Right
Color
   Black-white, reverse video
   Gray values
   Monochromatic
   Polychromatic
Textual/graphic form
   Sign: symbol (ideogram),
      icon (pictogram)
   Text
   Table or form
   Chart
   Map
   Diagram
   Illustration
   Photograph (e.g., the authors)

Hierarchy of Comments

A generic page of textual comments might include the possibility for three levels of comments within three areas of the page: the main text area, the narrow column marginalia, and the footnote zone at the bottom of the page. The components of the comment hierarchy for the different areas might be the following:

Main column
   Titling
   Subtitling
   Comments
   Indented comments
Minor column
   Titling
   Subtitling
   Comments
   Indented comments
Footnotes
   Titling
   Subtitling
   Comments
   Indented comments

These areas are indicated schematically in Figure C.2.

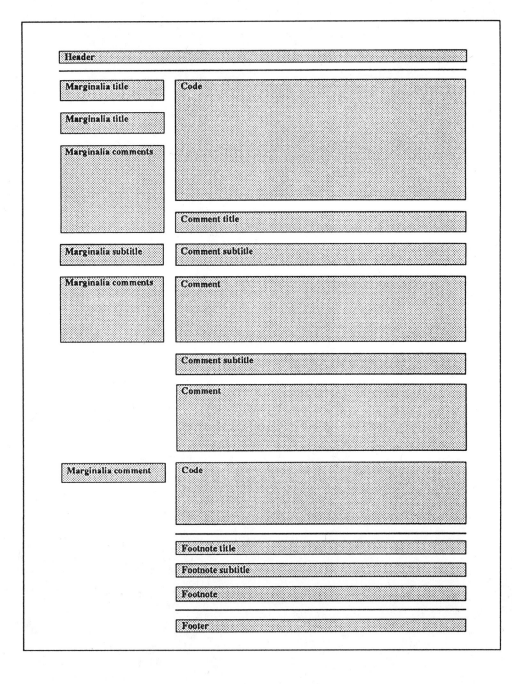

Figure C.2: *Typical zones of layout for code and comments.*

Appendix D
Graphic Design Specifications for C Programs

Section D.1
Program Structure

Definition: A C program consists of one or more source files. Each source file contains some part of the entire program, typically one or more *top level declarations*. Top level declarations can be either declarations or definitions of either identifiers or functions. A declaration (see Section D.4) is a statement that you will use an object that is defined elsewhere. A definition is the statement that actually "creates" the object (see Section D.3 on Function Definitions and Section D.4 on Declarations). Interspersed among lines of C code proper are comments (see Section D.2) and preprocessor commands (see Section D.5).

The function *main* must be defined in one of the program source files. It is the first function called when the program is started.

Format: Harbison and Steele (1984), Section 1.2. Throughout the remainder of the chapter, such references will be abbreviated as follows: H and S (1984).

Specification: The listing for each source file begins on a new page. The file name appears as a chapter title in 18 point Helvetica bold, regular. Underneath the file name is a 6-point rule 31 picas long.

Specifications for function definitions and identifier declarations appear in Sections D.3 and D.4, respectively.

Two blank lines of vertical white space are introduced at every transition between top-level declarations and function definitions, and between each pair of function definitions.

The programmer's blocking of code into logical sections is preserved. Two consecutive newlines, i.e., a blank line, is considered as a request for a half blank line of white space in the typeset output.

A formfeed character is taken to mean a request for a new page. If possible, SEE avoids breaking a page in the middle of a comment, function header, type definition, or structure definition.

Footnotes are used to assist with navigation among files. On a page where a global or a file static variable is defined, a footnote lists the identifier followed by a forward-pointing arrow followed by the page numbers of every location of a reference to that variable. On a page where a reference occurs, a footnote lists the identifier followed by a backward-pointing arrow followed by the page number of the location of the variable definition. Global variables appear in 8/9-point Helvetica Bold, roman. File static variables appear in 8/9-point Helvetica Regular, roman. Page numbers appear in 8/9-point Times Roman Regular, roman.

Example and Depiction: See Eliza program book.

Section D.2

Comments

Definition: Comments are ignored by C language processors, but are often an important part of the C program for the human reader. They express, it is hoped in plain English, what some portion of the program is intended to do, design decisions made in developing the program, or essential notes for program maintenance.

Format: H and S (1984), Section 2.2.

Specification: See the specifications in the following sub-sections.

Notes: It is possible to characterize and distinguish comments along a number of dimensions of variation (see Appendix C) and to display these distinctions with different methods of presentation. Currently, we make only four distinctions, shown in the following four sub-sections.

Prologue Comments

Definition: A *prologue comment* is a descriptive or narrative comment that appears at the beginning of a C file.

Specification: A prologue comment appears as one or more lines of text in the main program text column. Text is set at 10/12-point Times Roman Regular, roman, upper- and lowercase, normal letterspacing, 3-to-the-em wordspacing. The text is set inside and over a 10% rectangular gray screen tint area.

Notes: Instead of using the gray screen tint area, the comment can be separated from the code by surrounding it with a hairline-rule box (see Figure 3.7).

Example and Depiction: See Eliza program book, beginning of each file.

External Comments

Definition: An *external comment* is a descriptive or narrative comment that appears on its own line outside of a C function definition.

Specification: An external comment appears as one or more lines of text in the main program text column. Text is set at 10/12-point Times Roman Regular, roman, upper- and lowercase, normal letterspacing, 3-to-the-em wordspacing. The text is set

inside and over a 10% rectangular gray screen tint area.

Notes: Instead of using the gray screen tint area, the comment can be separated from the code by surrounding it with a hairline-rule box (see Figure 3.7).

Example and Depiction: See Eliza program book.

Internal Comments

Definition: An *internal comment* is a descriptive or narrative comment that appears on its own line inside of a function definition.

Specification: An internal comment appears as one or more lines of text in the main program text column. Text is set at 10/12-point Times Roman Regular, roman, upper- and lowercase, normal letterspacing, 3-to-the-em wordspacing. The text is set inside and over a 10% rectangular gray screen tint area. The comments and gray area are indented to the same level as the code in which they are embedded.

Notes: Instead of using the gray screen tint area, the comment can be separated from the code by surrounding it with hairline-rule brackets (see Figures 3.7 and 3.8).

Example and Depiction: See Eliza program book.

Marginalia Comments

Definition: A *marginalia comment* is a concise (usually one line) phrase that appears on the same line in the input text as the program source code to which it refers.

Specification: Marginalia comments reside in a dedicated margin area to the left of the primary text column. This text is set 8/12-point Times Roman Regular, roman, upper- and lowercase, normal letterspacing, 3-to-the-em wordspacing.

Notes: For reference to deeply indented source code, marginalia comments can be linked to the code to which they refer by use of rules (see Figure 3.9) or leader lines (see Figure 3.10).

Example and Depiction: See Eliza program book.

Section D.3

Function Definitions

Definition: A function definition is used to define a group of statements that conceptually form a separate complete action. The function can then be invoked (executed) as a single unit.

Format: H and S (1984), Chapter 9.

Specification: If a function definition does not terminate on the page on which it begins, an ellipsis (...) is introduced as the last line of code on that page. Its horizontal position indicates the nesting level of the code continuation on the next page. The control constructs in which this code continuation is embedded (the "nesting context") are shown in the header on the following page (see Figure 1.3).

The remainder of the specification appears in the following subsections.

Example and Depiction: See Eliza program book, pages E21/177, E23/179, and E25/181.

Static Functions

Definition: If the storage class specifier *static* is used in a function definition (as the first word in the definition) the function may not be referenced by other C files.

Format: H and S (1984), Section 9.1.

Specification: The storage class specifier is set in 10-point Helvetica Bold, roman, upper- and lowercase, normal letterspacing. It will appear on the line immediately preceding the line containing the function name, as the first token on the line.

Function Type Specifiers and Declarators

Definition: In a function definition, as in a declaration, the type of the function is determined by the type specifier and the declarator.

The type specifier gives the type of the value that the function will return when it is called. The declarator determines the function name, which can be any arbitrary identifier. The function name may be followed by a *formal parameter list*, which gives the names of each of the function's formal parameters, or arguments.

Format: H and S (1984), Section 9.2.

Specification: The type specifier is set in 10-point Helvetica Bold, roman, upper- and lowercase, normal letterspacing, separated from the storage class specifier (e.g., *static*), if it exists, by 3-to-the-em wordspacing. The type specifier is placed on the line immediately preceding the function name. Any extra declarator parts (generally the pointer symbol "*") are also placed on that line. The function name follows on the next line, flush to the margin, followed by its formal parameter list.

The function name is set in 14-point Helvetica Bold, roman, upper- and lowercase, normal letterspacing. The formal parameter list is set in 10-point Helvetica Regular, roman, upper- and lowercase, normal letterspacing. The function definition is underscored by a 1/2-point rule by 31 picas, which lies 4 points down from the baseline of the declarator to the top of the ruled line.

Formal Parameter Declarations

Definition: The formal parameter declarations give the names of each of the parameters to the function preceded by their types. When the function is called (or "invoked"), actual values must be supplied for each of these entries. The declarations specify the type expected for each of the parameters.

Format: H and S (1984), Section 9.3.

Specification: Formal parameter declarations (if any exist) are separated from the variables declared immediately upon entrance to the function compound statement by a hairline rule extending from 2 picas from the margin to the end of the text line. See also Section D.4 on Declarations.

Function Body

Definition: The function body is a compound statement that performs the work of the function when it is called.

Format: H and S (1984), Chapter 9.

Specification: 10/12-point Helvetica Regular, roman, upper- and lowercase, normal letterspacing, 3-to-the em wordspacing with 2-pica indentation levels.

Section D.4

Declaration of Identifiers

Definition: C allows identifiers to represent a number of possible objects. There exist a number of built in data *types*, each of which has a set of possible values and a set of operations on those values. As well, there are functions which can be executed and otherwise referred to. The *declaration statement* is used to associate an identifier with an object of a given type, and to perhaps define the object or give it a value. Declarations are constructed from:
• Storage class specifiers
• Type specifiers
• Declarators
• Initializers.

Format: H and S (1984), Sections 4.1–4.2.

Specification: See the specifications in the following subsections.

Storage Class Specifiers

Definition: Data items stored in different areas of a C program's memory have different properties. Storage classes specify these properties and also determine which portions of computer memory are used for which items of data.

Universe: A variable which is declared *auto* is newly created each time the compound statement that it is defined in is entered, and it is destroyed when the compound statement is exited. Note that a function body is just a compound statement.

A declaration of *extern* states that although this variable may be used in the current file or function, its actual definition occurs elsewhere. Therefore no storage is reserved for it here. A declaration of a variable to be *extern* does not actually create that variable. Instead it informs C that the variable is defined elsewhere as a *global variable* and that it will be used in the same context in which the *extern* declaration occurred (globally or in a compound statement). A global variable is a variable that is declared outside of any function without the storage class specifier *extern*.

The *register* storage class can be used in formal parameter declarations and in compound statement declarations to indicate that variables will be used frequently and should be allocated in registers or fast memory. Otherwise they have the same properties as *auto* variables.

A *static* declaration occurring outside any function bodies declares a global variable whose name will not be defined in any file but its own (normally a global variable's name is known everywhere in a program that it is part of). A *static* declaration occurring inside a compound statement declares a variable that will not be destroyed when the block is exited, and it will have its old value when the block is re-entered.

The storage class *typedef* is only that by courtesy: it is a statement for creating synonyms of C types.

Format: H and S (1984), Section 4.3.

Specification: The storage class specifier is set in 10-point Helvetica italic, upper- and lowercase, normal letterspacing. It is set flush left with respect to the main code column.

Example and Depiction: See Eliza program book, page E23/179.

Type Specifiers and Declarators

Definition: A *type specifier* declares the data type of the variables being declared. A *declarator* contains the name of the variable being declared, as well as modifiers to the basic type ("array of...," "pointer to...," "function returning...").

Format: H and S (1984), Sections 4.4–4.5.

Specification: The type specifier is set 10-point Helvetica Regular, italic, upper- and lowercase, normal letterspacing. The declarator is set in 10-point Helvetica Regular, roman, upper- and lowercase, normal letterspacing and is aligned flush left at the 16-pica tab stop.

Example and Depiction: See Eliza program book.

Integer Declarations

Definition: Integer data types are basic C types that are used to represent signed integer numbers. There are several sizes of integer, based on the largest number that can be represented. An integer type declarator may in most cases be preceeded by the modifier *unsigned* which will cause the computer to shift the range of the integer to store only positive values.

Universe: The following are the integer type declarators:

char　　　*short*　　　*int*　　　*long*

Format: H and S (1984), Section 5.2.

Specification: See under "Type Specifiers and Declarators."

Floating Point Declarations

Definition: Floating point variables are used to hold approximations to real numbers. The computer holds a fixed number of digits of precision and a limited range of exponent. Double precision floating point variables allow for more digits of precision and on some computers a wider range of exponent values.

Universe: The following are the floating point declarators:

float　　　*double*

Format: H and S (1984), Section 5.3.

Specification: See under "Type Specifiers and Declarators."

Pointer Declarations

Definition: A pointer variable is used to store the address of another variable in memory. The type of data to which it may point is specified in the declaration of the pointer.

Format: H and S (1984), Section 5.4.

Specification: See under "Type Specifiers and Declarators." The pointer declarator symbol "*" is set in 12-point Helvetica Regular, roman and is raised so that the top of the symbol aligns flush with the top of the capital-letter height of the source code.

Example and Depiction: See Eliza program book, page E28/184.

Array Declarations

Definition: An array is a collection of some other type where the individual members of the collection can be numerically selected (*indexed*).

Universe: A declaration for an array contains a set of square brackets in the declarator section of the declaration. The position of the brackets indicates exactly what kind of array is being declared, and they may contain a constant to indicate the size of the array. There may be more that one set of brackets in a declarator.

Format: H and S (1984), Section 5.5.

Specification: See under "Type Specifiers and Declarators." The brackets should be set in 10-point Helvetica Regular, roman, normal letterspacing.

Example and Depiction: See Eliza program book, page E28/184.

Enumeration Declarations

Definition: An enumeration is a type consisting of a set of values represented by identifiers called enumeration constants. The declarative keyword for enumerated types is *enum*.

Format: H and S (1984), Section 5.6.

Specification: The *enum* token is set in 10-point Helvetica italic, upper- and lowercase, normal letterspacing. The enumeration tag, enumeration constant, and declarators are set in 10-point Helvetica Regular, roman, upper- and lowercase, normal letterspacing. The enumeration constants are aligned flush left at tab stop 10. The declarator is aligned flush left at the 16-pica tab stop.

Example and Depiction: See Eliza program book, page E28/184.

Structure Declarations

Definition: A structure is a collection of data elements which are individually referred to by name, as structure members. Structures are used to bundle together conceptually related, but different, data.

Format: H and S (1984), Section 5.7.

Specification: The *struct* token, the structure tag, and the type specifiers of the components are set in 10-point Helvetica italic, upper- and lowercase, normal letterspacing. The structure components and the declarators are set in Helvetica Regular, roman, upper- and lowercase, normal letterspacing. The structure tag follows the *struct* token with 3-to-the-em wordspacing. The structure components are aligned flush left at tab stop 10. If there are embedded components of substructures, each outermost level is pushed 2 picas further to the right. The declarators are aligned flush left at the 16-pica tab stop.

Notes: Currently, structure definitions are set with braces in the usual way. These could be removed and replaced with systematic indentation and the use of enclosing brackets. For an example of the recommended style see Figure 3.30.

Example and Depiction: See Figures 3.26 and 3.30.

Union Declarations

Definition: A union is a single piece of data which may be accessed as more than one type. Unions are used for memory areas which will need to have different types of data stored in them at different points of a program's execution.

Format: H and S (1984), Section 5.8.

Specification: The specification is identical to that for "Structure Declarations."

Function Declarations

Definition: A *function* is a group of statements that conceptually form a separate complete action. Due to the nature of the compiler, if there is a reference to a function before the place in the file where is is defined, the compiler assumes that it is of type "function returning *int*." This will cause errors if it is of some other type. A function declaration is available to declare the type of a function before its actual definition. This facility is also used for non-integer functions defined in separate files or in the system library. See also Section D.3 on "Function Definitions."

Format: H and S (1984), Section 5.9.

Specification: See under "Type Specifiers and Declarators."

Example and Depiction: See Eliza program book.

Defined Types (Using *typedef*)

Definition: A *typedef* allows a C programmer to create a synonym for a type. They are frequently used for portability and modularity.

Format: H and S (1984), Section 5.11.

Specification: The *typedef* specifier is set in 10-point Helvetica Regular, italic, upper- and lowercase, normal letterspacing. The declarator is set in 10-point Helvetica Regular, roman, upper- and lowercase, normal letterspacing, and is aligned flush left at the 16-pica tab stop. Subsequent uses of the declarator once the type has been defined appear in 10-point Helvetica Regular, italic.

Example and Depiction: See Eliza program book, page E28/184.

Initializers

Definition: An initializer is an optional part of a variable declaration that assigns an initial value to the variable.

Format: H and S (1984), Section 4.6.

Specification: In general, the initializer is set in 10-point Helvetica Regular, roman, upper- and lowercase, normal letterspacing. This expression is set similar to other expressions (see Section D.7).

Notes: Initializers are surrounded by braces. The braces are used as syntactic sugar as well as to indicate hierarchy when initializing multi-dimensional arrays and structures. Formatting of initializers is controlled by the user through the inclusion of spaces, tabs (relative to tab stops set at 2-pica intervals), and carriage returns (linefeeds) appearing after the commas which follow individual initializer elements. SEE formats the output in such a way as to obey these controls.

Example and Depiction: See Figures 3.31 and 3.32.

Section D.5

The C Preprocessor

Definition: The C preprocessor is a simple macro processor whose semantics and operation are distinct from the actual C language processor itself. It is considered to be an integral part of C, though. It processes the source text of a C program before the compiler proper parses the source program and outputs its translation.

The C preprocessor performs expansion of macros, interpolation of other files (*file inclusion*), and selection of optional lines in the source file (*conditional compilation*). *Macro expansion* is performed upon any *macro names* encountered in the C program source. Macros may have parameters associated with them (see below).

Format: H and S (1984), Chapter 3.

Preprocessor Commands

Definition: A preprocessor command is a line beginning with a "#" that is executed by the preprocessor before the program is compiled.

Universe: The following are the preprocessor command names:

#define	#undef	#include	#if
#ifdef	#ifndef	#else	#endif

Format: H and S (1984), Section 3.1.

Specification: 10-point Helvetica Bold, roman, lowercase, normal letterspacing. The preprocessor statement should be shifted left, so that the preprocessor symbol is exdented to reside flush left in the 1-pica margin between the primary text column and the marginalia comment column. The preprocessor command name to the right of the "#" symbol should be aligned flush left with the left side of the primary text column.

Example and Depiction: See Eliza program book, page E20.

Simple Macro Definitions

Definition: Simple macro definitions allow constant values, small expressions, and (although it is considered poor style) arbitrary C constructs to be given names to make them more meaningful to the programmer.

Format: H and S (1984), Section 3.3.1.

Specification: By convention, macro names should be in uppercase only. The macro name is set in 8-point Helvetica Regular, roman, normal letterspacing, with the first character in 10-point type. The value of the macro name is set in 10-point Helvetica Regular, roman, normal letterspacing. The macro name is set flush left, ragged right, aligned at the 8-pica tab stop. The value is set flush left, ragged right, aligned at the 16-pica tab stop.

Notes: See page 84 and Figure 3.35 for a discussion of problems introduced by certain kinds of macros.

Example and Depiction: See Eliza program book, page E20/176.

Definitions of Macros with Parameters

Definition: Macros can also be defined with parameters. When macros are called, their arguments will be substituted for the parameters during macro expansion.

Format: H and S (1984), Section 3.3.2.

Specification: The macro name and its parameters are set in 10-point Helvetica Regular, roman, upper- and lowercase, normal letterspacing. The macro definition is set in 10-point Helvetica Bold, roman, upper- and lowercase, normal letterspacing. The macro name and its parameters are set flush left, ragged right, aligned at the 8-pica tab stop. The macro body is set flush left, ragged right, aligned at the 16-pica tab stop.

Notes: See page 84 and Figure 3.35 for a discussion of problems introduced by certain kinds of macros.

Example and Depiction: See Eliza program book, page E20/176.

File Inclusion

Definition: The file inclusion mechanism allows code from other files to be inserted into the current program. This is often used to include common declarations and macro definitions.

There are two ways of specifying include file names in an **#include** command. The file name is surrounded either by double quotation marks or by angle brackets. The difference is that the double quotation mark will search the local directory as well as the standard directories for the include file. The angle bracket form is most often used for including system files.

Format: H and S (1984), Section 3.4.

Specification: The names of the include files are set in 10-point Helvetica Regular, roman, upper- and lowercase, normal letter-spacing, flush left, ragged right, aligned at the 8-pica tab stop.

Example and Depiction: See Eliza program book, page E21/177.

Conditional Compilation

Definition: Conditional compilation allows several variations of a program to be kept in a single file. By defining various macros C code can be selected or rejected, depending on need. The conditional usually used is the **#ifdef** statement. If, and only if, the macro named by the identifier following the **#ifdef** part is defined at that point, the C program text between the statement and the next matching **#endif** statement is included into the compilation.

Universe: The following are the conditional compilation commands:
#if   #ifdef   #ifndef   #else
#endif

Format: H and S (1984), Section 3.5.

Specification: The macro name is set according to the rules given above.

Notes: See page 84 and Figure 3.36 for a discussion of problems introduced by the use of conditional compilation.

Example and Depiction: See Figure 3.36.

Section D.6

Statements

Definition: As in natural languages, statements in C are the basic units of thought that express actions upon objects. In C, statements are sequences of tokens (see Section D.8) and are normally terminated by semicolons.

Format: H and S (1984), Chapter 8.

Specification: 10-point Helvetica regular, roman, upper- and lowercase, normal letter-spacing with 2-pica indentation levels.

Lines are broken by an algorithm that tries to break at certain operators of low precedence, or at places where programmers have indicated break permission by entering a line break such as a carriage return (newline) in the input source text. See pages 90 and 133 and Figures 3.44 and 3.45.

Expression Statements

Definition: An expression statement is simply an expression that is terminated by a semicolon. An expression statement would be meaningless if it had no effect, so it usually contains some kind of assignment or procedure call. Assignment statements and procedure calls by themselves are expression statements.

Format: H and S (1984), Section 8.2.

Example and Depiction: See Figure 3.47.

Labeled Statements

Definition: A labeled statement is a statement prefixed with a *label* so that control may be transferred to it with a *goto* statement.

Format: H and S (1984), Section 8.3.

Specification: The label is set in 10-point Helvetica Regular, roman, exdented 2 picas from the current nest level.

Example and Depiction: See Figure 3.47.

Compound Statements

Definition: A compound statement (or *block*) is a number of statements grouped together between braces and treated as a single statement. This construct is used for two reasons. Many places in the C language allow only one statement, and the use of a block enables the programmer to perform an action that requires multiple statements. In addition, new identifiers that are not required elsewhere may be declared inside a block. Blocks may be nested within each other to any depth.

Format: H and S (1984), Section 8.4.

Notes: The braces have been removed, except in the case of "just-for-scope" blocks (see Figure 3.38). This is because rigorous, systematic indentation is sufficient to convey program hierarchy.

Example and Depiction: See Figure 3.38.

Conditional Statements

Definition: Conditional statements allow a decision to be made (based on a logical value) whether or not to execute a block of statements, or which of 2 blocks of statements to execute.

Format: H and S (1984), Section 8.5.

Specification: The statements of *if* and *else* parts are indented 2 picas.

Notes: The braces have been removed because rigorous, systematic indentation is sufficient to convey program hierarchy.

Example and Depiction: See Eliza program book.

Iterative Statements

Definition: *while* statements repeat a statement or compound statement (the *body*) as long as a logical expression has nonzero value. The expression is tested before the body is executed, so the body may never execute.

do statements are similar to *while* statements except that the test of the logical expression takes place after the body has been executed. The body is therefore always executed at least once.

for statements are a more generalized form of *while* statements which provide a handy way of specifying an initial (only happens once) action as well as an action that is performed after each execution of the body.

Format: H and S (1984), Section 8.6.

Specification: The statements comprising the body are indented 2 picas.

Notes: The braces have been removed because rigorous, systematic indentation is sufficient to convey program hierarchy.

Example and Depiction: See Eliza program book.

Switch Statements

Definition: A *switch* statement provides a mechanism for selecting one alternative action out of several, based on the value of an integer expression. *case* labels are used to indicate the various actions (which are statement lists) and the expression value that causes each action to be performed. As well, the special *default* case specifies an action to be performed if the expression does not match any of the *case* label values.

Format: H and S (1984), Section 8.7.

Specification: The *case* labels are set flush left with the *switch* token, and the statement lists are indented 2 picas.

Notes: The braces have been removed because rigorous, systematic indentation is sufficient to convey program hierarchy. An alternative format would be to indent the *case* labels 2 picas and the statement lists 4 picas.

Example and Depiction: See Figure 3.47.

Control Flow Altering Statements

Universe: A *break* statement is used to escape from the bounds of the immediately surrounding *while*, *do*, *for*, or *switch* statement.

A *continue* statement is used to skip over processing the current pass through a *while*, *do* or *for* statement and continue with the next repetition.

A *return* statement is used to exit from the current function and continue execution from where that function was called. A *return* statement may also supply the *return value* of the function. This is the value of the function if it is used in an expression.

A *goto* statement causes execution of the program to continue at the statement with the specified label.

Format: H and S (1984), Sections 8.8–8.10.

Notes: All suspicious and potentially dangerous control statements could be flagged in the visualized source with small symbols placed flush right in the marginalia column opposite the construct referred to (see Figure 3.47). One possible definition of "suspicious" control constructs includes every label, *continue*, and *goto*, any *break* not at the end of a *case*, any *case* that may fall through to the next *case*, and any *return* not at the end of a function definition.

Example and Depiction: See Eliza program book.

Null Statements

Definition: A null statement is a semicolon with no action preceding it.

Format: H and S (1984), Section 8.11.

Example and Depiction: See Eliza program book, page E27.

Section D.7

Expressions

Definition: New values can be calculated by combining constants and variables with a wide variety of operators to form expressions.

The *precedence* (priority or binding power) of an operator defines at what point it is evaluated when it is used in combination with other operators. Operators with higher precedence are evaluated first. Parentheses may be used to change or emphasize the default ordering.

Universe: Figure D.1 is a list of C operators and other expression elements. Operators are listed from highest to lowest precedence, with operators on the same line having equal precedence. Precedence values are given in the rightmost column. "L" and "R" indicate left associative and right associative operators, respectively.

Format: H and S (1984), Section 7.2.

Specification: A number of techniques are employed to enhance the readability of complex C expressions. Unary operators are raised and turned into superscripts. Additional space is added around binary operators to indicate the order in which subexpressions are evaluated. The two components of the conditional (ternary) operator, the "?" and the ":" are treated as binary operators. More details may be found in the appropriate specification subsections below.

Notes: See Section D.9 on Containment Symbols for notes on brackets and parentheses.

Example and Depiction: See Figures 3.48 through 3.53.

Primary Expressions

Definition: Primary expressions are conceptually the most basic ways of accessing values. They consist of using constants or variables directly, extracting single elements from arrays or structures, or performing function calls. When an expression is enclosed in parentheses, it is again considered to be a primary expression.

Universe:

Simple tokens	*identifiers*
	constants
Subscripting	a[k]
Function call	func()
Direct selection	.
Indirect selection	–>

Format: H and S (1984), Section 7.3.

Specification: Letterspacing should be normal and wordspacing should be 3-to-the-em.

Example and Depiction: See Eliza program book.

Unary Operator Expressions

Definition: Unary operators take only one argument.

Universe:

Postfix incr./decr.	++	––
Prefix incr./decr.	++	––
Size	*sizeof*	
Casts (type conv.)	(*type-name*)	
Bitwise not	~	
Logical not	!	
Arithmetic negation	–	
Address of	&	
Indirection	*	

Format: H and S (1984), Section 7.4.

Specification: All unary operators should be raised so that the top of the operator aligns flush with the top of the capital-letter height of the surrounding source code.

Notes: The increment (++) and decrement (––) operators are the only operators other than the assignment operators that can change the value of an identifier. They are also the only operators that can be placed after their operand. In this case they return the value of the operand before they perform the increment or decrement operation.

Example and Depiction: See Figure 3.49.

Primary Expressions

Simple tokens	identifiers/constants	16
Subscripting	a[k]	16
Function call	func()	16
Direct selection	.	16
Indirect selection	–>	16

Unary Operators

Postfix increment/decrement	++	––		15
Prefix increment/decrement	++	––		14
Size	*sizeof*			14
Casts (type conversion)	(*type-name*)			14
Bitwise not	~			14
Logical not	!			14
Arithmetic negation	–			14
Address of	&			14
Indirection	*			14

Binary and Ternary Operators

Multiplicative	*	/	%	13L
Additive	+	–		12L
Left and right shift	<<	>>		11L
Inequality	<	>	<=	10L
	>=			
Equality/inequality	==		!=	9L
Bitwise and	&			8L
Bitwise xor	^			7L
Bitwise or	|			6L
Logical and	&&			5L
Logical or	||			4L
Conditional (ternary)	? :			3R
Assignment	=	+=	–=	2R
	*=	/=	%=	
	<<=	>>=	&=	
	^=	|=		
Sequential evaluation	,			1L

Figure D.1: *C operators classified and listed in order of precedence.*

Binary Operator Expressions

Definition: Binary operators take two arguments and produce one result.

The multiplicative, additive, and shift operators consist of the arithmetic operations and the shift operations (which can be considered equivalent to multiplying numbers by powers of 2).

The relational and equality operators consist of the set of operations for comparing two numbers or expressions.

Bitwise operators treat their numeric operands as fixed-length sets of bits. The result is a sequence of bits produced by performing the given logical operation on each corresponding pair of bits.

The logical operators are used to write logical expressions.

Universe:

Multiplicative	*	/	%
Additive	+	−	
Left and right shift	<<	>>	
Inequality	<	>	<= >=
Equality/inequality	==	!=	
Bitwise and	&		
Bitwise xor	^		
Bitwise or	|		
Logical and	&&		
Logical or	||		

Format: H and S (1984), Sections 7.5–7.6.

Specification: The algorithm for adding space around binary operators in expressions works as follows: The lower the precedence of the operator, and the higher it occurs in the parse tree of the expression (i.e., closer to the root), the greater the space that is added. More specifically, space is added around binary operators based on the height of the taller of the left and right subtrees below the operator (Figure 3.52). The occurrence of parentheses in an expression resets the algorithm so that the parenthesized sub-expression acts as a leaf in the parent expression, and so that the algorithm begins anew on the sub-expression (Figure 3.51). Sequences of operators of identical precedence are treated as a single "n-ary" operator with identical spacing around each operator (Figure 3.51). Assuming no more than six levels of spacing to be added in an expression, these levels are 0 em, 0.2 em, 0.4 em, 0.6 em, 0.8 em, and 1.0 em (Figure 3.53). If more than six levels are required, which is almost inconceivable for reasonable C given the "parenthesis reset" and "n-ary operator" strategies just described, then the levels are scaled so that the largest space is 1.0 em.

Example and Depiction: See Figures 3.49 through 3.53.

Conditional Expressions

Definition: A conditional expression consists of three expressions. Depending upon the truth or falsehood of the first expression, the result is the value of either the second expression or the third expression.

Format: H and S (1984), Section 7.7.

Specification: Both the "?" and the ":" are treated as binary operators and set according to the specification given above.

Assignment Expressions

Definition: The assignment operators are short forms of an assignment statement of the form "*result = result op value*," where almost any binary operator can be substituted for *op*. Essentially an operation is performed on a variable and the result is stored back into the variable.

Universe:

=	+=	−=	*=
/=	%=	<<=	>>=
&=	^=	|=	

Format: H and S (1984), Section 7.8.

Specification: All the assignment operators are treated as low-priority binary operators and set according to the specification given above.

Sequential Expressions

Definition: The comma operator allows a sequence of operations to be performed where normally only one is allowed. The result of the comma operator is the right hand operand. This operation also guarantees left-to-right evaluation of its two operands.

Format: H and S (1984), Section 7.9.

Specification: The comma operator is treated as a low-priority binary operator.

Example and Depiction: See Eliza program book, page E33/189.

Section D.8

Tokens

Definition: *Tokens* are the "words" of the C language. We have separated out one special kind, punctuation tokens, which we cover in the next section. Ignoring punctuation, tokens may be:

- Reserved words
- Variables
- Other identifiers
- Constants.

Specification: The appearance of individual tokens is documented below and in Section D.9. In addition to any space attached to the token (see Section D.9), readability of pairs of tokens can be enhanced by adding more space between pairs of tokens from certain token classes.

When two symbols are to be placed next to each other, the space between them is adjusted based on an "after" attribute of the first (which affects space after the symbol) and a 'before' attribute of the second, according to the following algorithm:

- If the "after rank" (RA) of the first is greater than the "before rank" (RB) of the second, the "after spacing" (SA) of the first is used; otherwise,
- If the after rank of the first is less than the before rank of the second, the "before spacing" (SB) of the second is used; otherwise,
- The longer of the after spacing of the first and the before spacing of the second is used.

Ranks and spacings for token classes have been derived through an iterative design process, and are documented below. Spacings are in hundredths of an em.

Token Spacing	SB	RB	SA	RA
Const., misc. names	0	50	0	50
Non-decl. res. wds.	40	56	70	55
Open braces/bracks.	10	50	10	95
Close braces/bracks.	10	95	10	50
Misc punc., commas	0	50	0	50
N-space	20	50	20	50
Decl. res. words	40	55	50	50
Names and lexvals	50	10	50	10
For statement ";"	5	75	99	70
Open parenthesis	0	50	10	95
Close parenthesis	10	95	30	40
Semicolon	0	99	0	50
Selection ops	0	50	0	50
Unary operators	0	50	0	50
Binary operators	20	50	20	50
Conditional ops	20	50	20	50

Token Spacing	SB	RB	SA	RA
Assignment ops	20	50	20	50
Comma operator	20	50	20	50

Reserved Words

Definition: We distinguish five kinds of reserved words:

- Preprocessor reserved words (commands) (already discussed in Section D.5)
- Declarative reserved words
- Control reserved words
- Control flow altering reserved words
- The *sizeof* operator.

Specification: 10-point Helvetica Regular, italic, lowercase, normal letterspacing.

Example and Depiction: See Eliza program book.

Declarative Reserved Words

Definition: A declarative reserved word is a reserved word that is used in the declarations and definitions of C variables, functions, and types.

Universe:

auto	*char*	*double*	*enum*
extern	*float*	*int*	*long*
register	*short*	*static*	*struct*
typedef	*union*	*unsigned*	*void*

Format: H and S (1984), Section 2.6.

Control Reserved Words

Definition: A control reserved word is a reserved word naming a C control structure.

Universe:

case	*default*	*do*	*else*
for	*if*	*switch*	*while*

Format: H and S (1984), Section 2.6.

Control Flow Altering Reserved Words

Definition: A control flow altering reserved word is a reserved word that names a C statement used to specify control flow more complex than selection of blocks of statements and looping.

Universe:

break	*continue*	*goto*	*return*

Format: H and S (1984), Section 2.6.

The *Sizeof* Operator

Definition: The *sizeof* operator is used to obtain the size of a type or instance of a type.

Format: H and S (1984), Section 7.4.2.

Variables

Definition: A variable is a name that represents a data item or collection of data items within the computer. A variable is one kind of identifier in C. Other kinds are described in the following sub-section.

Universe: An identifier is a sequence of letters, digits, and underscores, not beginning with a digit and not having the same spelling as a reserved word.

Format: H and S (1984), Section 2.5.

Specification: See specifications in following sub-sections.

Global Variables

Definition: A global variable is a variable that is defined in all functions. Global variables typically are defined or declared by using the storage class *extern* (see Section D.4).

Specification: 10-point Helvetica Bold, roman, upper- and lowercase, normal letter-spacing.

Notes: Global variables are set in boldface to make them more readily apparent. This is done because a global variable is the secondary mechanism for inter-procedural dataflow (in addition to the primary one, the procedure parameter and result mechanism), and because the semantics of global variables is dangerous enough that it is valuable to highlight and call attention to them.

Example and Depiction: See Eliza program book.

File Static Variables

Definition: File static variables behave like global variables, but each variable is defined only within its C source file. They are declared by using the storage class *static* outside of any function definitions in the file (see Section D.4).

Specification: 10-point Helvetica Regular, roman, upper- and lowercase, normal letter-spacing.

Example and Depiction: See Eliza program book, page E28/184.

Local Variables

Definition: A local variable is a variable that is defined only within a given C function. Variables declared within function bodies not using the storage class *extern* are local. This includes those declared *auto*, *register*, and *static* within the function.

Automatic variables are local to a function and are initialized anew at each invocation of the function. A static variable (sometimes called a "function static") is local to a function but retains its value across instances of the function in which it is defined. Thus there is exactly one instance of a static variable, which is shared among recursive instances of the function.

The formal parameters of a function are local to the function.

Specification: 10-point Helvetica Regular, roman, upper- and lowercase, normal letter-spacing.

Example and Depiction: See Eliza program book.

Other Identifiers

Definition: Other identifiers appear in the C language as names for some C object, such as a function or a type. There are:
• Function names
• Typedef names
• Structure and union tags
• Structure and union member names
• Enumeration tags
• Enumeration constants
• Statement labels
• Preprocessor macro names (already discussed in Section D.5).

Universe: An identifier is a sequence of letters, digits, and underscores, not beginning with a digit and not having the same spelling as a reserved word.

Function Names

Definition: A function is an encapsulated section of a program. An identifier is used to name the function. Function names occur in general use and also in the definition of the function. Function names in definitions are handled according to the specification given in Section D.4. Function names in general use are set according to this specification. "General use" is defined as any reference to a function other than that in its definition.

Format: H and S (1984), Section 5.9 and Chapter 9.

Specification: 10-point Helvetica Regular, roman, upper- and lowercase, normal letterspacing.

Notes: A valuable variant is to typeset all function names in general use in boldface (see Figure 3.56, top). This adds in browsing and navigating through the code, and in familiarization with the way in which functions are defined in terms of other functions.

   Another option would be to distinguish typographically function calls from references to the address of a function.

Example and Depiction: See Eliza program book.

Typedef Names

Definition: A *typedef name* is a programmer defined synonym for a C data type. Every data object has a type, which determines the set of values this object can assume and the set of operations that may be applied to these values. See also Section D.4.

Format: H and S (1984), Section 5.11.

Specification: See Section D.4.

Example and Depiction: See Eliza program book, page E28/184.

Structure and Union Tags

Definition: A structure, called a *record* in some programming languages, is a collection of data elements which are treated as a single unit. The elements of a *struct* are called *members*. The name of a kind of structure is called a *structure tag*. A union, called a *variant record* in other languages, is a single data element which has multiple types (a union of types). The name of a kind of union is the *union tag*.

Format: H and S (1984), Sections 5.7–5.8.

Specification: 10-point Helvetica Regular, italic, upper- and lowercase, normal letterspacing.

Notes: See also Section D.4.

Example and Depiction: See Figures 3.26 and 3.30.

Structure and Union Member Names

Definition: The individual data elements of a structure and the various names for the single piece of data in a union are called *member names*.

Format: H and S (1984), Sections 5.7 and 5.8.

Specification: 10-point Helvetica Regular, roman, upper- and lowercase, normal letterspacing.

Notes: For further information, see Section D.4 on Declarations.

Example and Depiction: See Figures 3.26 and 3.30.

Enumeration Tags

Definition: An enumeration type is a type whose set of values is a finite, programmer-defined set. The name of an enumeration type is an identifier called the *enumeration tag*.

Format: H and S (1984), Section 5.6.

Specification: 10-point Helvetica Regular, roman, upper- and lowercase, normal letterspacing.

Notes: For further information, see Section D.4 on Declarations.

Example and Depiction: See Eliza program book, page E28/184.

Enumeration Constants

Definition: The values that can be assumed by an object of enumeration type are called *enumeration constants*.

Format: H and S (1984), Section 5.6.

Specification: 10-point Helvetica Regular, roman, upper- and lowercase, normal letterspacing.

Notes: For further information, see Section D.4 on Declarations.

Example and Depiction: See Eliza program book, page E28/184.

Statement Labels

Definition: A *label* is an identifier used to mark any statement so that control may be transferred to it by a *goto* statement.

Format: H and S (1984), Section 8.3.

Specification: 10-point Helvetica Regular, italic, upper- and lowercase, normal letterspacing.

Example and Depiction: See Figure 3.47.

Constants

A constant is a data item that represents an actual *value* of a particular data type. There are a number of different kinds of constants in C:
- Integer constants
- Floating point constants
- Character constants
- String constants.

Specification: See specifications in following subsections.

Integer Constants

Definition: An integer constant represents a specific integer value.

Universe: Integer constants may be specified in decimal, octal, or hexadecimal. As well, an integer may be given as a *long integer*, which some C systems may allow to be a larger number than the regular integer.

Format: H and S (1984), Section 2.7.1.

Specification: 10-point Helvetica Regular, roman, upper- or lowercase (alphabetic character), normal letterspacing.

Example and Depiction: See Eliza program book.

Floating Point Constants

Definition: A floating point constant represents an approximation to a real number in the form $m \times 10^e$ (scientific notation) where m is the mantissa and e is the exponent.

Universe: The possible formats of a floating point constant are:

$$d \qquad\qquad m\,E\,e$$

where m is a signed decimal number with optional decimal point and fraction or a signed integer, e is a signed integer, and d is a signed decimal number with decimal point and optional fraction. The case of the "E" is irrelevant.

Format: H and S (1984), Section 2.7.2.

Specification: 10-point Helvetica Regular, roman, upper- or lowercase (alphabetic character), normal letterspacing.

Example and Depiction: See Eliza program book.

Character Constants

Definition: A character constant represents the numeric value of a single character in the machines character set.

Universe: A character constant is a character enclosed in single quotes. Special names have been given to certain non-printing characters. These characters are obtained by preceding the name with a backslash. For example, '\n' is a *newline* and '\t' is a *tab*.

Format: H and S (1984), Section 2.7.3.

Specification: 10-point Times Roman Regular, roman, upper- or lowercase, normal letterspacing.

Example and Depiction: See Eliza program book.

String Constants

Definition: A string constant represents an array of characters followed by a *null* character in the computer's memory.

Universe: A string is a sequence of (zero or more) characters surrounded by double quotes. The same use of the backslash for representing special characters in character constants may also be used in strings.

Format: H and S (1984), Section 2.7.4.

Specification: 8-point Courier Regular, roman, upper- or lowercase, normal letterspacing. Wordspacing is determined by the blanks and tabs that appear in the string.

Example and Depiction: See Eliza program book.

Section D.9   **Punctuation Tokens**

Definition: We divide punctuation tokens into three groups:
- Separator symbols
- Containment symbols
- Operators.

Separator Symbols

Definition: Separator symbols are used to separate different items at the same syntactic level.

Universe:
A ";" (semicolon) is used to separate statements and declarations and the three components within a *for* statement.

A ":" (colon) is used after labels in labeled statements, after case labels in *switch* statements, and in conditional expressions.

A "," (comma) is used to separate items in declaration lists, formal parameter lists in function declarations, argument lists to function calls, and initializers. The comma is also the sequential evaluation operator.

Format: H and S (1984), Section 2.4.

Specification: Certain separators have special fonts (F) and point sizes (P) or have additional space (S) always inserted after them:

Symbol		F	P	S
;	all	HR	10p	———
:	cond. exp.	HB	10p	———
:	all other	HR	10p	———
,	declar.	HR	10p	———
,	functions	HR	14p	———
,	initializers	HR	14p	0.5em
,	seq. eval.	HB	10p	———

Example and Depiction: See Figures 3.60 and 3.61.

Containment Symbols

Definition: Containment symbols are tokens that "group" a set of tokens in some way.

Universe:
"(" and ")" (parentheses) are used around expressions and declarators to override precedence, to surround a function argument list, and in certain kinds of statements such as *if*'s and *for*'s.

"[" and "]" (brackets) are used to denote an array subscript.

"{" and "}" (braces, called *curly braces* by C programmers) are used to group statements into compound statements, and they are used to indicate the organizations of elements in structure declarations and initializers.

"<" and ">" (angle brackets) may enclose file names in an *#include* preprocessor command.

A " " " (double quotation mark) is used on either side of a string constant and is used to enclose file names in an *#include* preprocessor command.

" ' " (single quotation mark) is used to enclose a character constant.

Format: H and S (1984), Section 2.4.

Specification: Certain containment symbols have special fonts (F) and point sizes (P) or have additional space (S) always inserted before or after them:

Symbol		F	P	S
(	all	HR	10p	———
)	all	HR	10p	———
[	all	HR	10p	———
]	all	HR	10p	———
{	all	HR	10p	———
}	all	HR	10p	———
<	all	HR	10p	———
>	all	HR	10p	———
"	strings	CR	8p	———
"	all other	HR	10p	———
'	all	HR	10p	———

Parentheses should be set in three sizes only: 14 point, 12 point, and 10 point. In expressions containing nested parentheses, the innermost pair should be set in the smallest point size, and each successive pair going outwards should be set in a larger point size. If there are more than three pair, the third and each outermost pair should be set in 14-point type.

As was mentioned previously, in Section D.6 on Statements, we recommend that braces in statements usually be eliminated and be replaced with systematic indentation.

Example and Depiction: See Figures 3.60 and 3.61.

Operators

Definition: An operator is a punctuation token that represents some operation to be performed on an instance of a C data type. Operators, identifiers, constants and containment symbols are combined according to the grammar of C to form expressions. We distinguish two kinds of operators:
• Simple operators, which consist of single character
• Compound operators, which consist of multiple characters.

Format: H and S (1984), Section 2.4.

Specification: See specifications in following subsections.

Simple Operators

Definition: A simple operator is an operator consisting of a single character.

Universe:

```
!   %   ^   &   &   *   *   -
+   =   ~   |   .   <   >   /
?   :
```

Specification: Assuming that the first "&" is the "address of" operator, and the first "*" is the "indirection" operator, the appearance of simple operators should be the following:

```
!   %   ^   &   &   *   *   -
+   =   ~   |   .   <   >   /
?   :
```

This is achieved through the use of 10-point Helvetica Regular, roman, except as indicated in the following table. Idiosyncratic positioning of the symbols upwards or downwards is sometimes required.

Operator	Font	Size	Position
!	HB	10p	2p up
%	HR	10p	
^	HB	16p	7p down
&	HR	8p	2p up
&	HR	9p	
*	HR	12p	1p down
*	HR	10p	
–	HR	10p	
+	HR	10p	
=	HR	10p	
~	HB	14p	3p down
		HB	9p	0.5p up
.	HB	12p	

Operator	Font	Size	Position
<	HR	10p	
>	HR	10p	
/	HR	10p	
?	HNB	10p	
:	HB	12p	

Example and Depiction: See Figures 3.60 and 3.61.

Compound Operators

Definition: A compound operator is an operator formed from two or three characters.

Universe:

```
->   ++   --   <<   >>   <=   >=   ==
!=   &&   ||   +=   -=   *=   /=   %=
<<=  >>=  &=   ^=   |=
```

Specification: The appearance of compound operators should be the following:

```
->   ++   --   <<   >>   <=   >=   ==
!=   &&   ||   +=   -=   *=   /=   %=
<<=  >>=  &=   ^=   |=
```

This is achieved through the use of 10-point Helvetica Regular, roman, with 1 point of space between the operators, except as indicated in the following table:

Operator	Font	Size	Space
->	HR	10p	-3p
++	HR	8p	
--	HR	8p	1p
<<	HR	10p	-2p
>>	HR	10p	-2p
<=	HR	10p	-1p
>=	HR	10p	
==	HR	10p	
!=	HR	10p	-0.5p
&&	HR	9p	-0.5p
||	HB	9p	
+=	HR	10p	
-=	HR	10p	
*=	HR	10p	-1p
/=	HR	10p	-1p
%=	HR	10p	-0.5p
<<=	HR	10p	-1p
>>=	HR	10p	-0.5p
&=	HR	10p	-0.5p
^=	HR	10p	-0.5p
|=	HR	10p	-0.3p

Example and Depiction: See Figures 3.60 and 3.61.

Appendix E

Index

Appendix F

Discussion of Color Plates

The color examples shown on the inside front and back covers depict a fragment of C code that was previously shown at the bottom of Figure 3.58. The color design evolved from numerous trial prototypes.

We began by postulating multi-color assignments for token classes:

1 color	1) The entire program.
2 colors	1) Code. 2) Comments and preprocessor commands.
3 colors	1) Comments, preprocessor commands, strings.
	2) Reserved words. 3) All other tokens and punctuation.
4 colors	1) Comments, preprocessor commands, strings.
	2) Reserved words, defined types, structure tags, library functions.
	3) Functions, global variables. 4) Identifiers, macros, punctuation.
5 colors	1) Comments, strings. 2) Preprocessor commands.
	3) Reserved words, defined types, structure tags, library functions.
	4) Functions, global variables. 5) Identifiers, macros, punctuation.

In our first study of the use of color for typographic encoding, we chose a code sample to allow comparison with the series in Figures 3.54–3.58. It contains no preprocessor commands. We therefore experimented with four colors in the following manner:

Color 1	Defined and called functions, global variables
Color 2	Comments and strings
Color 3	Reserved words, defined types, structure tags, library functions
Color 4	Identifiers, macros, punctuation

Because red is the strongest and most noticeable color, we used it for color 1, to denote functions and global variables, the semantically most important components. We then experimented with variations in the choice and assignment of black, blue, and green to the other categories.

The two color plates (A: inside front cover; B: inside back cover) are based on the following color assignments:

Token class	A:Top	Middle	Bottom	B:Top	Middle	Bottom
Functions/globals	Red	Red	Red	Dark red	Red	Dark red
Comments/strings	Blue	Black	Black	Black	Black	Black
Reserved words...	Green	Blue	Green	Green	Dk green	Dk green
Identifiers...	Black	Green	Blue	Blue	Blue	Blue

Based on the first three variations (as well as others, not shown here), we felt that the third variation (Color Plate A, inside front cover, bottom) presented a meaningful palette of colors. The use of black for comments and for ASCII strings harks back to traditional monochrome text display. Blue rather than green is chosen for identifiers because it appears strange to see large bodies of text in green.

Yet the red appeared too bright, so we decided to darken it in the fourth variation and make it more subdued. The green seemed stronger than the blue, so we decided to darken it in the fifth variation. These two variations appear on the inside back cover, as does a final variation in which we darken both red and green. The choices represented in this last variation (Color Plate B, inside back cover, bottom) present what we feel is the optimum tuning of colors we have achieved in research to date.